T.. POLITICS AND HUMAN RIG..
Southeast Asia and Universalist Theo. y

This important new book makes a major contribution to the theory and practice of human rights, engaging in particular with the 'Asian values' debates of the 1990s. It is especially concerned with the tension between a universal regime of human rights and its ability to accommodate diversity. Incorporating original fieldwork from Malaysia, Singapore and Indonesia, the book also draws out the significance of Southeast Asian developments for the international human rights discourse. The book advances beyond the stalemate that the 'Asian values' debate has reached, developing an intermediary stance between the competing claims of universalism and relativism. Drawing on the work of Cass Sunstein and Chantal Mouffe, the theoretical contribution of the book will ensure its relevance to readers with a general interest in human rights. This book is likely to become a definitive account of contemporary political discussions of human rights in Southeast Asia and an important contribution to the development of human rights theory.

Anthony J. Langlois was educated at the University of Tasmania and the Australian National University. He is presently a lecturer in International Relations at the School of Political and International Studies, The Flinders University of South Australia.

CAMBRIDGE ASIA–PACIFIC STUDIES

Cambridge Asia–Pacific Studies aims to provide a focus and forum for scholarly work on the Asia–Pacific region as a whole, and its component sub-regions, namely Northeast Asia, Southeast Asia and the Pacific Islands. The series is produced in association with the Research School of Pacific and Asian Studies at the Australian National University and the Australian Institute of International Affairs.

Editor: John Ravenhill

Editorial Board: James Cotton, Donald Denoon, Mark Elvin, Hal Hill, Ron May, Anthony Milner, Tessa Morris-Suzuki, Anthony Low

To Amanda

THE POLITICS OF JUSTICE AND HUMAN RIGHTS

Southeast Asia and Universalist Theory

ANTHONY J. LANGLOIS
The Flinders University of South Australia

CAMBRIDGE
UNIVERSITY PRESS

PUBLISHED BY THE PRESS SYNDICATE OF THE UNIVERSITY OF CAMBRIDGE
The Pitt Building, Trumpington Street, Cambridge, United Kingdom

CAMBRIDGE UNIVERSITY PRESS
The Edinburgh Building, Cambridge CB2 2RU, UK
40 West 20th Street, New York, NY 10011–4211, USA
10 Stamford Road, Oakleigh, VIC 3166, Australia
Ruiz de Alarcón 13, 28014 Madrid, Spain
Dock House, The Waterfront, Cape Town 8001, South Africa

http://www.cambridge.org

First published 2001

Printed in Singapore by Craft Print Pte Ltd

Typeface New Baskerville (*Adobe*) 10/12 pt.   *System* QuarkXPress®   [PK]

A catalogue record for this book is available from the British Library

National Library of Australia Cataloguing in Publication data

Langlois, Anthony J.
The politics of justice and human rights: Southeast Asia
and universalist theory.
Includes index.
ISBN 0 521 80785 9.
ISBN 0 521 00347 4 (pbk.).
1. Human rights – Asia, Southeastern. 2. Asia,
Southeastern – Politics and government. I. Title.
323.0959

ISBN 0 521 80785 9 hardback
ISBN 0 521 00347 4 paperback

Contents

Acknowledgements

This book emerged out of my doctoral studies in the Department of International Relations, Research School of Pacific and Asian Studies, Australian National University. Despite the vicissitudes of academic existence in Australia at the turn of the millennium, the department, led by Andrew Mack, Jim Richardson and John Ravenhill, provided a milieu second to none in which to further one's intellectual development. I wish to thank – from across the ANU – Stephanie Lawson (now at East Anglia), Peter Dauvergne (now at Sydney), Jeremy Shearmur, Harold Crouch, Anthony Milner, and Robert McCorquodale, for their involvement with the various stages of the development of my arguments. Many thanks also to Chris Brown (LSE), Daniel Bell (Hong Kong) and Peter Van Ness (Denver/ANU) for providing advice and encouragement as I set about reconstructing the PhD thesis as a book. The School of Political and International Studies at Flinders University (under its Head, David Plant) has provided a congenial environment in which to conclude this task. In particular, thanks to Martin Griffiths, George Crowder and Rick DeAngelis for friendship, encouragement and intellectual stimulation. It has been a pleasure and privilege to work with Phillipa McGuinness, Paul Watt, Raylee Singh and the team at Cambridge University Press.

I have been accompanied on my intellectual journey by many good friends: Jonathan Hattrell, Paul Van Emmerick, Wynne Russell, Gavin Mount, Jacinta O'Hagan, Hiroyasu Akutsu, Hazel Lang, Fiona Terry, Abubakar Eby Hara, Craig Meer, Sonia Wu, Pru Grist, David Cooper, Peter Doering, Jennifer Collier, Brian Wixted, Frank and Heather Stootman, Patrick and Wendy Marman, Darrell Furgason, Tim Willson. I am grateful for the church communities in which I have found fellowship and hope, and to the One beyond us all. My beloved family remain constant to the last: John and Roslyn Langlois; Ruth, Wayne, Jessica and Caleb Amos; Catherine-Joy and Ricardo Munoz; Doris Phillips and Joan Langlois.

In the course of writing I met the beautiful Amanda Lopes, now my life companion and most intimate friend. Winter was replaced by spring and the whole world was filled with the fragrance and colour of new love and new life. Words cannot express my gratitude that our separate journeys have been thus joined; that we can love, laugh, cry and play as we together walk on and make our way.

Southeast Asia and the Asian Region

Introduction

The discourse of human rights exhibits and exemplifies two tendencies which many commentators have seen as the defining features of international politics during the transition to a new millennium: globalisation and fragmentation. In its historical origin and philosophical milieu a Western idea, the concept of human rights has become an international language of emancipation. It is spoken in its heartland, Europe and North America, and it is spoken in those places which often are silently missing from standard accounts of globalisation, notable among them Africa. The concept of human rights is appealed to by the international elite of educationalists, philosophers, theologians, social scientists, intellectuals and academics. It is forever strong in the rhetoric of world leaders and national politicians seeking appeal to the moral sentiment of their constituencies. It is a credo for non-government organisation (NGO) workers involved in relief and development, education, religious instruction and political emancipation. And 'human rights' has even become a language of legitimation for those who by their actions most belie the meaning of the term: despots, dictators, authoritarian regimes and a range of economically powerful actors.

One of the effects of describing human rights as a universal language is to reinforce belief in a universal moral order. Such a moral order is often taken to be that which is articulated by the language of human rights. What we observe from today's global languages – English, for example – is that they are spoken in many different ways around the world. English, even within the British Isles, has such variation that communication does not always ensue. There are other varieties of English – Chinese, American, Latino, African, ni-Vanuatu, Australian, and so on – where idiom, tone of voice, the local redefinition of words, and other factors change the way the language is used and make communication hazardous. I develop this

1

image because it places an imaginative hold on the nature of the human rights discourse, which can serve to illustrate the analysis presented in this book. It is in seeing that a language like English is at once global and fragmented that the nature of the human rights discourse can be imaginatively ascertained.

The question of diversity within the unity of the human rights discourse, however, presents many difficulties, some of which are seen to threaten the coherence of the idea of *universal* human rights. This is at its most acute when agents, using the human rights discourse as their language of legitimation, advocate mutually incompatible forms of behaviour. Such controversies are familiar to Australians, for a war of words has been interminable within the Southeast Asian region with respect to what practices are and are not human rights and about who has the determining authority. Political leaders of countries such as Malaysia, Indonesia and Singapore have been far from reticent in their advocacy of certain values and in their claim that those values are human rights as understood through their Asian cultural heritage. Thus Southeast Asian state elites claim their own interpretations of human rights, going so far as to suggest a rewriting of the United Nations Declaration on Human Rights because of its alleged Western bias. International NGOs such as Amnesty International and Human Rights Watch condemn the same states for human rights abuses. Regional NGOs such as JUST World Trust speak out against both the aforementioned, apparently using the same language of human rights.

It is this conflict of values which generates complexities for understanding human rights. If these and other actors in international politics use the same discourse with such apparently different objectives in mind, can it be plausibly argued that the discourse has something in common – namely, a unified and universal conception of human rights? Are these rights really there, in some natural law, metaphysical or contractual sense? Or is the term merely a linguistic trope, which is being used politically by different groups and therefore has no meaning in itself, or, alternatively, has various meanings depending on the context? In this book I argue for an understanding of human rights which is able to encompass both the fragmented and the global nature of the discourse of human rights. It is a model which allows for diversity and unity without reducing the moral force for emancipation that lies behind the adjective 'universal'. It thus does not reduce to yet another ideology of emancipation and, by so doing, close down on the diversity of human life and experience. It is possible to develop an understanding of human rights which provides for the pluralistic social practice of human rights in the world today and is consequently free from philosophical bankruptcy and inapplicability.

The diversity displayed by human cultures is genuine in its difference and this, from the start, led anthropologists to be sceptical about the claims to universality made by proponents of human rights. It is this awareness of cultural difference which is used, inter alia, by politicians, religious leaders, NGO workers, theologians, philosophers and others as a justification for dissent to directives based on the discourse of human rights. From the vantage point of Australia, these issues are raised most vocally and polemically by political leaders in the region, in what has become known as the 'Asian values debate'. In this debate, the idea of Asian values is systematically used to challenge what are perceived by Asian state elites to be the prevailing Western views on matters such as human rights, democracy and economic development.

The Asian values debate has precipitated the publication of a considerable quantity of political speeches and apologia; official state documentation; submissions to international conferences from governments, NGOs and other bodies; much media coverage; a considerable number of academic books, articles, theses and essays; and so on. Much of what has been written has focused on the claims of the elite political class within Asia, figures such as Prime Minister Dr Mahathir of Malaysia, former president Suharto of Indonesia, and former prime minister, now senior minister, Lee Kuan Yew of Singapore – and their deputies and public relations officers. Leaders from China, Burma, Thailand and other countries have also been outspoken in their support of one version or another of the Asian values position. The positions represented by Malaysia, Indonesia and Singapore serve conveniently as the starting-point for the argument of this book: their positions are well articulated and easily accessible and have been vocally and forcefully presented.

The book opens, then, with a discussion of the positions presented by the proponents of a set of distinctively Asian values, represented by Malaysia, Indonesia and Singapore, with particular attention being paid to the implications of Asian values for the human rights discourse. Malaysia, in the person of Mahathir, is seen to be the most brazen advocate of Asian values. Mahathir crusades against Western political hypocrisy and moral decadence, and on the crest of what till recently was a wave of economic success confidently looked forward to what his former deputy leader (now unjustly imprisoned rival) Anwar Ibrahim termed 'the Asian renaissance'. Indonesia's approach has been to work within the system, turning the Western system of states with its doctrines of state sovereignty and non-intervention to its own advantage. International law allows for the particularities of culture, and Indonesia has largely based its defence of its human rights interpretations on these allowances. Singapore, with its economic success, international reputation, and slick political machinery, has presented its case in measured tones, using elite political speeches, academic journals and popular current affairs publications as the forum for its views. While the Asian economic miracle lasted, it acted as a moral and strategic high ground from which these positions could be argued. It should not be thought, however, that the present regional economic crisis has permanently ended the debate. On the one hand, it may be assumed that economies will eventually recover and the state elites will return to defending the validity of their political ways. On the other, the issues raised by the genuine debate over human rights are not affected by the whims of the international capital markets.

Having allowed these voices to speak for themselves, I explore the critiques that have been levelled against the arguments and practices of the Southeast Asian state elites. This exploration elucidates four main lines of critique. The first pertains to arguments from culture; it is these arguments which form the bulk of the Asian values debate. A particular stress is laid on the dichotomisation of Western and Asian culture, which along with the general use and conceptualisation of culture is demonstrably flawed. Second, the claim that authoritarian governmental practices are justified on the basis that economic development comes before civil and political rights is shown to be fallacious. The third line of critique is directed against attempts to use the doctrines of the international system of states in the defence of authoritarian practices. Finally, it is argued, *pace* the regional state elites, that, inasmuch as they might be legitimately said to exist, Asian values are not simply to be confined to those values espoused by the ruling state elites. This is clearly exemplified in that it is the citizens of the region who condemn the authoritarian practices of the region's government in the name of human rights.

There is, however, an ambiguity here which is not resolved by merely presenting a critique of the regional governments in the name of universal human rights. While it is the case that regional human rights activists identify themselves as such, this is not seen to be the same as identifying themselves unequivocally with the human rights discourse as it is thought to be received in the West. Regional activists who go to jail for defending human rights do not necessarily identify fully with the Western human rights discourse. I argue, then, that inasmuch as the literature on the Asian values debate reduces the issues to defenders of human rights versus authoritarian governments it does an injustice to the issues at stake. The immediate way in which this can be ascertained is to consider the actors in the debate: here a simple dichotomy becomes impossible. It is true that those actors representing the state elites have a relatively homogenous position. Those in opposition do not. The opposition comprises NGO workers, religious leaders, academics, public intellectuals, dissidents, prisoners of conscience, politicians, foreign and expatriate representatives of all the previous, and so on. It is not possible to reduce the views of such a gathering into one unified set. The differences between them are multiple and, while these do not always affect their united opposition to state elites, at times they do. Thus, what is often depicted as a unified opposition is only ever unified on specific points at specific times and, depending on the issue, the composition of this opposition will vary.

It is out of a concern to elaborate this flux of positions that the argument of chapter 2 emerges. This chapter, drawing from both the literature and from primary research, addresses the fundamental questions which are determinative of the form of the human rights discourse within Southeast Asia. Thus, the chapter examines whether, and if so why, human rights in Asia are different from those elsewhere. The answers to these questions lead directly to the question of the source and nature of human rights as such in the understanding of people from the region. These answers dictate the values imputed to human rights. And it is to the extent that these values are different from those thought to be held in or by 'the West' that the above ambiguities in the human rights discourse in the region emerge. When a conservative Indonesian Muslim, for example, perceives himself as a creation of Allah and as responsible before Allah to live according to the Koran, then, inasmuch as he speaks in human rights terms, the values and specific rights that are defined must be consonant with his religious beliefs. Such an account of human rights may be markedly different, both theoretically and in the behaviour it allows or to which it gives rise, from, for example, the account given by a Javanese secular nationalist.

It is in this local sense that we can discuss Asian values: local religious and cultural beliefs do constitute the values which people hold. From this it flows that the contents of human rights will differ between religions and cultures, to the extent that these latter are what constitute people's values. This immediately raises complex issues for the human rights discourse, particularly for the claim that human rights are universal. I demonstrate that the values imputed to human rights are not universally held. Thus, the Asian values debate serves to direct us to some of the fundamental questions of political philosophy: with which values are we to constitute the formal structure for expressing legitimate behaviour to other persons and groups of persons which we term the human rights discourse? Who should decide which way the controversy is resolved on matters like abortion or religious freedom?

The two strategies which are developed later in the book for understanding such controversies and disagreements in the context of a discourse which claims universality are presaged by the discussions in this chapter. These concern the respective ways in which people within the region justify whether and why they have specific human rights. Reflection on these discussions suggested two observations. First, that people's understandings of the source and nature of human rights are dependent on the human traditions – religious, philosophical, political – which form their worldviews. Often, these different traditions substantially agree at an ethical level, while disagreeing about epistemology, metaphysics, ontology, and so forth. Second, the substantive rights which people understand themselves to have depend on the particularities of the tradition from which they emerge. Again, inasmuch as these traditions overlap, there is agreement on substantive rights. But there is also significant difference, and it is this difference which does harm to a simple notion of universality for human rights. This difference is not reducible, nor can it be rationalised away, for it is formed by the human traditions through which people receive their identity: it is constitutive. The implications of these two observations for the theory and philosophy of human rights are elaborated, respectively, in chapters 4 and 5. These implications cannot be fully understood, however, without first reviewing the way in which the concept of human rights has been theorised in the past, and how it is presently debated in contemporary political philosophy.

For this reason, chapter 3 comprises a change of scene from contemporary Southeast Asia to the history of the human rights idea. Here I argue that the way in which to approach the universality of human rights is to examine the philosophical and historical milieu from which it emerged. This provides insight into the development of the idea, furnishes material for critique, and explains much of what is behind the process of a particularist concept such as human rights being willed and socialised into being as a universal. In addressing the issue of universalism, then, I do not proceed from the assumption of universal human rights and attempt a philosophical apologia, as is the practice of much contemporary thought. Rather, I examine the assumptions and presuppositions which gave rise to the concept of universal human rights (in its various historical forms). This furnishes us with the resources to proceed with formulating a theory that is able to make sense of what has become a shared practice of living and meaning at the beginning of the twenty-first century: the human rights discourse and praxis.

Jeremy Bentham famously referred to what we now call human rights as 'nonsense upon stilts'. Like much nonsense, however, it has proved a powerful force in the world of politics, and as a motivator for the emancipation of the poor and oppressed. However, the philosophical questions which raised doubts for Bentham (among others) have never been adequately addressed. The concept of human rights is witnessed to have emerged from particular traditions of thought, and the idea has only ever had hegemony and persuasive power to the extent that the assumptions embodied in these traditions were commonly shared. It is with the political thought of the Enlightenment that the understanding of human rights common in contemporary Western political philosophy was established. In short, this means that human rights are the outcome of a political theory which seeks to establish a universal civilisation based on an autonomous and critical rational morality. Through the Enlightenment, rights moved from being premised on the natural law given by the divine lawgiver, to being secular, rational, universal, individual, democratic and radical. They become one of the grand narratives that emerge out of Enlightenment historiography. This shows us that phrases such as 'men are born, and always continue, free and equal in respect of their rights' can only ever be true and self-evident if the philosophical frameworks which inform such assertions are uncritically accepted.

The grand project of the Enlightenment failed because it was unable to sustain the claims it made on behalf of autonomous human reason: that it could ascertain and justify an independent rational morality. The consequences of this for human rights are profound, as they are profound for the whole of the political philosophy in which human rights were grounded and elaborated, that of liberalism. Liberalism is commonly characterised as philosophically dependent upon a conception of the individual self possessed of a universal faculty of reason, which could dwell within a neutral state consensually supported by all other individuals because of their common universal rationality. These assumptions support the doctrine of human rights and are widely so used in contemporary political thought. However, such formulations of liberalism fail to do justice to the plurality of ways of being as a self within a community, to the plurality of traditions of reason – among which liberalism is itself only one – and to the plurality of values exhibited in social organisation around the world. I conclude that 'human rights' should not be thought to exert a universal claim on reason such that it has universal moral, social and institutional application. For as long as human rights is centred around a particular non-universal tradition – Western liberalism (in all its variety) – it cannot be universal: it fails on its own terms. For while espousing universality it is limited by a particularist rationality; while espousing egalitarianism it judges other ways of thought and practices as unequal; while espousing freedom it forces silence on non-liberal voices.

In chapters 4 and 5, I address the question of how the human rights discourse, now so well entrenched in international law and politics and the law and politics of most states, may be reconceptualised such that its rhetoric of universality, freedom and egalitarianism is not undermined, as at present, by an inadequate theoretical framework. These chapters respectively explore the two observations derived from chapter 2: that among the human traditions there is often ethical overlap about the substantive content of human rights values, despite fundamentally anti-thetical philosophical groundings; and, second, that the diverse human traditions which people use to ground their understandings of human rights often lead to great difference about the proper substantive content of human rights and that this difference is non-reducible and intransigent.

Chapter 4 develops the implications of the first of these positions for general theories of human rights. Within the Western philosophical tra-dition the way of approaching human rights has been to develop 'a' the-ory of rights which will be universally applicable – this is done as much by postmodernist critics of foundationalist thinkers as by the founda-tionalists themselves. However, a theory of human rights will continue to be elusive for as long as the theorists operate on the assumption that one universal theory can be found which will garner support from everyone, across the human traditions. Such a theory is impossible because of the diversity in and often antithetical nature of human traditions. At best, such a theory can hope to become yet another particularist tradition, with, perhaps, widespread support.

An alternative model is to argue for a theory of human rights the focus of which is the shared ethical commitments we already have, not the way in which these are derived. A secularist and a theist can both affirm many of the same values, though for different and often antithetical reasons. Inasmuch as the organisation of society is dependent on shared ethical beliefs, the differences are of no immediate political consequence. This approach is developed in the chapter through the use of a model derived from the work of the legal theorist Cass Sunstein, an approach called 'incompletely theorised agreement'. Sunstein argues that it is through the mechanism of incompletely theorised agreement that parties to a legal judgement are able to accept the judge's sentence, despite coming from greatly diverse backgrounds and having different worldviews. To the extent, then, that there already exists widespread agreement on the human rights discourse, such an approach to the theorisation of social practice will be more insightful than the more traditional attempt to find one singular theory capable of comprehensively explaining the dis-course. Further, such an approach proves useful in explaining many of the problems which have developed for human rights theorists with the changes in human rights practices which inevitably precede human rights theory, such as the development by the United Nations of addi-tional generations of rights.

The great virtue of an incompletely theorised model of human rights theory is that it allows for any given ethical position, or substantive human rights value, to be indigenously justified by the various human traditions. It does not require people to assent to one specific political philosophy in order to arrive at a human rights conclusion, although, of course, people do have to be prepared to talk in the language of human rights. However, the limitation of the incompletely theorised model is that it does not speak to the issue of which substantive values are included and which are not included as human rights values. As it stands, the incompletely theorised agreement model views the human rights discourse as relatively fixed: certain values have been privileged; by affirming those values you join the discourse, regardless of which resource you use to affirm the values. The human rights discourse, however, is not static and fixed. Even in the short half-century of the UN's work with human rights, dramatic changes and extensions of the discourse have been observed. The question then becomes: on what grounds are new substantive human rights values determined? If it is admitted that there cannot be one single theory of human rights, and if it is admitted, following this, that human traditions at times disagree violently about ethical matters, who is to arbitrate as to which ethical standards are embodied in 'new' human rights? This question is the subject of chapter 5.

I contend that a *political* model of human rights serves to ensure justice in a way which the traditional legal–rational model cannot. The latter model, with its roots in natural law and right, ascertained by the proper use of right reason and enshrined in positive law, is the model which underlies most contemporary thought on human rights theory. It presupposes a fixed body of normative and universal principles which enlightened individuals and societies can discern and organise around. This account is found to have severe difficulties with respect to its philosophical defence on its own terms, and with respect to its correlation to the diversity of the world as we observe it. The alternative political model advocated does not rule out the possibility of there being what the legal–rational model is premised upon: a fixed set of universal normative principles. Indeed, many of the human traditions uphold such an account. What it does rule out is that proponents of the legal–rational model can be justified in asserting that their account of the substance of these principles is in fact the final account, the one which 'trumps' all other traditions.

The political model of human rights theorisation is built around what Chantal Mouffe has called, in the title of her book, *The Return of the Political*. Mouffe argues that much contemporary political philosophy has ignored the political, that aspect of our relations which involves power, authority, conflict, antagonism and, if 'undomesticated', violence. This is epitomised in the works of theorists such as Rawls and Habermas who attempt to do away with the political by constructing 'original positions' or 'conditions of perfect communication'. She argues that political philosophy proceeding in this manner towards the hope of a transparent society reconciled with itself will end by harming its objective of justice for all. This is precisely because such a methodology fails to recognise the discursive nature of justice, and consequently our lack of agreement with respect to what constitutes justice.

This disagreement is what makes the political model of human rights valuable as a way of ensuring the emancipatory nature of the human rights discourse. It does this by reconceptualising human rights such that, rather than being a fixed and immutable law which regulates human conduct, it becomes instead a contestable statement of identity and aspiration. This change attempts to bring theory in line with practice. The determination of what rights were in or out of the Universal Declaration on Human Rights was a political process. The establishment of the Right to Development, similarly, was the end of a period of consultation, lobbying, conflict, antagonism and discussion. This period was ended when a political body made a decision, and a new right was declared, signalling a change in the understanding and operation of the human rights discourse. This is seen also among groups who dissent from dominant positions within the human rights discourse, who issue different lists of human rights according to religious, political or other traditions. Here also is a statement of identity, and of intention to lobby for change within the discourse.

Thus, I argue that, by advocating a political model of human rights, the universality of human rights may be salvaged from its intellectual troubles. Neither the substantive values of the discourse nor its underlying philosophical assumptions could be said to have universal applicability or normativity. What *is* universal, however, is that the varying human traditions lay claim to an understanding of justice, and outline what it means, in their respective understandings, for human persons to be moral in their behaviour. The political model argues that the human rights discourse is the forum in which our competing accounts of justice and morality can play against each other and compete for hegemony. It is a model which allows radically different traditions to speak and be heard, and which does not demand that they alter their views to be included. Yet it provides the opportunity for the communication and discussion which may lead towards common ground. It is by being a forum in which our intractable disagreements about what we universally agree on – the need for justice to be done – can be discussed, debated, and decided, revised, redescribed and redecided, that genuine justice has the chance to be realised.

The model is political because it affirms that it is part of the human condition that there will be disagreement, power plays, authority relations, conflict and antagonism as we seek to live together. It contends, however, that it is by being open about this at the level of theory as well as at the level of practice, that we will best understand ourselves and those with whom we live. The political model acknowledges that decisions must be made about justice and that these will not satisfy everyone. But by making human rights a discourse in which persuasion, debate and conflict are permanent features, there is always the opportunity for a given minority voice, decided against, to start a process of revision, redescription and redecision – if the politics are played felicitously. The alternative is a covertly political model, where the discourse is dominated by a powerful set of arguments and positions which claim to be, but are in fact not, neutral. By failing to recognise the discursive nature of justice, such a 'neutral' model reduces to a vicious circle, in which the dominant theoretical and political positions define the timeless Truths of the discourse. By overtly recognising the political nature of the human rights discourse, however, this vicious circle can be made a virtuous circle. Thus, it is not by constructing a utopian original position or perfect communications community that justice is done, but by recognising the impossibility of these and by developing, encouraging and conspiring towards the theory and practice of human rights which will ensure a virtuously political and discursive justice.

CHAPTER 1

The Asian Values Discourse

Is there a distinctively 'Asian' concept of human rights? This question arises out of a debate that has been conducted in the international media, academic journals and political forums in response to claims made by political leaders within Asia that there are indeed distinctly Asian values. These values are said to have various sources – Confucianism and Asian interpretations of Islam prominent among them, along with more particularist cultural heritages such as those of Java and other sub-national groups. The values are said to be *cultural* values, and are understood to be at the heart of the 'Asian worldview'. All aspects of life are thus informed by these values: family relationships, educational methods, social structures, political institutions and the process of politics itself are all nurtured, it is claimed, under the umbrella of Asian values.

This claim extends to concepts such as democracy and human rights and therefore has great significance because these are concepts which claim forms of universal normative applicability. It is then of importance to promoters of democracy and human rights to assess the challenge issued by the Asian values debate. The first part of this chapter reports in detail the claims made by the political elites of Malaysia, Indonesia and Singapore with respect to Asian values. To this end, the speeches and writings of various representatives of the political elites will be quoted, sometimes at length. The result is a pastiche of the views generally referred to as 'Asian values'. The second part of this chapter serves to summarise the criticisms that have been directed at Asian values, so conceived, by addressing the three principal types of arguments presented by state elites in favour of such values. I suggest that there are alternative Asian values to those espoused by state elites.

Malaysia

The wider debate about Asian values is replicated within Malaysia in the debate about 'Malaysian values'. This debate, and the justification for the dominant set of values within the debate, find their original impetus in the communalist conflict that Malaysia experienced in 1969.[1] The Asian values which Prime Minister Mahathir preaches are but the most recent articulation and popularisation of a deliberate policy which seeks to counter this by uniting Malaysia as a nation. Mahathir also uses it as a platform from which to defend the 'East' or the 'South' against the imperialistic designs of a morally bankrupt and 'wicked West'.[2] This 'Mahathirism' can be summarised as combining a universalist Islam, a developmental nationalism, a more laissez-faire approach to the market and an attempt at mass appeal.[3]

Three main claims emerge clearly from the Malaysian debate. First, the placing of authority and order above democracy. Second, the critique of the West, put forward as an assault against liberal democracy, with its associated radically rugged individualism and lackadaisical moral values. Third, an account of a public culture that serves in Asia as an alternative to the liberal democracy of the West. This public culture is holistic, and its distinguishing feature is its reliance on the various religious traditions and formulations of transcendent moral values for its foundation and purpose. In what follows, each of these three aspects of Asian values Malaysian style will be elucidated using extracts from the writings and speeches of Mahathir, along with other less extreme sources.

The authoritarian nature of Mahathir's Asian values is demonstrated by the nature of the state over which he presides. The government has dominating powers over many aspects of life which Westerners would perceive as inappropriate. Freedom of religion, speech, association and assembly are all significantly regulated. A pronounced aspect of Malaysia's experience in this regard is the way in which its parliament has been ready to forgo its (potential) clout and acquiesce before the executive. In addition, the judiciary (despite regularly ruling against the government) has been deprived of much of its independence and power. As a consequence of these factors the individual is no longer able to adequately challenge the role of the executive.

Mahathir has said, 'Let us not be slaves to democracy … if by practising certain aspects of democracy we run the risk of causing chaos in our party and country, we have to choose our party and country above democracy'.[4] Quite explicitly, the national interest as defined by state elites is elevated over democratic rights for the people. Mahathir protests that he does not advocate authoritarian rule, merely 'democracy as it was practised by the

Western democrats during their democratic infancy'. His argument is that in democratic infancy the development of political stability is the overriding concern, not democracy for its own sake: 'The democratic system is not divine law. It is concocted by very human and fallible people. We cannot be accused of heresy if we disagree and reject some of the interpretations of the new prophets.' There is, however, little consistent promise of democracy once infancy is over: 'Once we are politically stable then only can we focus seriously on economic growth and the welfare of our people'.[5] Mahathir is not enamoured of democracy. It was, he says, foisted upon cultures who had no experience of it by their departing colonial masters. Further, he argues that it impedes the efficient working of government because of the necessity of maintaining popularity with the people.[6] Even when espousing democracy, Mahathir's rhetoric betrays a consciously chosen paternalistic approach to the people. Indeed, the prime minister has gone so far as to say that 'there is not going to be a democracy in Malaysia; there never was and there never will be'. Consequently, 'why not say that we need some form of authoritarian rule? We are doing that anyway ... Why not call a spade a spade?'[7]

The second thrust of Malaysia's Asian values is a critique of the West, and the rhetorical ploy of identifying the maladies of Western society as the logical consequences of its dominant political tradition: liberalism. In Mahathir's critique, the failure of the West (particularly America) to maintain a public morality based on its Christian (and, in America, specifically Puritan) tradition is conflated with the theoretical and philosophical primacy increasingly given to notions of freedom in Western (liberal) political thought. The primacy of freedom is interpreted by Mahathir and others as unfettered freedom or complete autonomy. This allegedly gives individuals licence to reject constricting traditional moralities and to give free rein to their passions, base or otherwise. This development in Western thought and practice is allegedly epitomised by Western approaches to human rights, particularly individual rights, as is demonstrated by the following extract from a speech given by Mahathir as he opened a conference dedicated to exposing Western hypocrisy in its pursuit of human rights:

> The West's interpretation of human rights is that every individual can do what he likes, free from any restraint by governments ... The result is perhaps not quite what the original liberal democrats expected. Individuals soon decided that they should break every rule and code governing their society. Beginning with simple things like dress codes, they went on to disregard marriage as an institution. Extra marital sex became the norm. The family was redefined to mean cohabitation between a man and a woman, with frequent changes of partners, or between a man and a man or a woman and a woman. Children were begotten without known fathers, which in time will lead to incest

between brothers and sisters and even father and daughter or mother and son. But then incest is not wrong either, if that is what is desired by the individual ... Clearly, Western society is confused as to what it wants. It wants absolute freedom for everyone but no freedom when individuals or society objects. If individuals or society can object to sexual harassment or infidelity among their leaders then there cannot be absolute freedom. And yet the West insists that freedom must in no way be fettered and that everyone must accept Western norms. They see nothing contradictory in their contrary attitudes.[8]

While Mahathir continues to maintain his political notoriety for speaking out in this fashion and enjoys the self-appointed role of spokesperson against the West for the 'global opposition', his former deputy, Anwar Ibrahim, operates on the basis of a more holistic political agenda.[9] This agenda embraces the critique Mahathir articulates (although with more insight and less hyperbole) but goes beyond it to suggest a way forward which takes what is precious from the Western tradition, fuses it with the excellences of the various Asian heritages, and storms the world with a new optimism born out of an Asian renaissance. Anwar says:

The fact that democracy is often abused, leading to chaos and paralysis, does not mean that dictatorship is the answer. Rather, the solution lies in purging democracy of its excesses, such as unbridled individualism at the expense of the rights and the interests of the majority. Thus democracy must be revitalised by infusing it with ethical principles and moral uprightness ... We must therefore reacquaint ourselves with the Asian civilisational ideals and intellectual legacies ... The Asian way is to reach consensus on national goals within the democratic framework, to take the middle path, the Confucian Chun Yung or the Islamic awsatuha, to exercise tolerance and sensitivity towards others.[10]

Thus it is that Anwar argues against a view of Asian values perceived as essentially authoritarian. He claims to have a different emphasis from Mahathir's: 'I emphasise the issues of civil society, fundamental liberties and the trust and wisdom that the public, with exposure to education and knowledge, should be able to exercise'.[11]

Anwar comments that it is most unusual, in the present day, for 'ethics and transcendent principles' to have relevance to state-craft. This is attributed to the dominance of the secular West and its ideologies of Enlightenment, which exalt reason as the sole guide to civilisation over and above the transcendent. This then is the third thrust of Malaysia's Asian values doctrine: the need for a religious public culture. The Asian 'man [sic]', says Anwar, 'at heart is persona religiosus'. This faith is not, as in the West, personal and private but 'permeates the life of the community'.[12] Chandra Muzaffar would have such a view universalised and made normative for all people.[13]

In the Malaysian context, and in the political application of these sentiments within Malaysia, the faith in question, of course, is the faith of the political elites in Malaysia: Islam. It has been a conscious policy on the part of Mahathir and his government to encourage the development of a modern and pragmatic Islam of the Sunni sect, with the threefold aim of providing a religious basis for public social values, retaining control over Islamic resurgence and extremism and encouraging modernisation.[14] Mahathir's rhetoric insists that it is the loss of such public religion which is at the root of most, if not all, of the West's problems – that this, in fact, is the Western *problematique*:

> Western societies have witnessed an almost completed separation of religion from secular life and the gradual replacement of religion with hedonistic values. Materialism, sensual gratification and selfishness are rife. The community has given way to the individual and his desires [leading to] … the breakdown of established institutions and diminished respect for marriage, family values, elders and important customs, conventions and traditions.[15]

Anwar speaks of Malaysia's adoption of a modern and pragmatic Islam that can speak to the social, political and economic spheres of life, providing a cohesiveness for a society confronted with modernity and postmodernity.[16] He says, 'We need to reassert the universalism of Islam, its values of justice, compassion and tolerance in a world that is yearning for a sense of direction and for genuine peace. If this could be achieved, Muslims can truly contribute to the shaping of a new world.'[17]

In a world that has been darkened by the Enlightenment critique of religion, the rise of individualism, the moral decadence that has flowed from the absolutisation of personal autonomy, the dislocation and alienation of globalisation and the possibilities of unethical uses of new technology, the spokesmen of Malaysian values preach a return to civilisational heritage and transcendence. In such a return, the three elements of Asian values as enunciated by the 'Malaysian School' are complete: a recognition of authority and order, to which democracy must submit; the recognition of community and universal moral principles, to which individuals must submit; and the re-emergence of the 'persona religiosus', with a concomitant and prerequisite recognition of the transcendent.

Indonesia

Until 1998 Indonesia, with Malaysia and Singapore, spear-headed the debate about Asian values under Suharto. In May 1998, Indonesia unexpectedly found itself with a new political order, with the consequence that in the space of two years it has had two new presidents.

The first hand-over of the presidency, forced by popular unrest and protest, was to the then vice-president, B. J. Habibie. While Habibie was pleased to release some political prisoners, and generally moved towards less oppressive government, he nonetheless maintained Indonesia's claims about its own cultural values, continuing – perhaps with less conviction – in the mainstream of Suharto's version of Asian values. As he put it, there is agreement on human rights, but 'the difference is in its translation and implementation'.[18] In the absence of evidence to the contrary, it can be claimed that Habibie's erratic nature did not change Indonesia's institutional position within the Asian values debate.

With the election of Indonesia's fourth president in October 1999, this has begun to change. Abdurrahman Wahid (also known affectionately as Gus Dur) surprised most pundits by winning against the competition, particularly against Megawati Sukarnoputri, who has become his deputy. Most commentators are full of hope. Human rights supporters may be encouraged by the appointment of Marzuki Darusman, former head of Indonesia's Human Rights Commission, to the new cabinet as attorney-general. In addition, a human rights portfolio has been created in the cabinet, initially filled by Hasbalah M. Saad from Aceh. However, not all are satisfied by such moves. Some reformists fear that Wahid will not be sufficiently hard on those who have given the nation the legacy it presently experiences.[19] While the future has yet to unfold, we will turn here to examine the role that Indonesia has played within the Asian values debate thus far.

Indonesia characteristically endorsed universal norms for humane treatment of citizens, such as those found in the Universal Declaration on Human Rights. It has been, however, an endorsement with two fundamental qualifications: first, the right to interpret such norms according to local culture and custom; and, second, the right to just political treatment by Western critics in the face of the hypocrisy and double standards from the West on contemporary human rights issues and in relation to the West's historical record – colonialism, slavery, political, cultural and religious imperialism, and so forth. Indonesia appeared to hope that these reminders of the West's excesses would reduce the severity of the West's assessment of Indonesia's practices.

Indonesia found it strategic to maintain a position which stressed agreement with one's critics, while pointing out the critics' own failures and arguing for allowances based on historical and economic factors. This, rather than the more difficult claims of cultural exceptionalism engaged in by Malaysia and Singapore, enabled Indonesia to capitalise on the political gains its neighbours made without having to engage in either the politics or intellectual games engendered by a cultural exceptionalism which goes beyond the mutually agreed rules of state-centric *realpolitik* to the more ephemeral discourses of culture. (It should be noted, however, that Indonesia was as willing as Singapore and Malaysia to use the resources of culture in its internal nation-building discourse; the point is not that Indonesia did not employ such tactics but that its external defence of its human rights record principally used other means.)

Former president Suharto, in addressing the Non-Aligned Movement in 1992, included a statement about human rights which illustrates the way in which the Indonesian regime used existing conventions about human rights as a means of defending its own position. He noted that human rights issues had begun to receive more international attention, although they had been a part of international concerns since 1949: 'Basic human rights and fundamental freedoms are unquestionably of universal validity'. This position is contested openly by other Southeast Asian nations. Indonesia has also been involved in attempts to redraft the UN human rights principles but has been much less confrontational in its approach. Rather than polemically denouncing the West's hypocrisy, Suharto used internationally credited notions about human rights to justify his own position:

> The principle of the indivisibility of all the various categories of rights ... should be fully acknowledged and adhered to. There should be no selectivity or undue emphasis ... Indivisibility also implies the need for a balanced relationship between individual and community rights. Such a balance is critical for its absence can lead to a denial of the rights of a society as a whole and can lead to instability and anarchy.[20]

Here Suharto endorsed a political approach similar to that of Lee Kuan Yew and Mahathir. But rather than justifying it by reference to Confucianism, Islam, or other Oriental communitarian traditions, he appealed to the UN human rights system:

> In the United Nations it has also been commonly agreed that the implementation of human rights in the national context should remain the competence and responsibility of each government while taking into account the complex variety of problems, of diverse value systems, of *differing economic, social and cultural realities prevailing in each country*. This national competence not only derives from the principle of sovereignty but is also a logical consequence of the fundamental rights of nations to their *national and cultural identity and to develop their own social and economic systems*. In promoting and protecting human rights, therefore, the basic aim ... should be to cooperate in improving the observance and protection of these rights rather than to accuse, to impose incompatible values or, worse, to explicit [*sic*] the issue of human rights by making it a political conditionality in economic and development cooperation.[21] [Emphasis added.]

It is clear that, while form is maintained by rhetorical agreement with the UN stipulations concerning human rights, Indonesia was determined to argue, on the basis of the UN system, that its 'own way of doing things' and, in particular, its own judgements about national priorities and values were paramount.

A further demonstration of Indonesia's strategy was witnessed in the statement given to the 1993 World Conference on Human Rights held in Vienna, as it was addressed by Indonesia's foreign minister, Ali Alatas. Alatas commenced by voicing concern at international media reports of 'a clash of values' between the countries of the North and the South: 'This depiction is not only erroneous but also unwarranted and counterproductive'. All participants were motivated by 'our shared view on the universal validity of basic human rights and fundamental freedoms'.[22] Alatas made the argument, common with Malaysia and Singapore, that Indonesian culture was not as individualistic as the West's and that this had consequences for human rights, democracy and societal organisation:

> In Indonesia, as in many other developing countries, the rights of the individual are balanced by the rights of the community, in other words, balanced by the obligation equally to respect the rights of others, the rights of society and the rights of the nation. Indonesian culture as well as its ancient well-developed customary laws have traditionally put high priority on the rights and interests of the society or nation, without, however, in any way minimising or ignoring the rights and interests of individuals and groups. Indeed, the interests of the latter are always fully taken into account based on the principles of 'musyawarah-mufakat' (deliberations in order to obtain consensus), which is firmly embedded in the nation's socio-political system and form of democracy.[23]

Alatas also reiterated Suharto's point that, at the national level, expression and implementation of human rights 'should remain the competence and responsibility of each government'. Thus, the 'unique value systems prevailing in each country should be taken into consideration',[24] including, as Wiryono, former ambassador to Australia, put it, Indonesia being a 'thoroughly ... oriental nation, which is communistic'.[25] And, once again, Alatas' justification was drawn from the principle of the sovereignty of states and was supported as a logical consequence of the right to self-determination.

As indicated above, a significant part of Indonesia's defence on the issue of human rights was to remind its accusers of their own record, and to suggest by this that we are all doing the best we can given the circumstances. Wiryono expressed 'surprise' at the ease with which Australians accused Indonesia of human rights violations, especially given Australia's track record with Aboriginal peoples and the Asian immigration debate:

'In Indonesia we believe that when we point a finger at people, three of our own fingers point at ourselves. So in Indonesia we place more stress on humility, rather than arrogance.'[26] Indonesia, said Wiryono, is happy to receive 'concern expressed in an enlightened, non-judgemental, and non-condescending fashion'.[27]

Juwono Sudarsono, in papers endorsed by the Suharto Administration, elaborated on the political uses of human rights: 'In the absence of communism as an adversarial focus, advanced industrialised countries turned their fixation on Asian "authoritarianism" and "repression"'. This is evidenced in the addition of a 'social clause' to trade and the mobilisation of international media in the development of a 'thriving conscience industry'. Sudarsono identified three main failings which invalidate the 'noble' side of the West's international human rights agenda. First there is the international economic dimension: 'Because human rights is a nebulous concept, its use as a political weapon in diplomacy and international business has led to it being applied more often by developed nations facing growing economic competition from emerging markets'.[28] Second, it is objected that the West only focuses on political and civil rights in its concern for human rights. Despite the adoption in 1966 of the International Covenant on Economic, Social and Cultural Rights, and the 1986 adoption of the 'right to development' with its focus on basic resources, food, health, education, and so forth, over 80 per cent of advanced industrialised countries continue to neglect the realm of economic, cultural and development rights. Third, Sudarsono, with government endorsement, objects to the manner in which the West purports to set the standard for Asia with respect to Asia's political and civil rights: 'The hypocrisy of governments and rights activists in industrialised countries is particularly stark in their assumption that civil and political rights in their countries are irreproachable and must become the benchmarks by which developing countries are judged'. Sudarsono concludes, on a height of rhetorical anguish, that 'human rights in international diplomacy should be affirmed for what it really is: A big scam that seems destined to last as long as nations compete for economic advantage through political subterfuge on behalf of noble ideals'.[29]

Such strong language was rarely seen in the Suharto Government's speeches or documents, although in this instance it was clearly supported by the government. Alatas' ironic comment, that 'as a people who have suffered colonial oppression for centuries, we know only too well the vital importance of human rights',[30] was more in keeping with the Suharto Government's desire to undermine the position from which accusations were being levelled, while at the same time asserting their commitment to embrace these 'noble ideals' in their own cultural, national and sovereign manner.

Singapore

Kishore Mahbubani commences his article 'The West and the Rest' by reciting the 'conventional wisdom' that the Cold War was won by the West not because of military considerations but 'because of the strength of its social, economic and political institutions'.[31] These institutions are given the shorthand 'liberal democracy' by analysts, and it is liberal democracy which is seen by the Western political and intellectual leaders to be the most just means of governing any given society. Lee Kuan Yew, Singapore's elder statesman, is direct in expressing his disagreement with this Western view. He claims that the liberal intellectual tradition posited that 'human beings had arrived at this perfect state where every-body would be better off if they were allowed to do their own thing and flourish. It has not worked out, and I doubt if it will.'[32] On Lee's view, good government understood as value-neutral government, which allows individuals to determine their own conception of the 'good life' and per-mits them the freedom to pursue the good life so defined, misunder-stands the nature of 'man' (sic). 'Mankind' (sic) partly comprises a certain sense of right and wrong, and also a propensity to do evil, which must be controlled. Liberal democracy, because it relegates such theo-rising to the private sphere, has lost sight of both the 'ethical basis for society' and the recognition that 'there is such a thing called evil, [which] is not the result of being a victim of society'. Society's problems will only be solved as people take personal responsibility; the view that good government means personal autonomy for the individual, problem solving by the government, and welfare as practised in the USA is, on Lee's assessment, erroneous.

This is not the only way of construing good government and is not the way it is construed by the so-called Singapore School. This school com-prises leaders who have articulated a defence of the Singaporean regime, either in their personal or official capacities. Lee Kuan Yew (Senior Min-ister of State), Goh Chok Tong (Prime Minister), George Yeo (Minister for Information, Arts and Health), Kishore Mahbubani (diplomat and former representative to the UN), Bilahari Kausikan (Singapore's perma-nent representative to the UN) and Tommy Koh (ambassador at large) have been most prominent in the Singapore School's publicity drive.

Mahbubani says, 'The crucial variable in determining whether a Third World society will progress is not whether its government is democratic but whether, to put it simply, it has "good government"'.[33] Good govern-ment comprises five characteristics: '(1) political stability, (2) sound bureaucracies based on meritocracy, (3) economic growth with equity, (4) fiscal prudence, and (5) relative lack of corruption'.[34] Lee claims that what is sought is a form of government that is comfortable, need-meeting, not oppressive and maximising of opportunities. Thus, according to the government's Shared Values White Paper:

> the concept of government by honourable men (*junzi*) who have a duty to do right for the people, and who have the trust and respect of the population, fits us better than the Western idea that a government should be given as limited powers as possible, and should always be treated with suspicion unless proven otherwise.[35]

Kausikan, with unintended irony, refers to the popular pressures exerted on governments from East and Southeast Asia by way of defending this account. Good government, he says, consists in 'effective, efficient, and honest administrations able to provide security and basic needs with good opportunities for an improved standard of living'.[36] It is these qualities which the people of the region want to experience in their lives, over and above the democratic virtues propounded by the West. Indeed, the crux of the argument is that economic development lays the foundation for democracy and must thus be developed first.

The Singapore model of government is one of paternalistic trusteeship: the people entrust their well-being to a government that 'exercises independent judgement', as Goh puts it, to ascertain what decisions should be made for the best interests of the community. Kausikan quotes Goh:

> The trustee model of democracy that Singapore has subscribed to enabled it to pursue the tough policies necessary for economic development. Indeed, the concept of government as trustee went hand in hand with democratic accountability. Because the Government has acted as an honest and competent trustee of the people, we have been returned to power in every general election since self-government in 1959.[37]

Policy decisions taken in the economic realm will inevitably affect the private lives of citizens. The government, however, is not averse to intervening directly in the lives of citizens. While in the West the political system is (at least rhetorically) designed around the freedom of the individual, this is confessedly not the case in Singapore. Senior Minister Lee Kuan Yew says, 'Whether in periods of golden prosperity or in the depths of disorder, Asia has never valued the individual over society. The society has always been more important.'[38]

It is often at this point where some defenders of Singapore will explicitly make links between its policy of good government and Asian values. In the Shared Values White Paper it is the different societal balance between community and individual that is the crucial difference between 'Asian' and 'Western' values. It is the emphasis on community which has been 'a key survival value for Singapore'. Then follows the increasingly familiar litany of ills caused by the West's excessive individualism. These problems are said to be in large measure prevented by taking the Confucian option of soft-authoritarian government, where a strong moral state champions order.[39]

Those who support this view argue that the egalitarian individualism of the West, demonstrated by such concepts as human rights, emerged out of an adversarial culture historically dominated by patrimonialism and feudalism and presently characterised by adversarial political and judicial processes. In contrast, they posit that their own societies have a consensual tradition, and that the institutional and social forces at work within the West to produce an adversarial and highly individualistic society were not operative or present in the Asian countries.[40]

The contrast is with a strong moral state which enables people to fulfil their duties to society, persuades the people of what is good for them, provides for them economically, and oversees a moral tradition in which the virtues of filial piety, chastity, industry, selflessness and the like are championed.[41] These are what Lee Kuan Yew terms the 'core cultural values, those dynamic parts of Confucian culture which if lost will lower our performance'.[42] Thus, it is traditional Confucian ideas of 'firm direction' which are often seen by the West to be a form of soft authoritarianism: 'Firm government is part of this model. You've got to take tough decisions. We had to change people's habits', says Lee.[43] To Goh Chok Tong, such authoritarianism is part of what it means to be the aforementioned *junzi* – that is, the 'Confucian gentleman' leader, morally righteous, trusted by the people and committed to the public good.[44] It is this Confucian commitment to the public good which, following the argument, inclines the people to accept constraints on their individual democratic rights in return for economic prosperity and security. The Internal Security Act is one example of this trade-off: Goh Chok Tong opines that the ISA keeps the streets safe, and a correspondent to the *Straits Times* claims that the ISA is no more irritating than is wearing a condom and that it has analogous preventative benefits.[45]

Other representatives of the Singapore Government do not see the justification of Asian values as subsisting in cultural traditions which find their expression in societal organisation. Rather, as Kausikan argues, the debate is properly about which values Asia sees fit to adopt, given the goals of good governance.[46] Thus, the 'erudite games' involved in demonstrating links between modes of political practice and a Confucian cultural tradition are of little relevance: 'Most Asian societies have such long histories and rich cultures that it is possible to "prove" nearly anything about them if the context of the recovered references is ignored'.[47] Instead of playing such games, Kausikan advocates thinking about which values can sustain the development which Singapore has experienced, in such a way that it does not fall into the 'pitfalls and dead ends' which have confronted developed Western societies. It is because the overemphasis placed on liberal values and individual rights has failed in the West that they are not appropriate as adoptive values for nations such as Singapore. 'A small library' of critiques of this nature from within the West exists, which leads Kausikan to say: 'Whatever the debate over "Asian values" may be, then, it is not a clash of civilisations ... The real debate is not about values of any particular geographic area, but values per se.'[48] The argument, according to this defence of Singapore, is that the values chosen by the government and agreed to by the people through popular election are values which lead to a healthy and prosperous society.

This defence of Singapore is one that cuts away much of the rhetoric of culture which has been in the main the substance of the Asian values debate, as a fair survey of the literature demonstrates. Culture moves from being determinative of social institutions to being the result of consciously chosen social arrangements. It is at this point that the debate begins to be useful and the genuine issues are identified.

Critical evaluation of the Asian values discourse

As we have seen, Malaysia, Indonesia and Singapore have presented a range of arguments which have in common the rhetorical term 'Asian values'. These arguments can be divided into three broad arenas of debate: culture, economics, and the role of the state.

First, and most significantly, is the claim shared by all three states with varying degrees of rhetorical brinkmanship: that Asia has, or specific regions within Asia have, distinctive cultural traditions which are different from, perhaps even opposed to, those of the West. These traditions legitimate a soft-authoritarian style of leadership in which the individual is subservient to the good of the community, and the good of the community is determined through various mechanisms of consensus by the elders (in practice, almost invariably men) of society. It is claimed that these cultural traditions have been authentically maintained and have thus not fallen into the decadence and moral bankruptcy exhibited in the West. In addition, it is argued that the nations of Asia have the right to choose to maintain the cultural values they see fit, in the process preserving and building on their cultural heritage.

The second form of argument is based on a model for the achievement of human rights which is sequential. It is argued that the civil and political classes of human rights – and thus full democracy – are dependent for their realisation upon a degree of economic development. Thus, economic and cultural rights are prioritised over civil and political rights. Western countries are exhorted to provide aid for development

and to be patient because, as their own history allegedly attests, industri-
alisation and economic development precede the full realisation of
democracy. Similarly, it is argued that strong and paternalistic government is needed to provide the right environment for economic development, to ensure law and order and to make the economy attractive to
investors and developers.

Finally, arguments are made on the basis of the role of the state in society. A soft-authoritarian mode of government is defended not just on the
economic grounds expressed in the previous point, but also on the
grounds that without such authoritarianism the internal centrifugal
forces of religion, race, ethnicity and economic disparity, if not controlled, would tear the countries apart. National integrity, which is after
all in the interests of all citizens, compels governments to use authoritative means to preserve unity. It is argued, further, according to the principles of the international system as exported by the West, that states are
sovereign and have rights of self-determination and non-intervention
with respect to their internal affairs. Western states assume these rights
for themselves and only disallow them to non-Western states because the
latter are still viewed as subservient, in practice, if not in the rhetoric of
international politics. The West should be consistent and respect the
integrity and competence of Asia's states.

These, then, are the principal arguments that are used in the various
Asian values discourses. In each of these primary areas – culture, economic development and the role of the state – the state elites have used
the argument as a means of justifying the status quo, particularly of
power relations.

Arguments from culture

The use of culture by the political elites of Southeast Asia to legitimise
the public values that are enshrined in their policies and practices is
endemic. This use of culture has come under severe criticism by outside
observers and internal dissidents, particularly in those contexts where
culture is used to provide sets of Asian values which then act as qualifications on notions of human rights and democracy. I contend that it is not
legitimate for regimes to use (allegedly communitarian) culture as a
basis for questioning the (allegedly individualistic) values associated with
human rights and democracy.

Culture is an unfortunately broad term with which to work, and it is
partly this broadness which gives rise to the critiques presented below.
Culture can be used to denote particular practices, such as the way in
which the Chinese serve green tea, or 'the' Great Australian Barbecue.
At the other extreme it is used as a broad-brush term to refer to long-

standing religious or philosophical traditions, Islam or Confucianism, for example. That culture is such an amorphous term is to the advantage of those who would use it to further a particular socio-political agenda. Culture involves a feeling of belonging, of being distinct, although not necessarily exclusive, as a consequence of being a practitioner of the shared forms of being which make up a culture.[49] The idea of culture is both useful and dangerous for state elites because one of the ways in which people feel included or that they 'belong' is by identification with a particular culture. Authority figures can persuade, direct and manipulate individuals, and in the aggregate, groups, into obedience to a certain social agenda – in the name of culture. Thus, culture may be subsumed by the state, with the concept of 'national identity' being used to regulate cultural difference.[50] Culture, *when used to this end*, becomes more than a set of practices which are the outworking of a worldview, participation in which develops a sense of belonging and identity. Culture becomes, in addition, a form of ideology, a means of exerting power.[51]

Various questions need to be answered when the term 'culture' starts being used as a justification for the policies and practices of states and their governing elites: 'To what extent is culture seized "from above" by state elites? Is it deployed as an instrument of social and political control? Is the idea of culture used to empower, legitimate and authorise some at the expense of others?'[52] Many pronounce a resounding yes, for the state elites in the region have argued that to question the veracity of Asian values is to question existing political structures (which, incidentally, they control). For governments, the mechanism of posturing as guardians of a cultural heritage turns any critique of the government into an assault on the collective culture, silencing internal and external criticism and creating anti-Western sentiment.[53]

Culture, like the concept of history, has been the subject of a certain presumption of universalisation.[54] Consequently, a certain epistemology and content are made normative and essential. Given this assumed base, the spokespeople of the culture in question are then represented as pure channels for the universal articulation of what it means to belong to that particular cultural entity. The role of the spokespersons in this process is crucial, for it is they who make pronouncements regarding identity and destiny – those troublesome issues of who we are and where we are going. Thus, the issue of cultural authenticity becomes profoundly political. This is particularly so given the socially constructed nature of cultures. Cultures are not there – pre-existent – to be represented; rather, it is by representing ourselves and others that cultures are created and constructed. A culture may well provide a constraint as to who is permitted to represent it; for example, traditional religious norms in many religions stipulate that women are not permitted to teach. But the reflexive argument is that these norms were created because men did not want to lose their position and interpreted the religious culture in such a way that maintained their position of privilege. The suspicion that this operates in the Asian values case is reinforced by the 'smorgasbord' or 'pick and choose' approach to identifying the features of a culture. That Asian values are only ever those values which are positive and produce a 'warm inner glow', and that Western values bespeak a society in terminal decline, induces a suspicion of 'interest' on the part of the cultural interpreters.[55]

We must therefore ask who it is that claims the authority to interpret cultural frameworks. The answer here is immediate: as we have seen, the state elites have claimed this authority. In what follows, the legitimacy of this claim will be examined and denied: the claim that the content of Asian values, as articulated by the state elites of Malaysia, Indonesia and Singapore, represents the cultures of the people living within these states is false.

What is Asian? What is Asia?

A first way in which this may be demonstrated is to critique the use of the term 'Asian values' as a representation of a set of cultural and moral norms. The region of 'Asia' grew from what was initially called the Near East or Asia Minor to what we now think of when someone refers to Asia: a vast portion of the map from forty or even fifty degrees north longitude to ten degrees south, stretching from the Indian Ocean through to the Pacific. It is often commented that it is from Asia that all of the great world religions have developed. This in itself, aside from all other factors, points to tremendous diversity.

The irony is that it is not, in this instance, the people on the European side of the Bosporus who are making these heroic generalisations, but Asian political leaders themselves. Geo-cultural models of what it means to be Asian, as opposed to Western, have been rhetorically established by leaders from Malaysia, Indonesia and Singapore, and others besides. The discourse thus established is a curiously inverted form of the Orientalism outlined by Edward Said; this inverted form of Orientalism has been termed 'Occidentalism' by international relations scholars.[56] Cultural criteria are seized upon from above by state elites, 'packaged in an homogenised, unitary and ultimately essentialised form',[57] and used as a means for differentiating the policies and practices of these elites in contrast to those of Western democracies. The purveyors of the package deal of Asian values all too often reduce culture to the state, and then proceed to use this 'culture' or set of values as a device for delegitimising internal or indigenous critics of the regimes in question, aided by the use of draconian legislation such as the Internal Security Acts of Malaysia and Singapore. That the state elites have to *impose* their interpretation of Asian culture on their populations, through means moving incrementally from speeches to ISA laws, ironically suggests that the cultural construct they are using is not at all universal or representative of a homogenous culture. David Birch says:

> This is the point, there is not a cultural, political or economic homogeneity in those various countries seeking to put an 'Asian values' issue on the agenda … We are dealing with societies, like Indonesia, Malaysia and Singapore, which are themselves multicultural and multi-ethnic, with the development of national ideologies like *Pancasila, Rukun Negara* and shared values, put into place in order to build a single, unified, nation.[58]

These national ideologies are claimed to be the Asian values which stand out as the unifying feature across the heterogeneity of Asia. This claim rests on the common rejection, demonstrated earlier in this chapter, of the West's autonomous freedom which is found in these ideologies and, allegedly, the broader cultures from which they draw, along with the common emphasis on community and consensus. It is ironic, therefore, that the official attempt to articulate Asian values sees them defined as a reaction to the West, a cultural *via negativa*, rather than a positive affirmation. Ironic, because the region is made up of political systems that are adaptations of communist and liberal democratic systems.[59] Asian values then appear as a reactionary move against subversive notions of freedom and emancipation, co-opting Asian traditions of authority as legitimating principles.

However, when we move back from the political debate and examine the Western and Asian traditions, we find classical thinkers in both who take authoritarian positions. Plato or St Augustine may be viewed in this manner equally with Confucius. The real question is whether perspectives of freedom and tolerance are *absent* in the Asian tradition.[60] The notion that freedom is only Western develops out of a twofold ahistorical approach dependent on, first, reifying the current dominant experience in Western democracies back into the past, and, second, assuming that the (apparent) absence of a Western-type liberal tradition in the East justifies authoritarianism. It ignores the key historical experiences of the West which have been both evolutionary and revolutionary in the development of democratic forms out of autocratic ones. It also denies the potential of traditional resources of Asian thought and present-day dissent in Asian society as a foundation for increased freedom and democracy.

While not all cultures and traditions can be thought to accommodate, pre-empt or otherwise be analogous to Western liberalism, it is nonetheless the case that these cultures and traditions do provide resources which can be used to legitimate the sorts of protections we call freedoms, liberties and human rights. What is needed is for those who are versed in our traditions and cultures to 'spell out' the contributions that they make to freedom, liberty and rights, 'starting from intrinsic themes and tendencies'.[61] While many would dispute the claim made by the state elites of Indonesia, Malaysia and Singapore to be the guardians of culture and tradition in those countries, they nonetheless do make the claim and, as we have seen, do 'spell out' their understandings of these cultures and traditions. If, as I have suggested, this claim is false, what does it represent?

Asian values as imposed neo-conservative state ideology

An alternative account of the Asian values discourse may be elucidated, one which holds that state elites are not representing 'an' Asian culture, or even various Asian cultures, but that they are using culture and values as 'noble lies', as means to justify state ideologies, in turn used to secure their own political position and longevity. On this account, the Asian values discourse of the state elites is not an Asian alternative to Western liberalism. Rather, it is an alternative in Asia to liberal government.[62]

This account offers a powerful critique of the definition and institutionalisation of culture presided over by state elites. The key point is the political nature of this process.[63] Pacific Asia's regimes are characterised by a fusion of state, party and bureaucratic authority. In Malaysia there is the United Malays National Organisation, in Singapore the People's Action Party and in Indonesia (till 1998) the added dimension of the Army joined in the fusion of these three elements presided over by Suharto and his Golkar party. It is because of these fusions that government elites assume the commonality of state and community. This conflation is highly destructive of the community. The community is based on norms which emerge through consensus, mediation and persuasion. The state, however, is an imposition on the community, which is why it needs to be humanised by procedures such as democracy and norms such as human rights. However, this has happened very little in Asia. Instead, governments have squeezed out the activities of non-government groups of all kinds (social, political, religious), in the name of community.[64] By conflating community and state and by using force, such as the military or political manipulation, state elites have retained their positions.[65] Equally clearly, their continued dominance has not been accepted in any universal sense by the people they govern. The regimes may perceive their mode of ascendancy as an 'Asian value', but it is far from the case that this is uncritically granted them by all the people under their jurisdiction, many of whom have utilised every avenue available to increase debate and contestation of the regime.

At this point in the analysis we can observe two streams of thought coming together to form the ideology of Asian values: a strong anti-Western sentiment on the one hand, and on the other the political praxis of organic statism. The former serves as a motivating force, akin to nationalism. The latter provides the alternative paradigm for identity. It is ironic that the sources for both these streams of thought have either direct analogues or their intellectual origins in the West. This genealogy of Asian values contributes to the invalidation of the claim that the doctrine is based on particularistic or exceptionalist Asian cultures which are differentiated from those of the West.

The case of Indonesia serves here as an example of how European theories of organic statism were internalised into the state elite's psyche, to be used later as resource material for the construction of an Asian cultural type, distinct from that of the West.[66] David Bourchier refers to this exceptionalist self-understanding by Indonesians as 'conservative indigenism'. His argument, in short, is that while in Indonesia this conservative indigenism has seen various reincarnations – as 'Guided democracy', *gotong royong, kekeluargaan* (familialism), *Pancasila, paham integralistik* (integralism), *negara kesatuan* (unitary state) or *negara kekeluargaan* (family state), *ketimuran* (Eastern-ness), and so on – despite these attempts to reinvent conservative indigenism as something essentially Indonesian, the whole scenario is nothing more than 'political thinking which has been deployed by specific groups at specific times to achieve specific political ends. It is a variety of conservatism which resembles, and is indeed indebted to, anti-enlightenment organicist political philosophies of 19th and early 20th century Europe and Japan.'[67] As such, it has been crucial to the process of delegitimising any form of political organisation outside that permitted by the state.

This cultural essentialist model has been replicated by Malaysia[68] and Singapore.[69] The *Pancasila* incarnation of Indonesian conservative indigenism proved an 'attractive model' for those regimes presiding over Malaysia and Singapore: 'The Malaysian government placed renewed emphasis on its *Rukunegara* "Articles of Faith of the State" (first proclaimed in 1970) emphasising consensus between all sections of society'. In Singapore a national ideology committee appointed by the government in 1988 developed the doctrine of 'Shared Values' which emphasised 'placing society above the self, upholding the family as the basic building block of society, resolving major issues through consensus instead of contentions, and stressing racial and religious tolerance and harmony'.[70]

This intellectual history gives an interesting twist to John Steadman's 1969 comment that 'the most obvious signs of unity in Asia are, paradoxically, those of Western influence'.[71] The region has adopted a Western form of government – the state – and precisely because the region is strongly influenced by Western liberal democratic and communist ideas it is very difficult to maintain the essential Asian-ness of government in Asia.[72] Malaysia and Singapore, for example, were not constructed according to a model of Asian values but were legatees of the British colonial state. In these nations, so-called 'Asian Authoritarianism' is nothing more than the outworking of the difficult project of building a nation and a national identity.[73] Thus, European political models for nation building are the real antecedent for the current debate. The twist continues when one moves from examining the origins of the notions of consensus and organic society to the anti-Western liberalism sentiment. It is this critique of liberalism which forms the basis for much of the Asian values rhetoric; it is because Asia disagrees with the values of liberalism that it is said to be different from the 'West' and so essentially Asian. The difficulty here is that the so-called Asian values critique of Western individualism is entrenched within the tradition of Western conservatism and, in more extreme forms, in the tradition of anti-Enlightenment thought.

This point can be elaborated by demonstrating the links between the anti-liberal critique of the Asian values spokespeople and the thought of Western conservatives and neo-conservatives in the present. These have been attracted to the focus on strong states, authority, social order, social discipline, the family and moral values provided by the purveyors of Asian values.[74] Richard Robison argues that there is a confluence of opinion between the views of Lee Kuan Yew and other Asian values spokespeople and those of Ronald Reagan and Margaret Thatcher and the socio-economic movement they embody, an amalgam of social conservatism with economic neo-liberalism. The neo-liberals of this amalgam hold that democracy, or, at least, excessive democracy, is an impediment to the development of free markets and the growth of economies. On the other hand, the role of the paternalistic government in ensuring law and order provides the security for investment and development which economic growth needs. While it would be incorrect to hold that there is no difference between those representing this 'new amalgam' and the proponents of Asian values, it is nonetheless the case that both hold that economic growth can be impeded by democracy, that social life should be guided by strong moral values and that a strong state is needed to preserve law and order.[75] Gary Rodan argues:

At their core, these challenges and debates centre around the fundamental and unresolved disputes over the relative rights and responsibilities of individuals and the state: precisely the same set of questions underlying the political and ideological contestation in Asia today and embodied in the content of 'Asian values'. It is the linking up of ideological forces across 'East' and 'West' in the prosecution of positions taken in these fundamental disputes, not a clash of cultures, which is unfolding.[76]

Although it cannot be claimed that there is an identical agenda being driven by the promoters of Asian values within Southeast Asia, and conservatives in the West, it is clear that there is a substantial convergence of ideas about the socio-political nature of human beings and society as an aggregate. Both see human nature as something which has a tendency to disorder and therefore needs clear social and political structures to prevent harm being done to others. Both champion order above autonomous freedom; family or traditional values are emphasised over and above individual freedom to choose one's 'values'.

The doctrine of Asian values therefore operates as a political myth which, inasmuch as it receives popular support, legitimises the polity-creation agendas of the governing elites. These agendas cannot be said to genuinely represent Asian cultures, traditional philosophies or religious values – although aspects of these have been purloined in an ad hoc fashion in order to produce a semblance of authenticity for those who are not motivated to look below the surface. As Yash Ghai says, 'The notion that distinct Western and Asian perspectives exist is inaccurate, ahistorical, and leads to unfruitful polarities. Equally it distorts the debate by suggesting that the key conflict is between the East and the West, rather than that it is within each.'[77] For example, little attention is paid to that strand of thought called democratic socialism which would appear to combine the elements of community which Asian leaders emphasise with those of individual freedom which Asian leaders argue have gone to seed in the West. Edward Friedman argues that 'the "other" of the "fascist" mind is the open, liberal and human rights oriented democrat, imagined by proto-fascist Europe as Asia, by proto-fascist Asia as Europe. An imaginatively divided geography hides a shared political problematique.'[78]

Thus, we can say that to the extent that regional governing elites identify a coherent communal culture which is then opposed to that of the West, and inasmuch as this culture purports to represent Asia – indeed, an Asia culturally superior to its opponents – the governing elites betray their real agenda: the ideological manipulation of populations so as to maintain the political and social status quo. The argument that governments are acting to preserve historic cultures and by so doing are acting in the best interests of their people is shown to be little more than an ideological smokescreen.

Arguments from economic development

There are two main elements involved in the economic arguments used by Asian state elites to justify their modes of governance. Both of these elements interact with the above cultural arguments for Asian values, and provide, so it is alleged, further grounds for an alternative, Asian,

interpretation and praxis of democracy and human rights. First, governments appeal to the long distance that lies between the West and Asia in
the process of economic development and modernisation. Democracy,
and the human rights which support it, they claim, are not natural rights
as such but depend on contingent variables which are specific to any
given country: history, culture, economics. It is because of the distance
between the conditions of Asia and the West, it is argued, that Asia is not
able to provide democracy and human rights to the West's standards.
The implementation of democracy and human rights requires economic
development; as Asia does not have this to the degree that the West does
(and, some add, at least partly because of the West's continued economic
imperialism), the West should be patient with Asia and help in providing
economic development so that the distance can be covered more quickly
and, as a consequence, rights bestowed more readily. The West should
remember that its democracy took a long time to develop, and so be both
patient with Asia and willing to help. Second, it is argued that for this economic development to take place, strong paternalistic government is
needed. Economic development needs investment, which only comes in
an environment of law and order. This can only be guaranteed by forms
of government which the Western human rights 'complex' insists on
referring to by the disparaging and derogatory term 'soft authoritarian'.

There is in the argument from economic development an implied
sequential opposition between political and civil rights such as free
speech, and the whole class of socio-economic rights. The former class is
thought to be less important than the latter, and, further, civil and political rights are thought to be a hindrance to economic development.[79] It
is ironic that such an opposition should be appealed to by the elites of
Asian countries, because one of their most commonly used arguments,
particularly when they are advocating economic and cultural rights, is
that rights come as a whole: they are indivisible, and so the West should
equally support economic, social and cultural rights as well as civil and
political rights. They are seen to champion the doctrine of the indivisi-
bility of rights when it appears useful as a tool to achieve recognition of
economic and cultural rights, but then clearly disown it in practice by the
unnecessary abrogation of other rights when it threatens their political
and social status quo.

These classes of rights, however, are not exclusive but complementary,
and they work together symbiotically. Governments may implement policies which are intended to provide economic rights but which, for example, end up widening the rich–poor divide. In such instances, political
and civil rights are needed so that citizens can report back and argue for
change. If free speech does not exist, the only report-back facility is that
appointed by government. In this manner, economic and cultural rights

are threatened by the non-existence of political and civil rights.[80] There is a severe flaw in the suggestion that governments will be able to address the development issues associated with poverty and institute and maintain other economic rights, without free speech. For these goals to be achieved there needs to be a free flow of information and public participation in the processes of decision making. Another flaw which vitiates the argument from economic development is the notion that one's capacity to utilise basic civil rights is dependent on education and economic status. The implication of such an assertion is that illiterate farmers (for example) are not able to have an opinion on those aspects of government action which impinge upon their lives.[81] Of course, they can and do. Kenneth Christie comments:

> Allowing fair, constructive political debate of major policy issues, protecting citizens from torture by state authorities and from imprisonment without fair trial, and permitting freedom of worship are not incompatible with economic development. Indeed, preservation of these rights is likely to increase a government's legitimacy and encourage hard work and sacrifice for national goals. In this light, Western-style human rights are seen as a benefit, even a necessity, for the poor, not a luxury of the rich.[82]

An additional problem with the argument that eventually economic development will arrive at a sufficiently advanced state to justify political liberalisation is that there is no overtly stated or theoretically recognised threshold level. How developed is developed enough? In this regard there are differences in the way the economic and cultural arguments are applied and stressed. Indonesia, a large country with, in 2000, up to one-half of its population living below the poverty line, is clearly not in the same category as Singapore, one of the world's most prosperous states. At this point Singapore's representatives revert back to the cultural arguments examined and critiqued above, arguing that their culture is such that they are predisposed to a more authoritarian political culture. This reversion to the cultural argument is the only avenue open to them at this juncture because, according to the economic argument, Singapore should be one of the most politically liberalised states in international society.[83] By contrast, and demonstrating that a liking of authoritarian government is far from essentially Asian, in Hong Kong vehement opposition can be expected in response to any suggestion that a patronising and paternalistic state which provides a high standard of living is sufficient without democracy.[84]

The second part of the argument from economic development maintains that the region's economic growth was dependent upon the authoritarianism which enabled governments to make propitious decisions; in other words, the suppression of opposition was deemed essential for economic progress.[85] However, while authoritarian means may be sufficient to the task of producing a growth-oriented economic climate, they can hardly be said to be necessary: there is no conclusively established link between authoritarian government and development. Many authoritarian regimes have failed to achieve economic development and social stability. The co-occurrence of political repression and economic success in some cases does not establish a necessary relationship between the two; nor should it constitute a model for others.[86]

Empirical counter-examples to the economic development claim are numerous: Marcos' rule over the Philippines, the State Law and Order Restoration Council's repressive regime in Burma, and the former Soviet Union, to name the most well known. As the *Economist* has somewhat facetiously noted, 'If dictators made countries rich, Africa would be an economic colossus'.[87] While such rhetorical manoeuvres may be discounted as 'straw men', more scholarly arguments pertain. Amartya Sen's research demonstrates that there has never been a substantial famine in a country that is democratic and has a 'relatively' free press. This is because the civil and political rights of a democratic system enable citizens – lay and specialist alike – to publicise social, economic and environmental problems and precipitate political response and intervention. The denial of such civil and political rights is then at great cost and can only result in 'a deeply unbalanced set of ground rules'.[88] An example here is Malaysia's suppression of political discussion of logging in Borneo's state of Sarawak, with the detention without trial of indigenous residents in order to prevent them speaking out. This is the dark side of Malaysia's 'consensus seeking' style of government.[89]

The argument that authoritarianism is necessary is problematically reductionist. It suggests that with sufficient social and economic control the government can turn poverty into prosperity and, moreover, that this is sufficient justification for any method that might be thought to induce such prosperity. There may, however, be other factors, besides authoritarianism, which explain why it is that the Asian tigers and similarly fast-growing regional economies attained the growth rates and developmental successes they did. This is indicated by the Asian financial crisis which began to unfold in mid-1997. In the region, economic development and growth has slowed, stopped, and for some countries, notably Indonesia, regressed rapidly. These changes were not precipitated by political liberalisation or any other change in socio-political and economic management by the nations in question. While the real causes of the economic crisis are immensely complex and perhaps unknown, it is quite clear that authoritarianism has not saved the day and may, in fact, have been one of the spoilers. The more cogent argument is that the growth exhibited by Asian countries owes its provenance to the conditions of the post-war modern world. This, rather than any supposed Asian-ness, is more credible as the decisive factor in Asia's sometime economic success.[90]

The conclusion to be drawn, then, is that the alleged need for strong government in order to advance economic development, which in turn encourages the observance of human rights and democracy, has in many cases acted as a pretext for the continued abuse of power by authorities in the attempt to maintain the political status quo. Indeed, the discussion, in this light, has proceeded on the basis that there is in fact a move towards the protection of human rights and the establishment of democracy which emerges out of economic growth and development.

However, Sidney Jones is sceptical of this view. It is, she says, a 'muddleheaded argument' and she proceeds to offer a critique, the main points of which I shall echo here.[91] The key variable in the economic growth argument is the middle class. It is thought that a middle class in possession of the economic means to become involved in society in ways other than those of subsistence level (such as education or business activities) will lead to increased involvement in existing political systems, which will then evolve in order to cope with the new demands. By this means the process of democratisation will take care of itself, and human rights will similarly be paid increasing respect.

However, democratisation does not equate directly with the observance of human rights. Historically, democracy has been used in the abuse of rights. It is because we expect democracy to be in the service of human rights that we think it a good thing; this cannot always be guaranteed to be the case. Second, Jones argues that 'the growth-equals-democracy argument is the classic "modernisation" theory of the late 1950s',[92] and as such has come in for a series of critiques, the upshot of which for our purposes is that, *contra* the accepted wisdom that economic growth leads to freedom, there is in fact a clear relationship between economic expansion and the growth of authoritarianism.[93] Singapore is the classic example: economic growth and modernisation have not led to increases in democracy or human rights. It is ironic, then, that Singapore, a country now richer than most Western liberal democracies, appeals to this argument to justify the need for the continued inhibition of democracy and human rights. Jones argues the case similarly for Indonesia and Malaysia. In Indonesia (particularly prior to the revolution in 1998), those benefiting from economic wealth are either directly linked to the familial system and to the administration, or they are, as with the Chinese, an ethnic minority suffering social alienation; neither group would benefit from democracy. Indonesia's Chinese, in particular, find themselves disqualified from political leadership because of ethnic discrimination. Otherwise, due to comprising a large portion of Indonesia's growing middle class, they might have been able to initiate reform.

Others in the middle class are either partners of the Chinese or are in some way linked to the patronage network.[94] Thus, in Indonesia, social limitations act as a strong qualifier for the 'economic development leads to democracy' argument.

In addition, recent research shows that the Jakarta middle class is reluctant to act as an agent for reform, to the extent that it sees a link between democratic reform and instability, uncertainty and upheaval. The middle class appears to view democracy as a good thing but, because it implies unrest, is inclined to hold that Indonesia is not ready for democracy now (by contrast to the students, who have been a catalyst for much of the change seen in the last two years). In this sense, the economic advancement of the middle class fosters a desire for an environment of order and security for the maintenance of economic well-being, rather than a striving for democracy.[95] The scenario is arguably the same for Singapore: middle-class people are sometimes irritated and even angered by the political elite's methods, but their material interests and social position are maintained by the regime's elitist policies.[96] In Malaysia, social changes have come as a direct result of government intervention, particularly after the race riots of 1969. However, these interventions strengthened the state rather than the polity. The new middle class does not generally function as a check on state power; indeed, it is often concerned to protect the status quo against the social changes stemming from government direction, the global economy and domestic proponents of democratisation.[97]

While Jones is prepared to concede that there is an 'uneven' relationship between economic development in Asia and the protection of economic, social and cultural rights, she argues that the relationship between growth and the improvement of political and civil rights is not very apparent.[98] In the cases where there have been changes in the treatment of people, positive changes in line with human rights standards, the evidence points to international political pressure, not internal economic growth.

In addition, she contends that the human rights concerns linked with specific political difficulties are rarely improved by economic growth. Here may be cited the issue of religious and ethnic discrimination in Malaysia, for example. The ethnically Malay Muslim half of the population is the clear beneficiary of much legislation pertaining to a range of activities, from the economic to overt religious preferences and family law.[99] Because of the legally and socially entrenched religious inequality between Muslim ethnic Malays and non-Muslims of other ethnicities, economic growth will not act as an equalising factor: that depends on overt political action. The situation is similar in Indonesia, where government regulations make interfaith marriages 'virtually impossible'.[100]

Jones' final two cases involve refugee flows and torture. With respect to the former, while economic growth may benefit the nationals of a country, it may have no effect whatsoever on the way in which refugees, migrant workers or foreigners are treated. Once again, this is a socio-political problem, not an economic one. Similarly, while those advocating soft authoritarianism as a means of ensuring rapid economic development do not advocate torture, it is nonetheless the case that, for example, in Indonesia, the routine use of torture by government officials as a way of extracting confessions and inflicting punishment did not change with the rising income levels of police. The only way in which changes will occur in relation to these issues is through systematic attempts at changing the mind-set of those who work in the police, and through public debate and exposure.[101]

We can conclude that in fact there is no *direct* correlation between economic development and the adoption of human rights and democracy. While it cannot be denied that soft-authoritarian modes of governance may aid governments in the advancement of economic development, it is clear that there is no necessary link between this advancement and the protection of human rights or the institution of democracy. Therefore, this avenue of argument must be seen for what it is: an attempt to retain unmediated control over economic development and the preservation of the political status quo.

Arguments from the role of the state

It is ironic, in a debate which revolves around ideas of cultural particularity and appeals to authentic traditions, and in which these ideas are used to erect a demarcation between that which is Asian and that which is Western, that one of the most effective tools used by the self-styled Asian cultural particularists and traditionalists is an undeniably Western invention: the nation-state. The twentieth century saw the map change, such that the international society of Europe with its imperial dominions has become a global if 'patchy' international society, wherein the rules and norms attendant upon the nation-state have been recognised across the board, even when flouted. Since the Second World War the non-West has had at its disposal the equipment of state-craft as a further means of protecting itself from or vindicating itself against the West. Foremost among this equipment is the notion of sovereignty, which has been the driving force behind traditional understandings of the state, of territoriality, of non-intervention, and of the mechanics of international law.

In line with this, the interpretation of human rights offered by the Asian governments is more concerned with the 'national interest' than with the welfare of the people. The protection of human rights is the preserve of the national government and state infrastructure. According to the Bangkok Declaration, 'states have the primary responsibility for the promotion and protection of human rights through appropriate infrastructure and mechanisms and also recognise that remedies must be sought and provided primarily through such mechanisms and procedures' (paragraph 5). The Bangkok Declaration omits any significantly detailed reference to civil or political rights and instead highlights state sovereignty, territorial integrity and non-interference in internal matters. By so doing it hopes to shield itself from the scrutiny of the international community. Thus, the Asian values discourse 'sanctifies sovereignty as an omnipotent talisman for silencing annoying human rights demands'.[102]

The states in the region represented by ASEAN (Association of South East Asian Nations) have secured their co-operation by turning a sovereignly blind eye on human rights matters internal to member nations which, in the West, have been denounced repeatedly. The trust and confidence of these relationships are thought too precious to jeopardise by issuing criticisms.[103] It is also because of the shared conviction that a certain amount of authoritarianism is needed for the nation-building process in radically divided societies with little internal social capital. Thus, in addition to the form of argument examined above which argues that an authoritarian approach is needed to ensure economic development, a parallel argument is put forward based on the need to promote national stability. Centrifugal forces exist, it is argued, which if given free rein might tear nations apart. Classic cases are Indonesia in 1965, Singapore in the late 1960s and Malaysia after the 1969 riots. It is not clear, however, that such emergency situations provide any justification for the ongoing suppression of civil society, nor that central authoritarian force is capable of securing the national stability appealed to in the argument.

By contrast, democratic and civil society political theorists argue that more important for a strong state is the relationship between society and the state. The ASEAN states may have a form of inter-state relational capital between them because of common aims, but this is apt to crumble if there is no capital between the individual states and 'their' societies – the absence of which is the original justification for authoritarianism.[104] The absence of civil society within states may contribute to governments' inability to control their population in a time of crisis, and this in turn may strain relations within organisations such as ASEAN.

Regarding human rights, as was indicated by the Bangkok Declaration and from which position there has been no indication of change, the appeal to the statist argument is a primary line of defence. It is important to note, however, and especially in the context of internal strains, that the argument thus formulated is not merely a response to Western criticisms but as significantly is also a response to the criticisms of Asian people themselves. The contrast between the Bangkok Government Declaration and the Vienna Declaration is instructive. While the latter, inevitably, also affirms the efficacy of national institutions in areas such as grievance redressal, information dissemination and advisory roles, it is clear that these functions are only fulfilled in the intended manner when the pertinent national institutions are genuinely independent from centres of power. Again, the difficulty is that, while the state is the most powerful agent we have for the advancement of human rights causes, it is also the most able to check any such advancement by virtue of the same power. Hence the import of external parties and institutional practices which are international, in the protection of human rights: the hands of the state may not be clean hands.[105]

> The pervasive use of draconian legislation like administrative detention, disestablishment of societies, press censorship, sedition, etc. belies claims to respect alternative views, promote dialogue, and seek consensus. The contemporary state intolerance of opposition is inconsistent with traditional communal values and processes. I fear that the contemporary state processes in Asia are worse than the much-derided adversarial processes of the West, which at least ensure that all parties get a fair hearing.[106]

The use which Asian state elites make of the argument from sovereignty or statehood can be interpreted as little more than the selective appropriation of an aspect of Western-originating ideas of international organisation, for the benefit of the position of the state elite in question. It is dubious intellectual practice to accept the Western tradition of the state without also accepting the same tradition's restraints on the state – which include the doctrine of human rights. This is particularly the case when states are members of the United Nations. To join the United Nations is to voluntarily relinquish certain aspects of state sovereignty in the interests of international law and accountability. States often give the impression, however, that the United Nations should not conduct activities which are predicated upon this voluntary suspension of their sovereign rights.[107]

The intellectual and moral critiques become particularly clear when one acknowledges that within the development of Western ideas of international organisation, from which such sovereign rights emerge, there are various other doctrines, granted at least equal status to that of sovereignty, which together form a regulative whole. Sovereignty may be seen as the driving force behind many of the concepts which are used to demarcate responsibility for populations and territory. However, this doctrine is balanced by others which recognise the perversities that can ensue if sovereignty is left as *the* final principle. Thus, the doctrine of state sovereignty is balanced by principles of the rule of law, of international law, of humanitarian intervention, and of human rights.

In choosing only to embrace one aspect of the tradition and praxis of international society, Asian state elites lay themselves open to the charge of opportunism – on two levels. First, if, in principle, they wish to function as a society according to their authentic traditions of 'Asian-ness', it is at best hypocritical to selectively appropriate from another tradition, particularly without acknowledgement. Second, this appropriation is rendered absurd when it can be demonstrated that the manner and intent of the appropriation contradict the traditions from which and for the preservation of which it has been appropriated. Thus, an exclusive emphasis on state sovereignty is inimical to the ideas of freedom, justice and accountability which emerge from the Asian traditions of Confucianism, Islam, Christianity, and so forth.

Not Asian values but Asians' values

In some discussions of Asian values, particularly those carried on in the popular press and political forums, critiques such as the foregoing are used to suggest that the debate is nothing more than an attempt by certain political leaders to maintain their position and prestige by using a conservative ideology dressed up as an authentically Asian tradition of political governance. But the question is considerably more complex than that. If it were merely authoritarian governments versus the people, with the former advocating Asian values and the latter insisting on liberal values – democracy and human rights – the debate would be short. However, while most of those opposed to the governments will support ideas of democracy and human rights, what they mean by these terms can be strongly divergent. There are Asian intellectuals, activists and others who are influenced by what Onuma Yasuaki has recently called 'West-centric' human rights perspectives, perspectives which often overrule and marginalise local perspectives.[108] Such perspectives often come into conflict with perspectives indigenous to the region. Sen argues that, in many of the concrete debates in the region, the parties are Asians of different convictions.[109] Many of the discussants are not liberals in any straightforwardly Western sense of the term and yet forcefully condemn the authoritarian practices of their country's leaders.[110]

The positions taken by regional NGOs are an excellent example of this complexity. The authoritative statement of their views is articulated in the NGO statement on human rights given prior to the Vienna world conference on human rights in 1993. On the one hand, they express views on human rights which are at variance with those of the governments in Southeast Asia. They state that human rights are universal, that they are equally rooted in different cultures, condemning those who abuse universally accepted human rights on the basis of cultural practices. The

NGO declaration recommends that organisations engage in international co-operation and expressions of solidarity as ways of refuting the claim that 'Asian nationalism' has precedence over human rights considerations. On the other hand, there is common ground between NGOs and the governments in the region in that they see a clear correlation between the state of the international economy and development as an important contributing factor in the continuation of human rights abuses.[111]

Many regional NGOs operate within the UN human rights context, so that their pursuit of improved human rights conditions has as its basis the international legal instruments developed under the UN system. However, such NGOs will often find themselves working in local situations where human rights abuses are carried out and where the people have no conception of the United Nations beyond that of white trucks, certainly not to the extent of understanding international legal instrumentalities and the philosophy upon which they are based (liberalism). For them, the justification for the work of the NGO people may be understood in very different terms. Indeed, it would rarely be true to say that human rights activists represent the will of the people as a whole.[112] It is more likely, then, that success in the promotion of human rights will come by building on local cultural traditions, rather than by mounting confrontational challenges to them.[113] In short, rights stand little chance of enforcement if they are not congruent with the worldview of those for whom they are to regulate justice.[114]

Diversity of views among local human rights organisations may become more of a factor than is suggested by the documents produced by global gatherings. It is common to assume that all human rights organisations have similar definitions and goals and that they all have the same fundamental ethical commitments. This, however, is not the case. Daniel Lev says that, while one may want to affirm that the basic values held by NGOs are the same, this view is more tenuous than 'anyone devoted to human rights wants to contemplate'. He argues that human rights NGOs in the region are based on ideological and political agendas which go beyond the observation of human rights, and that this has implications for the extent to which basic notions about human rights are shared across the board.[115]

This ambivalence to set notions about universal human rights is echoed among intellectuals in the region, who, while supporting democracy and human rights, are less committed to the intellectual traditions from which these ideas are derived.[116] Many argue that these traditions are flawed in various respects, and from some Western points of view the positions held in the region are too close to relativism or fundamentalism to be satisfactory. Traditional Western conceptualisations of human rights have not always been the convictions that have provided regional intellectuals with the tenacity and endurance they display while suffering human rights abuse from their own governments.[117]

It becomes apparent that there are Asian values other than those proposed by state elites, but which are sometimes closer to what is said by those elites than by their Western opponents. How can this be explained? One of the problems with anti-Asian values arguments is that they do not take seriously that a significant proportion of the non-state elite professes to hold to these distinctive Asian values. The turn to Asian values taken by the new middle classes in Southeast Asia seems to some commentators to be of considerably more interest than the more predictable claims of the ruling elites.[118] Ideologies such as Singapore's Shared Values are clearly invented, but they undoubtedly find some cultural resonance within sectors of the society.[119] This is because the Shared Values ideology draws upon the 'traditions' of the three component ethnic populations in Singapore. This gives it more 'resonance' than a merely invented tradition could have – and in turn, because of this resonance, it cannot be argued that Shared Values is *merely* foisted upon the people. While this ideology has helped many Singaporeans to essentialise themselves as 'Asians', this is only because of a pre-existing openness based on the various cultural heritages of Singapore's people. This openness to conceptions of essentially Asian values also follows from the simple recognition that, on many of the issues discussed under the rubric of human rights, many strongly disagree with commonly held liberal–Western positions. Issues such as religious freedom, marriage, homosexuality, the death penalty, abortion, freedom of expression, and minority rights are treated differently at the everyday citizen's commonsense level in many Asian countries. Violations of human rights in these categories (as opposed to violations such as arbitrary detention or political suppression) may well flow from genuine ideological, cultural and religious differences that must be taken seriously.[120]

It is going too far to say that certain positions on these issues are intrinsically or essentially Asian (these positions are prominent within some Western traditions also). It is nonetheless accurate to observe that in Asia there are dominant views on some of these issues which are radically opposed to the dominant views in the West. There are also minority views in Asia which are in agreement with the dominant views in the West. It is not the case that these are somehow essentially Western or Asian, as is demonstrated by the historical fact that the views on many of these matters have changed in the West. This occurred as the West changed from being a conglomeration of perfectionist religious societies identified together as Christendom, to being a set of anti-perfectionist secular liberal societies.

Nonetheless, it is the case that large numbers of Asians who struggle under the various types of oppression that their political leaders call Asian values are not Western liberals and will, however contingently, support political moralities which are paternalist and perfectionist to an extent with which most liberal human rights advocates in the West would not be comfortable. It is in this sense that we might meaningfully talk about Asian values – as the values which are held by Asians and which, for various contingent reasons, are different from those held by some Westerners and, ipso facto, similar to those held by others.[121] The two mistakes that are made on this matter are that either there is something essentially paternalistic and perfectionist about Asian cultures, or that this is not the case and that both cultural traditions and the everyday views of ordinary Asians are essentially liberal.

Osman Bakar argues that, because the Asian values debate has focused so much on the political issues involved with authoritarianism masquerading as Asian values, there has been little discussion of the real Asian values – that is, the values which are held by Asian democrats who do not want to be identified as liberals.[122] This middle range is not the preserve of any one political morality but is filled with differing positions, contingent upon many factors: religion, education, political practice, economics, philosophical traditions, and so on. It is only in this contingent sense that we can talk about Asian values, and only then with the recognition that these values are not in any sense a whole or monolithic but cross the whole spectrum of political values and often confound traditional classifications. Thus it is that, while Asians are often critics of their government elites, they nonetheless want to retain the idea that they are different from the West. It is felt to be legitimate that in Asia there need not be exactly the same balance between the role of the individual and the role of the community as there is in other parts of the world, and it is also felt to be legitimate that this is explained at least in part on cultural and religious grounds. As Daniel Bell points out, 'many otherwise progressive liberal voices in the West still seem compelled by a tradition of universalist moral reasoning that proposes one final solution to the question of the ideal polity, yet paradoxically draws only on the moral aspirations and political practices found in Western societies'.[123] It is in opposition to this sort of position, and with the other qualifications brought in this section, that Asian values may legitimately be discussed.

Conclusion

Two main conclusions can be drawn. The first is that the Asian values discourse as presented by the state elites of Southeast Asia is demonstrably politically self-interested, fails to genuinely represent the cultural traditions that do exist within Asia and is debilitated by major theoretical flaws. The use of culture is concluded to be a political ideology which gains legitimacy through a superficial resonance with cultural traditions. The prioritised need for economic development and the suggestion that this legitimates authoritarian policies and practices are shown to be misleading, with such practices identified as at least potential hindrances rather than aids to economic development. An unbalanced and opportunistic interpretation of state sovereignty is behind the manipulation of the norms of the international system of states in favour of allowing states carte blanche on matters of internal administration, justice and legitimacy. The second conclusion is that the view of Asia sustained by Lee Kuan Yew, Mahathir Mohamad and Suharto, their colleagues and their successors, is not the only possible way of conceptualising Asia or the values held by people who live in and identify with the region.

In fact, 'Asian values' are extraordinarily diverse, ranging across the political spectrum and drawing on religion, tradition, politics and culture in ways that make a definitive articulation of what characterises Asia's values clearly impossible in any overarchingly representative sense. It is precisely this diversity which makes the undertaking of an assessment of Asian values a particularly daunting task. In the following chapter, therefore, the focus will narrow to test claims of Asian values against their representation within the human rights discourse, a discourse which has been one of the favourite targets of the state elites' rhetoric and one which allows a relatively controlled assessment of a certain range of values.

CHAPTER 2

The Real Asian Values Debate

The debate over Asian values is often waged within the context of arguments over democracy and human rights. But, rather than there being *a singular* set of Asian values which opposes the values of the West, there are many Asian views, some of which contradict one another. These various views also pose questions about how the concept of human rights should be understood. These are questions about the ontological, epistemological and substantive axiological nature of human rights. Focusing this chapter on human rights thus problematises the notion of human rights, as well as the notion of Asian values.

Much has been claimed about the notion of Asian values. It is a significant observation that the great majority of these claims, whether they are made by proponents or critics of the notion, are generalisations which purport to speak on behalf of others, often all others, in the region. Senior political leaders speak of Asian culture in a way which suggests that the people under their leadership all share alike in this culture. Critics of Asian values deride this totalising representation and suggest instead that human rights are universal, the same for Asians as for Westerners. Much of the literature implicitly argues along this dichotomy: that proponents of Asian values are using the idea for political purposes and that the idea is demonstrably wrong; furthermore, that human rights are the same for all of us, that beyond our apparent differences the same universal and fundamental values are affirmed.

In-depth recognition of the existence of other significant views within Southeast Asia is often absent. It is not the case that the political elites in Southeast Asia speak for all people. Nor is it the case that the views of Western critics of Asian values necessarily coincide with views held in the region. When one reads the work of Asian non-political elite actors who talk about human rights in Southeast Asia, one finds views that are not easily accommodated by the pronouncements of their political leaders, nor by those of their Western critics. Such commentaries are often overlooked in the debate on Asian values within academic disciplines. One reason for this may be that these disciplines do not always recognise as valid the starting assumptions of many of the voices in the region. The Western academy, for instance, is prepared to 'research' views from the region that have a religious approach to life, such as those of Islam. It is rare, even in avowedly multicultural settings, that the Western academy will sanction theory, analysis and normative judgements that are based on explicitly religious assumptions.[1] Similarly, some voices in the region are not heard because they do not speak the correct conceptual language, such as that of human rights. While the Western academy and international political figures may assume the existence of such rights and seek to address all people using rights-talk, the 'little people' in some places have not heard the phrase, and in other places cannot own it for themselves despite acquaintance. Failing to take these points into account renders the debate impoverished and unable to address the concerns of Asian people, who become mere pawns in a game of rhetorical brinkmanship.

The research undertaken for this chapter was motivated by such concerns. Focusing on the concept of human rights, it sought to provide an account of Asian values which goes beyond the dichotomy examined above. It does not claim to be particularly, let alone comprehensively, *representative* of 'Southeast Asia', but it does provide an opportunity for voices which have not yet been adequately represented to speak to the debate.[2]

There was a need to provide evidence to support the argument that there is a philosophical problem within the discourse of human rights. The problem is in the supposed *universality* of human rights. The key question is: Is there diversity between and within understandings of human rights and is this diversity merely conceptual, leaving us agreed on actual behavioural norms, or does it range from fundamental philosophical commitments through to behavioural norms? Clearly, if the latter is the case, then the idea of *universal* human rights is challenged by a number of critical questions on ontological, epistemological and substantive grounds (that is, are there human rights, how do we know, and which rights are they?). In using the Asian values debate as the catalyst for this argument, the key objective of the research was to establish whether there are 'Asian' interpretations of human rights which are different from those espoused in the West, and which cannot be dismissed in the way that is possible with those claims made by political elites. The argument here is that there are multiple religious, philosophical and cultural approaches to human rights that have genuine claims to difference; further, that these multiple accounts are not just different conceptual schemes with common behavioural consequences, but that the various traditions define 'the good' differently and thus lead to different standards of behaviour, some of which are common, some of which are incommensurable. These findings, that different metaphysics lead to different ethics, support the view that there needs to be a major reconceptualisation of the notion of human rights.

Asian values

The academic critique of Asian values is largely written by Westerners, writing in English and publishing in Western-based journals and publishing houses. When one goes to Asia and evaluates the local critique of Asian values, one finds that while it is superficially similar, many of the voices heard are also critical, either explicitly or implicitly, of the assumptions employed in the standard liberal critique.

Asian values is 'a bogus political stunt on the government's part', a 'political tool used by Mahathir as an end to his political ambitions'. It is an 'ideological tool riddled with double standards' and comprises nothing more than 'the intellectual fallout from the economic miracle'. There is 'no such thing' as Asian values; despite the Asian values rhetoric, 'all people have the same rights', because, 'basically, we are all human'.[3] These sorts of responses represent a very common initial reaction to questions about the rhetoric that comes from elite political actors in Southeast Asia around the notion of Asian values. It is obvious to many, be they academics or NGO workers or public intellectuals, that the claims being made are driven by political motives.

Out of fifty interviews conducted throughout Indonesia, Malaysia and Singapore, not one participant was prepared to defend the argument of the political elites at face value. The wider irony of this is also not lost on 'the people'. As one interviewee said, 'In Singapore, the people know the government is repressive', this being a normative judgement, not merely a descriptive one, which stands against claims of authentic Confucian governance.[4] In Indonesia, lawyers, NGO activists, academics and public intellectuals use appeals to the cultural, political and legal 'other' that the regime defines itself against in their own fight against injustice. That is, those resisting the regime do not shirk from using Western resources as they find them appropriate. Many are unabashed about the geographical origin of the ideas to which they appeal. One NGO leader and women's advocate asserted unapologetically that ideas of gender equity and reproductive rights *do* come from the West.[5] They find their legitimacy in that they are good for women. Their origin, for this organisation, is of no consequence – except at a practical level, because the government and religious establishment are not so sanguine regarding originating locales. A similar point was made by a female government think-tank academic, namely that 'ideas are not geographically located' and that Asian countries must be able to assimilate Western concepts. The ambiguity here is important: that ideas are not geographically located and yet that some ideas are identified geographically as 'Western'. This ambiguity pervades the discussion of the universality of certain concepts like human rights, concepts that have entered the political discourses in Asia through Western colonialism and globalisation. Nonetheless, the point being made is significant: there is strong resistance to the national or cultural essentialism that is so often used to justify particular discourses of governance.[6]

It is, then, the case that the Asian values talk of the political elite does not appear to buy much legitimacy among important types of people within the region that the same elites call 'Asian'. Intellectuals, religious leaders, NGO participants, even members of government think-tanks, explicitly carry no brief for the idea, as it is propounded by the political elites. Do all such agents then take the view of the Indonesian feminist cited earlier, who is unabashed in sourcing her ideas to the West? A positive answer would clearly debunk the notion of Asian values. As will be shown, however, the answer is no, they do not. There is a wide range of issues where there is marked difference between the views held by Asian social actors and those held by their counterparts in the West. There are also significant areas of agreement. Again, as a brief empirical survey will demonstrate, there is no single set of Asian values, just as there is no single set of Western values. In the sets of values held by social actors in Asia, there are, however, certain areas of overlap which are significantly different (and differently represented numerically) to those commonly found in the West. It is these which end up telling the diverse and fragmented story of Asian values.

Source and nature of human rights

'What are human rights and why do we have them?' This double question is crucial for understanding the issue of human rights in Southeast Asia, and the various answers to it, as shown below, will provide a partial answer to the question posed at the beginning of this chapter as to the extent, nature and implications of diversity between and within understandings of human rights. It is possible, and useful for analysis, to group the answers into four categories: religion, existentialism, human essentialism and legal obligation. The first of these was overwhelmingly significant in conversation with interviewees and is thus treated at length.

Religious foundations for rights

Positions which draw on some formulation of religion (principally Islam) for understanding the origin and nature of human rights are placed in this category. There are ambiguities, however, which complicate the attempt at analysis. On the one hand, there are those who affirm the necessity of a sovereign God to the notion of human rights. On the other hand, many of the same also recognise other religious and even non-religious traditions of human rights. The ambiguity lies in how God-centred and non-God-centred views should relate. Is it the case that religion provides *a* justification or *the* justification? Is the God thesis necessary or merely sufficient? When it is said that 'people feel that they have rights and look to religion to justify this', what is the causal sequence (is it Islam which gives people the initial suspicion that they have rights or is it something more fundamental than religion?)[7] and is Islam just one of a number of valid justifications? It is an ambiguity reflected in the relation between the consciously articulated answer to the question of 'why, fundamentally, do we have rights?', and the role that religion plays when specific rights are discussed. Does the recognition of other traditions of thought about human rights mean that they are merely recognised as existing, but are mistaken; or that they are recognised as valid paths to the same end; or, again, that they are different paths to different ends, but confusingly use the same terminology?

One way to find possible answers to these questions is to consider both the stated relationship of religion to the question of why we have rights and what they are, and then to consider what people say about specific rights. If the former allows for diversity but the latter does not, then despite the use of pluralistic or compromising language, these religious approaches to human rights are perfectionist. That is, they posit *one* correct way of both deriving rights and of giving them content, and that this remains the case despite high levels of tact and diplomacy in discussing dissenting positions. I will focus first of all on the derivation of rights, and then return to the substantive question.

In articulating the role of religion in understanding human rights the fundamental presupposition is the sovereignty of God. This is central to the religious explication of human rights. The actual existence of 'mankind', let alone human dignity and notions of moral behaviour, are totally dependent on God. Indeed, according to the leader of an Islamic think-tank, concepts of human dignity and prescriptive normative standards for behaviour are inseparably related to the concept of the afterlife. At issue here is the existence of something bigger than 'man' by which 'man' is judged. It is this 'something bigger' which gives identity, which constrains behaviour towards others, which grounds dignity. As expressed by a representative of ICMI (the Indonesian Muslim Intellectuals Association), human rights are given by God, not by any human institution. This ensures that such rights are inalienable, to use the language of the Universal Declaration on Human Rights. If human rights are merely contingent on human thought and institutions, what is to be appealed to in preventing the justification of atrocities? No, the sover-

eign God stands over and above humanity in a relationship of divine rev-
elation, by virtue of which we know how to live. So, again, people find in
religion the explanation of the rights that they feel they have, an explanation which is secure and serves as a platform for judging themselves,
others and society as a whole: 'religion is basic to human rights'.[8]

However, interviewees were often reluctant to suppose that human
rights values could only be posited by traditions such as Islam which
depend centrally on the notion of God for their epistemic, ontological
and substantive categories. On the other hand, however, 'without belief
in God it is very hard to give account of human dignity. Christianity and
Islam provide an excellent foundation for good behaviour to one
another.'[9] One line of argument states categorically that, for Islam,
human rights depend on a theological context but what matters is that
the right is there, not where it comes from. Muslims, therefore, may well
have a different historical route to the formulation of human rights
because of the history and development of their religion. Thus, it is
alleged, there is one understanding of human rights for all, despite our
disparate backgrounds. This position rapidly resorts to casuistry when
instances of different values are raised, such as those examined in the
next section. But it does indicate on one level a notional belief in human
rights that are accessible by and thus behind all religious or other moral
systems of thought. This legitimises a certain degree of pluralism for the
recognition of those human rights values. A slightly different approach
to the matter is to suggest that Islam developed the substantive content
of human rights first and more extensively, if in a different conceptual
language. Thus, according to one conservative Muslim think-tank leader,
'women schooled in Islamic thinking think that women in Islam have a
lot more rights under Islam than any other culture'.[10] *His* examples
include divorce laws and the ownership of property.

There is for some an awareness that the modern development and
usage of human rights language is a non-religious phenomenon which to
an extent is consonant with religion and can thus be used, and may serve
as a valuable esperanto in a globalising world, given certain modifications. So, it is suggested that human rights be talked about in the context
of duties, or even *as* duties.[11] There is less of a tendency to assert the universality of human rights and to then seek to demonstrate how the particular religious worldview is validated in its normative position by these
rights. Rather, there is a recognition that the religious worldview brings
modifications to universal human rights themes with their liberal roots.
Here there is less of a need to seek the comfort of universality in justifying beliefs, moral and religious; rather, these beliefs take precedence
over and modify any external-to-tradition universal schema. So, Western
ideas can be imported selectively and 'proof texted' by Islam,[12] explained

to people by using the language that they already have, such as conceptually theological tools like creation, man being God's vice-regent, and so forth.[13] Thus, 'the human rights issue is a matter of social packaging. The ideas from the West can always be repackaged in Islamic or other forms'[14] – this was expressed as a negative reflection on a deeply conservative religion's failure to engage with and be reflexive about modernisation and globalisation, including the spread of the human rights culture.

Several conclusions may be drawn from this survey of religious bases for human rights. First, there are views of the nature that religion is the only adequate way of providing a basis for human rights, and that attempts to do so without religion will end in failure. Second, there are views that religion is one way and the best way to understand human rights, but that there are other ways which do satisfactorily account for human rights. This view is deeply ambiguous in its pluralism, however, because it still only allows conceptual pluralism, how we derive human rights, not normative pluralism, the substantive content of rights. Third, there are views which accept the use of human rights talk but which see this as a second-order language. Their own religion provides them with a doctrine of human dignity; this can be accounted for in human rights talk, although for some the translation causes distortions in meaning.

Human rights existentialism and humanism

After religious reasoning, the way in which answers to the question of why we have human rights were presented depended heavily on what may be called a type of existentialism and closely related to this, a form of intuitive humanism.

Human rights existentialism, as I term it, is expressed by people who do not have a foundationally religious or other rationalist explanation but who, instead, ground their conviction about human rights in their daily experience (hence 'existentialism') of human rights abuses and related suffering, and in what we experience in our own selves when we observe such abuse and suffering. One of the more poignant examples comes from a women's organisation worker. Her testimony is that, out in the field, women do not know about human rights. They do know, however, that violence is wrong and that they don't want to be battered. This is not something that needs cognitive justification: *people just know* that being battered is bad for you and thus is wrong. Similarly, a human rights activist and academic points out, when asked about philosophical justifications of human rights, that while such questions are interesting his time is fully occupied trying to help those who suffer because of being silenced in various ways by the government. The government causes intellectual, psychological-emotional and physical distress, and this is obviously wrong. Explaining why it is wrong in a philosophically rigorous manner requires time and energy, and what exists of both is being used to help people – one simply knows that one should.

An alternative way of expressing similar sentiments is to say that what is significant is to stop people from being excluded – excluded from economic, social and political goods.[15] Similarly, people have human rights because they have needs. Having seen needy people and having been prompted to ask 'why are they so?' has led to the conclusion that these people have human rights. Again, seeing needy people and feeling the satisfaction that comes from helping such people serves as an existential basis for using human rights language. It is not just seeing other people suffer that convinces us that people have rights. It is the alleged a priori knowledge within us that this is wrong which gives us the foundation for what we call human rights. This, it seems from people's testimony, is not merely the reflective rationalism of Descartes' *cogito* but is an intuitive experiential apprehension of what must not be done to others or ourselves.[16] Finally, an interesting perspective is brought to the notion of existential human rights by a long-time observer of the Javanese. His view was that 'the Javanese would not like this question ("What are human rights?"). They are reluctant (to answer) ontological questions. Truth is not something abstract – it is a feeling of fitting, psychological harmony. If you use a concept and it fits well, you don't need to ask why or what.'[17]

There is a sense in which this sums up what I have called existentialist human rights: you do not need to ask why we have human rights – it is self-evident, intuitive. It may well be significant, however, that, for a number of these interviewees, talking about this issue in terms of rights is already to translate the truth of the matter into more abstract language. Things that are wrong to do to people are translated into the positive language of rights (and sometime the corresponding language of duties) because of the paradigm from which the questioner is coming. For instance, the battered women's worker notes that talk of human rights is alien; even talk of women's rights is removed from the women themselves. What they know is that being battered is wrong. The much more appropriate term to use may be that of human dignity; talk of rights is the language that outsiders looking in are wont to use.

The other way of answering the what and why questions of human rights being treated in tandem here is what I have called 'intuitive humanism'. Interviewees simply assert that we have human rights *because we are human*. In some instances this is quite a different sort of answer to that given by the existentialist mode of understanding, because it is little more than the popularised Western humanism that members of the middle class have picked up through being educated in the West. They may or may not have studied philosophy, but there are overtones of the

European Enlightenment's universal 'rational man' heard in such discussions. Others have a more critical account of what it is to be human, giving the diversity of humanity its due, and yet still seeing something about us which, because we all share it, guarantees us human rights, something that is inherent in us.[18] That human rights are both found in us and made by us as humans also helps our understanding of what might be being suggested, because it is not naively universalist and takes certain account of our historicity. However, the way in which these might be consistently explicated is not clear.

Obligation derived from positive law

When interviewees were questioned about the nature and sources of human rights, most of their answers fell within the categories discussed above. This was in part because the question makes clear that the subject is not human rights law as such but rather the metaphysical question of what lies behind the law. Thus, responses making reference to international human rights law were few and did not, in any case, see international human rights law as the origin of human rights. As has traditionally been the case in Western political theory, positive law was seen to reflect something that exists behind it. International human rights law was not therefore used by any of the interviewees as a justification for understanding what human rights are or why we are said to have human rights. Rather, it is a convenient way of codifying moral norms.

The United Nations Universal Declaration on Human Rights (UDHR) was discussed by some interviewees.[19] These references usually had more to do with political than philosophical questions, though the two are not unrelated. For example, extremely conservative Muslims will generally not accept the UDHR. In some cases this will be because of a general anti-Western sentiment (referred to by one as their 'psychological problem').[20] In other cases it will be a principled rejection of the approach the UDHR takes to issues such as religious freedom (see below). For others it matters not whether the Declaration is Western in origin, it represents a good account of how we should behave towards one another and is something to which we should aspire.[21] There is no sense here, however, that the reason we have rights is because of the UDHR. The Declaration's role is merely a codification of values, values which lie behind human rights law. Similarly, an Indonesian bureaucrat says that, while the UN human rights framework is accepted in the main by Indonesian NGOs, it is local issues which influence the discourse on human rights.[22]

This account of people's responses to human rights demonstrates considerable conceptual diversity on the issue of what human rights are and why we have them. Without having yet examined the normative or substantive accounts of human rights that correspond to these conceptual discussions, it is nonetheless possible to infer from what has been reviewed above that any simple universalism in understanding what human rights are has to be ruled out. The positions are too varied and, while some nod towards ideas of simple universalism, in the end their manner of deriving human rights, their epistemology, puts in doubt whether compromise, let alone harmony, can be reached on substantive norms. As one interviewee noted, the issue with human rights is how injustice is defined.[23] The conceptual bases reviewed here give no indication that agreement can be found on this issue. In the end the question becomes: 'Whose justice, which rationality?'[24] The following examination of views about selected specific alleged human rights amply demonstrates the existence of this impasse.

Substantive disagreement on rights

The goal of much writing within the literature on human rights is to show that it is possible to come to widespread agreement on the content of human rights, because of widespread agreement across traditions. Much of the literature that makes passing or summary reference to human rights does so on the presumption that this goal has already been achieved or is, in principle, achievable. It is my contention that this conclusion is largely a result of methodological assumptions about how to establish the existence of substantive agreement on universal human rights. These assumptions privilege agreement on certain issues and, questionably, use this agreement as the basis for assertions about the probable success of the wider project of universal human rights. Even though it may be recognised that the agreement reached is only applicable to certain issues, it nonetheless seems to provide a psychological undergirding for confidence in the wider project; such a confidence, I suggest, is misplaced.

This is confirmed by the outcomes of attempts to find basic agreement: these outcomes focus on a small set of basic issues such as freedom from cruelty and the provision of subsistence-level economic resources. It is not at all clear that these conclusions can be used to build up, in the style of Euclidean geometry, a matrix of human rights such as that of the Universal Declaration on Human Rights. Rights to holidays with pay are a long way down the track from economic subsistence, and on a pragmatic level can be nothing more than wild dreams for much of the planet's population. Something as basic as the avoidance of pain does not apply to all cultures in the same manner. Dissent and mourning often receive expression through self-immolation or self-injury.[25] Despite this, articles and books continue to be written that are premised on the notion of common agreement being in principle attainable across cultures, religions, philosophical traditions, political institutions and civil traditions. The examination of the *controversial* issues between us shows that agreement is a lot more elusive than is claimed by the positions noted above. It may well be the case, to illustrate, that we find agreement on economic subsistence or, more controversially, on cruelty. However, the question of agreement on religious freedom, abortion or gender equity is radically negative. The critique implicitly levelled here is that the focus of universal human rights theorists on issues such as economic subsistence and cruelty is a form of wish fulfilment. By privileging those issues on which there is agreement and making them the foundation for human rights, their desire for a justification for universal human rights is, in appearance, that much closer to reality. Were they to make women's rights and religious freedom the basic axiomatic issues, universality would undoubtedly be out of the question. The methodology has therefore centred around the controversial issues in the discourses of rights claims, in an attempt to test the claim to universality in more difficult terrain. If genuine universality existed (universality that transcends the particularities of culture, religion, tradition, and so forth), there would be substantial agreement among positions. In the event, there is not.

The place and rights of women in society

There are many different ways in which to approach the issue of women and society. There are cultural factors, health issues, participation rates in civil and political institutions, education standards, reproductive rights, general employment issues, religious matters, and so on. It is beyond the scope of this survey, and unnecessary for the argument of the book, to deal comprehensively with all of these. The discussion here will focus on the debate to do with religion, particularly Islam, and women, both from the point of view of those observing the issues from various standpoints within Islam, and from those who are critiquing the debate from outside. There are quite distinct categories of representation in this debate. Within Islam there is a general division between types of traditionalists and types of modernists. Following that, there are those who do not accept that the religious voice should have a defining role in determining the role of women.

It should be parenthetically noted that these three categories correspond to three modes of understanding religion: the pre-modern religious, the modern religious and the 'post-public religion agnostic'. The first employs a literal hermeneutic in its interpretation of its conventions and canon; the second, a critical contextualist or historicist hermeneutic;

and the third, a historicist post-public religion moral philosophy. These fundamental philosophical commitments are significant as a means for understanding the nature and extent of substantive difference.

Representing traditionalism/conservatism

This view holds that, while before God there is no difference between men and women physically, emotionally and with respect to their role in society, men and women are indeed different. There is, on this account, no religious role for women in Islam.[26] A woman cannot, for example, become an imam. This is explained by and is a consequence of different biology: menstruation makes a woman ceremonially unclean, and an unclean person cannot play the role of the imam.[27] Similarly, men and women have different economic roles: the man is the breadwinner, and by virtue of this and his physical strength the man is entitled to be the head of the house. (There does appear to be a willingness to recognise that changing economic patterns may mean that the man is not the sole breadwinner; this may make space for negotiation among couples. It should be noted, however, that these arguments are all expressed by men and thus there appears to be a vested interest in how such socio-economic changes are interpreted.)[28]

In institutions of higher education, in more conservatively Muslim areas, educators find it difficult to discuss Islam and the treatment of women because the immediate response is the question: 'Are you being critical of my religion?' One issue that is shared by women's NGOs and educators has to do with the beating of women. In traditional Islam, the beating of women with a handkerchief is allowed. Yet those who come to the NGOs are sustaining significant bodily damage. An educator who works with such women resignedly concludes: 'Islam is not to be questioned'.[29] There is no room for critique or reflection, despite claims to the contrary. A positive response is gained from a progressive account of Islam, but there is strong resistance to claims of discrimination against women in Islam. In these situations, the rights of women are rejected because of 'a different concept of equality, a different concept of religion'.[30] As noted above, while there is spiritual equality between the sexes, 'the majority of scholars will not accept women in positions of final leadership'.[31] Nor will the conservative Islamic community accept certain social activities. For example, in 1997 a group of Malay women received considerable attention by virtue of having been involved in a beauty quest. Religious officers interrupted the end of the pageant and arrested two of the winners, both Malay women, who were taken away while still holding their awards. The overall winner was a Malaysian Chinese woman, who was not arrested. The pageant could not be countenanced by Islamic authorities, whose actions, based on a law forbidding Islamic women from 'parading in public', set in motion an international debate.[32]

Abortion is a practice which, particularly for conservative Muslims, is legitimate either not at all, or perhaps only within the first forty days. The reason for this ambiguity has to do with the question of when the foetus is granted its soul.[33] The principle the conservatives follow in this debate, which to them renders the otherwise arbitrary 'approximately four months' cut-off point legitimate, is that it is murder to destroy a person, and a person is that which has a soul. Once the foetus has a soul, abortion is murder.[34] There are possible exceptions to the general principle in the event of some instances of rape[35] or illness.[36] The issue of abortion is one on which there is quite a noticeable difference between Indonesia and Malaysia. For Malaysia, in general terms, abortion is openly rejected by Islam and, according to one account, even among the most progressive women there is no public discussion.[37] Within Indonesia, however, there is much more ambivalence. The conservative position, that abortion is wrong, is held less dogmatically, and many individuals and NGOs openly support the practice.

The progressive account of Islam and women

Any progressive account of women in Islam is premised on some notion of critique. This may be conceptualised as either intrinsic or extrinsic – critique originating from within Islam, or critique that originates from outside Islam and is then adopted by Muslims. Intrinsic critique argues that the Islamic tradition contains within it all that is needful for its own reformation on matters of injustice. The Koran is centrally concerned about the issue of injustice and advocates equality of all; thus, if it can be established that women are being treated unjustly, there are resources internal to the religion for addressing the matter.[38] It is argued that the roles that men and women play in society are conventional, that is, based on convention. Convention is not fixed and is open to evolution and change – thus, 'nothing can never be done [*sic*]'. The constraint, it is said, is the conservative orthodox religious establishment which prevents people from being aware of the conventional nature of their mores, and that dispute is legitimate.[39] Even representatives of that same establishment give a similar account of the nature of change within Islam. There is no pope or synod, says one such conservative representative: 'Authority is in the community itself … it is very difficult to make distinctions between those who are heretics and those who are initiating change – there are no criteria for judging'.[40] On this account, though, it is possible to initiate change if one can get over the initial obstacle of getting a hearing from the community.

The alternative approach is to adopt ideas that come from outside one's own religious tradition, but which one sees as being consonant with it, and use them as the engine to drive change. This is what one Indonesian women's NGO worker sees as the practice of her organisation. The program of the NGO in question (and others like it) is premised on ideas such as those of democratic theory and feminist theory which come from the West: 'Gender ideas do come from the West'.[41] As another Indonesian NGO worker explained, such an approach receives considerable hostility from the establishment. The common experience among women's groups is receipt of the accusation that they are not Asian or have capitulated to Western values (taken as a self-evidently bad move).

A highly public case of this debate has to do with the Malaysian organisation, Sisters in Islam,[42] which is accused by the conservative establishment of being a fifth column for the West: 'Sisters in Islam have many influences from perceptions of the West, and they have not studied the Koran deeply. This causes problems, because they use the perceptions of the West as an analytic tool. Islam has its own perceptions of itself.'[43] The following will make clear why conservatives claim the Sisters are westernising Islam. However, it is equally clear that this is not their self-perception. In print they have described themselves in this manner:

> We began meeting in 1987 as a support group for women and women's organisations regarding Women and Islam. The group grew out of a concern at the number of complaints we as individuals had received from women on the personal law (family law) of Muslims ... The sharing of those experiences prompted us to evolve into a study group to better understand the message of the *Qur'an* and to undertake action to promote equality and justice as envisaged by Islam. We hope our efforts will begin a new dialogue in the building of a framework on women's rights in Islam which takes into account women's experiences.[44]

The continuing research and publication agenda of Sisters in Islam is premised on the need to reformulate the received Islamic tradition according to the context and circumstances of Muslims today, 'based on modern understandings of eternal Qur'anic principles and Islamic teachings'.[45] This approach leads to a rejection of the view that the formulations of those closest in time to Islam's formative and 'authentic' phase are those which must be implemented today. It is this view which is the impetus behind the attempt to reinstate Islamic Shari'a law within the context of the modern nation-state. It is, in turn, this attempt which has galvanised the intellectual work of those such as Rose Ismail and Norani Othman in Sisters in Islam, Malaysia, to consider whether the injustices which they perceive to flow from such a process really are condoned or mandated by Islam. They seek to determine whether, instead, the ideas of justice and equality talked about in the Koran could not be resuscitated and used as support for the thesis that history, context and place have to be taken into consideration in interpreting Islam; and further, whether modern notions such as human rights or women's rights can be used as tools, supported by the Islamic religious tradition, for achieving Islamic goals of justice and equality.[46]

It is, however, precisely because of the repeated use of 'modern' in the discourse of Sisters in Islam, and because of the dependence their project of reinterpretations has on the distinctively modern tool of historicity, that their project is not welcomed by traditionalists and conservatives. The modern is all too often identifiable with the West, moreover with the Christian West.[47] The observed decadence of the West is sufficient to alienate some, in this connection. Others have made an assessment of the consequences of embracing the modern for the Christian religious tradition, and particularly the consequences of this in modernist theology, with its eventual undermining of the status of the Christian scriptures, the denial of the supernatural, and even the denial of the historicity of the central figure, Christ. Such a route they do not wish to travel, and thus modern historicist, contextualist methods remain unwelcome. Against the force of institutional orthodoxy it remains the case that, as Andree Feillard described the Indonesian situation, 'Muslim feminists have few means to propagate the "right" understanding of Islam'.[48] The Sisters, however, are not prepared to deny history in their attempt to be devout Muslims but see themselves as honouring their faith, its divine source and their fellow believers in their struggle. I close this section with Norani Othman's recognition of the ongoing challenge:

> The cultivation of internal discourse within Islamic civilisation about the meaning and interpretation of Islamic texts, as with all other texts, is fraught with many problems. For Muslims the *Qur'an* is the word of God, revealed by the prophet Muhammad as a guidance to all people. Contemporary Muslims have to acknowledge that there are problems with interpreting that message. The *Qur'an* is and gives a message to humans for all time, but it is also *immediately* concerned with and addressed to the Arabs of Muhammad's time. It has two needs to fulfil – as a guide during Muhammad's time and also for Muslims in the future. The historicity of the *Qur'an* does pose difficult problems to modern Muslims of conscience.[49]

Defining the place of women without religion

A first example of how the relationship between rights and women is defined without recourse to religion comes from the (non-Muslim) leader of a Malaysian women's NGO, who nominates a point of departure by saying that 'rights are inherent in you', and that fundamentally all humans are the same, across political borders and constructs such as the West or the East. Thus, our understanding of what human rights are, and which ones we have, should not be related to religion. Rather, the former should stand over and against religion as a measuring stick for justice. This statement is expanded and in part justified by reference to the role that religion, and the revivalism of religion in Asia but also world-wide, plays in relation to human rights. In particular, the growing strength of religion is related directly to the institutionalisation of patriarchy in society. This is particularly evident, the interviewee states, in relation to the role Islam plays among Malays in Malaysia. Religion is used by political, ethno-nationalist and religious elites as a tool for creating and thus controlling the identities of individuals and communities, the former in that they are members of the latter: 'In this process the women get controlled much more ... with identity and religion comes the issue of reproductive rights'.[50] And so the link between the worldview and specific behavioural outcomes, or constraints on specific behavioural freedoms, is observable once again.

Domestic violence is another women's issue which highlights the ways in which behavioural norms and social outcomes are directly affected by fundamental philosophical commitments. Proponents of women's rights sought to have a Domestic Violence Act adopted in Malaysia which would have application to all women. The only way to do this was to arrange for the Act to come under the Penal Code, otherwise the Act would have to go under two courts (the regular Court and the Shari'a courts) and face dilution and change in order to cover Islamic women.[51] However, this strategy also involved compromise: to qualify for recognition by the Penal Code any incident must involve grievous hurt, and domestic violence cannot be defined in its own terms, but rather those of the umbrella Act. Thus, because of 'religious and cultural factors, basic human rights have been given up'.[52] For the interviewee, this accommodation of cultural and religious factors is exactly the same violence at the legal level as that which women who are battered at home experience.

Because of compromised emancipatory struggles such as these, it is concluded that the religious framework is not a suitable one for the defence of women's rights. With religion, identity, social roles and rights are all a matter of interpretation – and 'whose interpretation is final at the end of the day?' What is the answer to the question: 'Can I refuse my husband sex?' The lived religious framework of women does not provide resources for them to answer this question in the affirmative.[53]

What of the attempt by those such as Sisters in Islam to reinterpret the faith such that it provides these resources? This approach is seen to be ineffectual and prone to failure. It works for those who already have substantial social capital and the intellectual prowess to defend themselves against their opponents. This is not the lived experience of the 'average' Islamic women. It is better to use religion to support human rights than to run the risk of compromising rights by grounding them in religion. This is not to condemn faith, but it is to express profound condemnation of the institutions of faith in society – as was demonstrated by the across-the-board opposition by religious as well as political leaders in Malaysia to the attempt to develop a Domestic Violence Act.

A second example comes from an NGO in Indonesia which seeks to transform society by encouraging the development of civil society.[54] As with the views expressed above, the position articulated by the spokesperson for this NGO started with the claim that human rights come from our nature as human beings and are thus universal and cannot be divided between people from the West and the East, even given consideration of cultural and religious specificities. This approach allows the interviewee to argue that the notion of human rights can be accepted by all people; thus, for example, traditionalists who wish to look at everything from a theological perspective can articulate rights through their theological frameworks. This admittedly proves difficult, because of the 'psychological' problems that such sections of Islamic thought have towards the West.

The traditionalist's approach, complete with its antipathy towards the West, belongs in one of three categories which together provide the framework through which the NGO sees the relationship of various Islamic approaches to social and political issues. This is the category where all lived experience must be interpreted through a theo-centric worldview, the outlook of classical Islam. A second category exists where there is some accommodation of difference. There is less religious control, less exclusivity, although Islamic groups and interpretations are the standard by which all else is to be judged, and there still exists discrimination against non-Muslims. In the final category, religion is purely a personal matter, its sphere is the private realm. Further, there is no formal or theocratic relationship between religion and politics, except inasmuch as the individuals involved derive their public values from the private realm of personal religion.

A consequence of holding the third position is that, whereas in the past religious views on the organisation of society have been de rigueur, they are now openly challenged by social actors who derive their sense of justice from a political ideal not necessarily directly related to religion, and at times construable as antithetical to religious orthodoxy and praxis. This, at any rate, is the experience of the NGO in question as it has set about its goal of empowering women in Indonesian society. This is so because, as was explained, in traditional Islam there are three domains to life: the very personal, the family, and public life. In practice the first two are often conflated, such that, for example, discussion of the role of women in the family becomes off-limits because it slips back into the category of those very personal things which are not discussed or questioned, but accepted. This, however, leaves the religious believer with no grounds from which to evaluate the religious beliefs they are encouraged to share. Consequently, the NGO also disseminates a methodology for evaluating the authenticity of the religious beliefs in which people are traditionally instructed. The methodology is simple and twofold: first, it asks questions about the authenticity of the transmission of religious dogma; second, it poses a distinction between fundamental dogma and instrumental dogma. Thus, by opening the door to ideas of contextuality and historicity in religious belief, the NGO seeks to bring human rights as a standard by which to judge religion, rather than the other, distinctly pre-modern way around. This methodology is employed as grounds for an understanding of human rights which is not theocratic, not dependent on religion, and thus able to bring an external and allegedly universal critique. Through this critique, a correct or right understanding of how religion should be practised can be developed, one which observes human rights.

I referred earlier to the relationship between religious hermeneutics and the treatment of women: the pre-modern religious, the modern religious and the 'post-public religion agnostic'. The discussion of this topic implicitly makes the case that it is at this level that change must be brought about in order for there to be changes in the way women are treated. These changes are not necessarily towards what the latter view would call 'progress'. The resurgence of conservative Islam means change at this level towards the restriction of women's freedoms. Simultaneously, the pressures of globalisation – of everything from dress styles to ideas – also cause change at this level, towards granting more freedom. This argument once again supports the overall thesis of this chapter that there is a direct connection between one's fundamental philosophical commitments and behavioural outcomes. It is this which causes tension in Islamic Southeast Asia. If different fundamental approaches to religion all issued in the same behavioural consequences, the societal status quo would remain, power interests would go unchanged (except perhaps among the theological elite) and there would be no impetus for heated political engagement. However, the status quo is threatened, power interests are changing as women gain influence, and political debate has been very heated. These factors help to establish the case.

Approaches to homosexuality

The battle fought by the homosexual lobby to have gay rights recognised and its cause incorporated within the mainstream of Western society has succeeded to the extent that the language of gay rights, its self-identification with the wider human rights movement, and general acceptance of the movement in (at least) left-liberal circles are established. By contrast, most Asian societies retain, at least in public, a strongly conservative attitude to homosexuality which with few exceptions, according to those interviewed in this study, ranges from rejection of its legitimacy as a form of human sexual expression to non-hostile but disinterested recognition of its existence. This is particularly the case when homosexuality is discussed in the context of human rights. The following quotation is illustrative:

> Another example is ... the recognition of same sex marriages ... we cannot project this as a universal human rights issue. This is relative to certain context in certain societies [sic]. In Asia, such an idea will not be tolerated ... Using the human rights banner in this way will distract attention and possibly create resistance against human rights.[55]

As above, the conclusions drawn about the legitimacy of homosexuality are often strongly determined by the role of religion in the worldview of the interviewees. Thus, interviewees state that they disagree with the type of view held by what I above described as a Western left-liberal position on the grounds that God has made us heterosexual: that we are designed to relate as heterosexual couples. To refuse this is to refuse God and the nature that He has created. Similarly, the religious point of view is placed in contradistinction to that of liberals in the West: they want abortion and homosexuality and other such 'freedoms' to be sanctioned by society and through human rights language, but in fact if you accept these values you jeopardise the future of civilisation.[56] Again, an Islamic think-tank director states that Islam has very rigid rules against all forms of pre- or extra-marital sex, including homosexuality; in addition, Islam finds it hard to understand why the West, possessing its own similar teachings in the Bible, refuses to live accordingly. As another commentator put it, in the Indonesian context, 'Indonesian Muslims view life through faith; they can't conceive of people who have no faith. They view "free sex" and so on as (the behaviour of) people with no faith, which is incomprehensible.'[57] Because of the relationship between faith and public life, therefore, homosexuality is not a public issue. In Malaysia it is illegal;[58] in Indonesia it is not, and is subject to less censure. One theory put forward by interviewees for why this is the case cites the influence of Javanese culture, which exerts a strong moderating influence on the fundamentalist tendencies of Islam. Thus, it is claimed, those Indonesian locales where Javanese culture was not strong have become hotbeds of fundamentalism; those where it was strong exert a moderating force on Islam. Homosexuality and other sexual freedoms are simply accepted as existing but are passed over in public life, providing no fuss is made about them.[59]

Some of the difficulties that have emerged within the human rights movement in Malaysia have been because of the relation between the worldview of a religious believer, wherein public values are to be directly informed by a similarly public religion, and those who either are not believers or hold to a privatised view of the relation between religion and morality.[60] This is illustrated by a series of meetings held in the lead-up to the Vienna 1993 world conference on human rights. In one meeting held in Kuala Lumpur, it was found that there was strong division between representatives of NGOs with respect to homosexuality. On the one hand were representatives who viewed the rights of homosexuals as one and the same with the various other sorts of rights that were being discussed and which would be promoted by the gathering. On the other hand were groups which were not prepared to accept homosexual practice as a legitimate form of sexual behaviour or identity. In the meeting all the groups were represented and contributed their views, which were subsequently included in the transcript. However, the dissenting views (those of the pro-homosexuals, as against the Hindus, Christians and Muslims) were edited out of the press statement for fear that the government would use those views as a justification for hindering participation in the Vienna meeting. The conclusion that the interviewee draws from these events is that there is very little agreement about the supposed universality of rights, particularly on these sorts of questions. The centrality of religion to this disagreement is important and should not be sidelined in favour of culture, politics or other factors.

Another respondent points to what may happen in the future with this issue as well as similar ones (abortion, euthanasia, women's rights, and so forth). This interviewee holds that values are decided sociologically and that the interplay of value systems, outside influences, social need and the like work together to produce the sort of society that is needed by its inhabitants. Thus, if it is needful that values change to encompass homosexuality, then they will change.

On a purely pragmatic level, influence for such change is already being felt in Malaysia, where opposition to homosexual practice is strongest at a national level on religious grounds, by virtue of international standards for human rights assistance. The United Nations, says one interviewee, includes homosexual rights within the package of standards which nations must meet in order to gain certain assistance and benefits. Because Malaysia does not recognise these rights, it must forgo the assistance and benefits. This stance, of attaching aid and other assistance to controversial rights, is one which generates much resistance and is seen as little more than politicking – particularly given other examples of Western double standards, a litany of which is not far from the lips of most commentators from the region.

Singapore also rejects homosexual rights as legitimate forms of sexual practice and identity, both at a national level and broadly among its population.[61] Chua Beng-Huat argues that Singaporean society has chosen to be a conservative society and that it is because of this that the authoritarian government has mass credibility despite its excesses.[62] The middle class are quite prepared to work with the government, if it can learn how to work with them. The issue of the place of homosexuality is just one example of how this process functions. The government does have laws which reject homosexual practice, but they are not used. Similarly, the recent attempt of the gay group 'People Like Us' (PLU) to be registered as an association, while in the end unsuccessful, was not, says Beng-Huat, a cut-and-dried case for the government. Thus it is that, while at a formal level the government might appear illiberal, at the pragmatic level it is surprisingly flexible and willing to be consonant with those values that resonate in society.[63]

In conversation with a representative of the gay community, the perception of the government as conservative but benign is not so much present; instead, the frustrations of being a queer minority are evident, as individuals and groups of individuals try to find what it means to live their self-created identity and values system within a wider community which, while perhaps not actively hostile, is nonetheless not prepared to embrace their lifestyle. A crucial difference here, from the point of view of the interviewee, was dependent on the way in which different cultures work, the values they apply to coping with unwanted difference. The way in which this difference was explained had to do with the manner in which a gay person 'comes out'. In the West, it is argued, this tends to be a very obvious, even confrontational process. Family and friends are told, and they have a choice to accept or reject. This, it is argued, is in line with the more confrontational and outspoken nature of Western culture. In Singapore, by contrast, the preferred model (preferred by the speaker, and to the extent that his claim to be representative is accepted, then by the wider movement) is one which depends on the subtle development of an understanding. There may not be a time when one 'comes out'; however, one has made clear by certain understood indications that the regular pattern of marriage and children would not be following, and that these indications were given in a way that granted understanding about sexual orientation. To the extent that this is representative it does give evidence of a different set of norms for communication about one's sexuality from that prevalent in 'the West'; this indeed was the self-perception of the interviewee, who was deliberately defining these practices as different from those which the Western homosexual movement espouses, and by so doing was seeking to differentiate Western practice from that of the Singaporean movement.[64]

Altman's research backs up this analysis:

> The last decade has seen a remarkable growth in most Asian countries of Western-style lesbian/gay identities, and small activist groups are now present in most countries in the region where sufficient political space exists. There are huge problems of interpretation, as surface similarities (designer clothes, discos and cafes etc.) can also cloak more significant differences. Gay worlds reflect the larger culture within which they develop and while the Reeboks may be the same the styles and manners of relating to each other will vary.[65]

Religious freedom or freedom of religion?

This issue, more than the others examined to this point – precisely because it includes the others – highlights the reasons why it is not possible to talk about 'universal' human rights in any of the traditional metaphysical, philosophical and political ways. It is beyond the scope of this section to treat the topic exhaustively, so, as above, the focus will rarely go beyond a discussion of the differences within Islam, and between Islam and the West (neither noun being intended in totalising senses). Similar accounts could be adduced in discussion of Christianity, Hinduism, Confucianism, liberalism and nationalism.

As we have observed with the issues already discussed, the logic of the differences that emerge depends on whether the standards for judging the issue in question come from within a tradition (such as Islam) or from without. Put differently, the issue is whether there is a universal standard across cultures, religions and thought traditions which can be applied to a religion such as Islam and be used to precipitate change; or whether such change is only finally legitimate if it can be generated from within a given tradition, from its own principles and practices, no matter to what extent that change may then be consonant with values and changes happening elsewhere.

In mainstream Western discourse, the quintessentially liberal idea that individuals can choose for themselves which religion, or none, they care to adhere to is virtually taken for granted. Those 'sects' or 'cults' where one is compelled to act on the basis of religious authority, not personal choice, are readily described as being on the margins, as authoritarian (where this is a negative normative judgement, not merely descriptive), as peripheral, 'on the edge' or 'lunar', in the vernacular. By contrast, the forms of religious experience that the variegated non-Western 'other' experience are largely the forms that a liberal sensibility would like to put and keep on the margins. Christianity itself was very much like this in its pre-modern form, and is still so in many places. Similarly with Islam, where the authority of the religious community in the various communal and institutional forms that it takes is perceived to 'trump' the autonomy of the individual. It is very much the reverse of the commonly heard liberal position that individual rights are 'trumps' and thus have precedence.

On the contrary, 'Muslims cannot interpret things any way they like. The United Nations may provide such human rights, but Islam does not.'[66] Similarly, there is not, within Islam, latitude such that people are 'free to get free' as they are in the West. On the contrary, the only freedom to be legitimately had is freedom within the ethics of Islam.[67] Both with respect to social practice and religious belief it is against the ethics of Islam to repudiate either. As one interviewee, a Muslim academic, said, it is not legitimate for Muslims to leave Islam.[68]

An alternative response to questions about the nature of religious freedom in Islam is to invoke the Koranic principle of freedom of conscience: 'We have the right to refuse God'.[69] Similarly, as discussed above, it is often asserted that there is no monopoly interpretation or office of pope to decide Islam's response to an issue;[70] therefore, orthodoxy can change and embrace values that are consonant with it, regardless of their source. This might be thought to bode well for notions of religious freedom.[71]

These approaches to the issue are satisfactory in the comfort of the theologian's study where all ideas might be openly discussed. The social and political reality of lived Islam is quite different, however, as the social stigma attached to leaving Islam is severe. The issue of freedom to leave Islam is what prevents Indonesia from ratifying UN human rights instrumentalities that deal with religious freedom; in particular, there is on the part of all the main Islamic organisations ('Muhammadiyah, perhaps NU, Republika', as they were cited) a fear of the 'Christianisation' of Indonesia. It is precisely because of the pre-modern nature of religious affiliation in Indonesia that religion and politics become thus intertwined. In classical Islamic thought there is no differentiation between the public and private spheres, between religion and politics, and so the status of an individual's religious affiliation is both a highly corporate matter and a highly political matter. It is because of this, and as Zifirdaus Adnan points out, that 'the major conflicts in Indonesian politics since independence are ... between those who struggle for the idea of an Islamic state or the implementation of Islamic teaching by the state ... and those who oppose it'.[72]

The situation is similar in Malaysia but, because of the nature of ethnic and identity politics there, the legal and socio-political consequences of a decision to leave Islam all but obliterate any principle of religious conscience.[73] One response to this is critical of Islam, saying that by being a religion of control, by not allowing adherents freedom to leave, the religious establishment that officiates over Islam betrays a lack of confidence that people will come to the faith voluntarily or return to it after a period away.[74]

Quite plainly, the worldview that allows for the use of the term 'adherents' to describe people who belong to a religion demonstrates an alternative understanding of the nature of religious obligation to that held by Islamic orthodoxy. Religion subsumes and incorporates the individual – it is not something to which an individual can autonomously choose to adhere. Thus it is that orthodox Islam in Indonesia and Malaysia cannot agree with an account of religious freedom as given by the UDHR. Similarly, when an Indonesian official endorses the view that it is wrong, as recognised by the Declaration, to cause one's children to follow one's religion,[75] he is immediately articulating a radically different notion of religion, religious affiliation and family life from that held by Islamic orthodoxy in the region.

Islamic orthodoxy itself is variable, as is evident by the disparate regional and organisational views on the role and place of the Shari'a law. If this law is followed with rigorous literalism, death is the just consequence for the apostate. Such a view was not advocated by any of those interviewed, although it was noted that there would be tension over the interpretation of these matters,[76] and little protection for religious minorities were the proponents of Shari'a law to gain strategic positions of power.[77]

There are, then, a variety of positions which respectively uphold or repudiate the notion that the individual has the freedom to nominate his or her religious affiliation. In most cases this difference can be analysed as a consequence of pre-modern versus modern approaches to society and religion. The characteristic difference between these is a reversal in the pre-eminence of society over the individual; the radical change is from the individual conceived as constituted by the social community and religion in which he or she is born to the individual conceived as one who at a certain time becomes responsible for deciding which social tradition will constitute his or her identity. To the extent that this latter process is conceived of as a reasoned evaluation of options against a universal set of standards of justice or rationality, it betrays the division of approaches to religion explicated above, where it was noted that the issue reduces to precisely this: a question of whether there are universal norms by which religions can be judged, or whether all norms are radically situated, and thus change and critique can only be legitimated if they come from within a tradition.

While not necessarily accepting the 'radically situated-ness' of all religions and traditions thesis, the Islamic organisation Sisters in Islam represents moves within Malaysian Islam (and consonant with some Indonesian approaches,[78] such as that of P3M and the Neo-Modernists[79]) to precipitate critique and change on the basis of the resources internal to the tradition, rather than on the basis of external critique (although it should be noted that much of their inspiration is derived from sources external to their religious tradition). As Norani Othman writes,

> the view of some human rights activists that woman's rights movements are better served by utilising the 'secular' approach – one which grounds its arguments upon the supposedly universal basis of the rule of law and democratisation – is not at all pragmatic, nor is it easily implemented as its proponents claim. The experience of many women's groups operating in Muslim countries these past two decades demonstrated that in their daily battles a great deal more progress is achieved by working within their respective religious and cultural paradigm [sic].[80]

Some women, who are by no means averse to identifying themselves with a faith tradition, have nonetheless concluded otherwise, namely that the religious traditions are too steeped in patriarchal thought and social forms to be useful for advancing the rights of women.[81] That there is great opposition to new ways of thinking about one's religious tradition is confirmed in the strongest possible terms by people such as Sisters in Islam and P3M. One of the Sisters related the lengths to which the local religious establishment had gone to prevent a seminar on the topic of emancipatory themes for women within Islam. These lengths included the somewhat casuistical (if technically correct) argument that the Sultan, nominally the head of religious affairs in the Sultanate, had the legal power to prevent the university in his Sultanate from holding seminars on religious topics if he so deemed – this despite prime-ministerial approval. The Sisters find that they are granted freedom to think and publish, so long as it is in English, and thus unlikely to develop a foothold in the general Islamic women population. Nonetheless, they are on the receiving end of harassment in all forms, from limited opportunities to be heard to personal abuse and threatening mail.

Limitations on religious freedom extend beyond women's issues. A certain type of Muslim orthodoxy runs the political establishment in Malaysia and, as two sets of non-orthodox thinkers have found in recent years, free thinking is not permitted. The first of these are members of the *Al Arqam* sect who were arrested under Malaysia's Internal Security Act (ISA) in their hundreds for so-called 'deviationist teaching'.[82] In this case, as in the next to be instanced, there is a combination of religious and political threat to the (once again combined) establishment.[83] On both religious and political grounds, free thinking ('deviationist teaching') is not acceptable. Similarly, in November 1997 ten men, a number of them university academics and lecturers, were arrested under the ISA for allegedly promoting the teachings of Islam's Shi'ite sect, which, authorities claimed to fear, could threaten national security.[84] The government has made clear its intention to prevent Muslims from practising any *mazhub* (sect) other than Sunni.[85]

The significance of these events for the discussion of religious freedom is multiple. The government's actions rest on a number of assumptions which are far from universal in thinking about religion: that religion is a matter for government regulation; that religion is a public not a private matter; that the way to prevent religious rivalry is to impose one interpretation on all. (This, it should be noted, is a logical consequence of a religious approach which does not allow for a private–public split and a non-religious public realm (such as that proposed by liberalism).) Much opposition has been expressed by intellectuals, religious leaders and political activists in the local newspapers and from abroad (such as Amnesty International and the European Parliament). The political (and behind it the religious) establishment nonetheless refuses to back down. An-Na'im raises a similar series of questions:

> The essential questions to be raised from an Islamic as well as a human rights point of view include these: On what basis does the government assume the mantle of the guardian of the beliefs of its citizens to adjudicate who is 'deviationist' and who is 'conformist'? Granted that the state is responsible for maintaining national security and public safety, how can it purport to do so on the basis of vague accusations and unsubstantiated claims? If it does have the evidence to support its allegations, why not present that before the courts in accordance with the rule of law? What is the meaning of constitutional civil liberties and fundamental human rights if the state can be exclusive judge in its own cause as to whether these safeguards are complied with under conditions of discretionary indefinite detention without charge or trial or judicial review?[86]

In sum, there are radically different notions of religious freedom in competition within Islamic Southeast Asia. These differences range across the areas of individual religious choice, theological interpretation on key social issues and public policy. There are attempts to critique the state of religious freedom on the basis of universal norms of human justice; and similar-minded attempts on the basis of the religious resources of the Islamic tradition. These differences illustrate the question stated in the title of this section: 'Religious Freedom or Freedom of Religion?' *Religious* freedom, that is, freedom as defined by a religious (or otherwise) tradition, is not necessarily the same as the freedom to choose between religions, which itself is a religious (in a wider sense) conception of freedom, but this time from the liberal tradition. It is with this that we see illustrated again the link between fundamental philosophical commitments and the outcomes of these in individuals' lives.

Conclusion

There are, then, significant conceptual differences between and within understandings of human rights. While the political argument for Asian values, and therefore Asian conceptions of human rights, by the political elite was firmly discounted as a legitimate account of human rights, it is nonetheless the case that located within Asia there are ways of conceptualising these rights that are different from those dominant in the West, and that differ among themselves. A principal cause of this difference is the role played by public religion.

Also, these conceptual differences are not limited to schools of thought. Rather, 'ideas have consequences', and this is demonstrated by the different prescriptive ends arrived at by the differing conceptual accounts of human rights. Thus it is that considerable diversity exists between non-religious and religious approaches, and also within each of these broad categories. If there is any encapsulating sense in which one is able to talk about 'Asian values', given these conclusions, it is simply that Asian values means diversity and, to some extent, unreconcilable diversity. In this regard, it represents its similarly totalised partner term 'the West' or 'Western values', which, on any standard account, will demonstrate radical diversity rather than being a monolithic bloc.

These conclusions have fundamentally important implications for notions of universality, such as that upon which the concept of universal human rights depends. Does this mean that talk of universal human rights is misguided? Is it possible still to argue beyond the conceptual and behavioural diversity demonstrated above to some universal which binds all human beings? I consider the answer to be yes. But this is not a simple yes; it demands paradigm shifts in the ways in which human rights and universality have hitherto been conceptualised.

CHAPTER 3

Human Rights: Political Reality, Philosophical Problem

Understanding the development of the idea of universal human rights is the first step in reconceptualising human rights. Only by facing the historical and contingent nature of the concept can we make use of it in a way that is both just and philosophically sound. This approach is taken to be just because it avoids two a priori assumptions. First, that intellectual constructs developed by one dominant culture emerging from its own historically and philosophically contingent milieu are necessarily applicable to all societies and cultures. This assumption ignores and disdains the possibility that in and from other less dominant societies and cultures equally valuable constructs might be found and used. Second, a historically aware approach cautions against the opposite assumption: that it is *not* possible for an intellectual construct from one specific culture and society to emerge as the most effective tool for achieving a particular goal across all cultures. This approach is also taken to be philosophically sound, because the assumption that the concept of universal human rights is ahistorical and evident in all cultures and societies is demonstrably false. Any argument supporting the use of the concept of universal human rights premised on assumptions that can be empirically proven false will not be sustainable and may subvert its own cause.

The argument developed in the remainder of the book is an attempt to construct a theoretical understanding of human rights that might act as a common framework in the context of pluralism. While the argument is premised on the recognition of the historicity and non-universality of concepts such as human rights, it is not an argument for cultural or philosophical relativism. Rather, it seeks to provide a framework within which competing non-relativist systems of thought and being can come to a place of agreement about how they live together.

In addressing the question of whether the notion of human rights can be conceptualised as a universal notion, I start with an examination of the development of the idea. This necessitates a discussion and critique of Enlightenment and liberal political thought. The outcome of this discussion is the recognition of the historical nature of the doctrine of human rights, and the failure of these traditions in their attempt to sustain (on their own terms) the universality of human rights. This critique prepares the way for a reconceptualisation of human rights, in the hope that the doctrine, as a political reality, may be stultified less by anachronism and ambiguity.

Human rights: useful nonsense?

The formulation of moral discourse in the language of rights is peculiar to the modern West, where it has been entrenched in political and legal arrangements. From the West it continues to spread around the globe.[1] The wider views of the person and society implied in the concept of human rights are views which in origin are unique to the development of the West. The concept of human rights, like the religious and philosophical traditions out of which it has grown, is a historically particularistic doctrine with universalist claims. These claims have in recent years been supported by much political and rhetorical activism, including the claim that 'human rights' is the first universal ideology, one which now has world-wide acceptance.[2]

World-wide acceptance is too strong a claim. However, it is the case that the human rights discourse became one of the most prominent discourses of late twentieth-century international politics. The story of its rise gained momentum in the inter-war period which saw increased interest in the problem of freedom due to the rise of the totalitarian state in the former USSR and under Nazi Germany. The term 'human rights', however, did not come into frequent use until after the outbreak of the Second World War. The immediate impetus for this was a publication by H. G. Wells, *The Rights of Man, or What Are We Fighting For?*, followed by President Roosevelt's formulation of the issues in his peroration on the Four Freedoms.[3] It is argued by many that the popular imagination caught the idea of human rights once the world began to understand the atrocities committed by Germany in the Jewish Holocaust.[4] Prior to this, the protection of individuals was seen as a domestic, not an international, concern.[5] With the Holocaust and the other tragedies of the war, however, the notion of a natural law that surpassed international boundaries was reclaimed by Europe from its Christian past. It was both invoked as a legal basis for indictments against Nazis in the Nuremberg trials and as the foundation for the rhetoric of human rights.[6] Growing out of this, the language of human rights has become commonplace. In the last sixty years it has undertaken the transition from a little-used historical and legal term to being an internationally recognised banner for emancipation and freedom.[7] The term has been powerfully efficacious as a rallying cry for political action on behalf of oppressed individuals and groups,[8] and 'the vast majority of independent states' have recognised what has come to be called the International Bill of Rights: the United Nations Universal Declaration on Human Rights, the International Covenant on Civil and Political Rights, and the International Covenant on Economic, Social and Cultural Rights.

The historical circumstances of the revitalisation of the term, however, have militated against an adequate conceptualisation of what is meant by human rights. The term dropped out of use in Europe for intellectual and sociological reasons. It is not clear that such reasons have been addressed, and the notion of human rights continues to sit uncomfortably in the surrounding intellectual and sociological environment. Human rights declare behavioural absolutes, moral universals and are at least suggestive of Truth: this, at a time when many are less certain about – and in some quarters absolutely refuse – the validity of such notions. As Simon Chesterman comments, 'The ends of modernity in securing universal recognition of norms born of the European Enlightenment have been subverted by the *end* of modernity and the concomitant scepticism of the power of reason to herald in a new World Order'.[9]

The starting-point for a history of human rights is to recognise the concept as a product of Western civilisation. This needs to be insisted upon, as there are many revisionist writers from non-Western cultural backgrounds who in the rush to justify the value of their background against the norms of suddenly popular human rights, vigorously disseminated by a victorious and powerful West after the Second World War, have gone as far as claiming that they invented rights first, apparently to show the equal standing of their own cultural history.[10] This is anachronistic. What may be said in such cases is that other cultures and religions have consonant values, perhaps even consonant mechanisms for their realisation. What they do not have is the confluence of historical and intellectual contingencies that gave rise to the concept of human rights.[11]

Richard Tuck identifies two periods during which the language of rights received its formative gestation: those of the early and high Middle Ages, and the period of 'the classic texts of rights theory' – that is, the period from Grotius to Locke.[12] Tuck identifies the medieval science of Roman law of the twelfth century as the temporal location of the first modern rights theory, considered to be so because it was the first theory built around the notion of a passive right.[13] The rights developed by these legal glossators of the Roman Digest were claim rights: they required others to act in a particular way towards the claimant, by granting something.[14]

Grotius' work *De Iure Belli* is another significant development in rights language, for in it is constructed for the first time a legal system based around rights, not laws. This is the decisive shift away from the Aristotelian theories of justice which had eclipsed the initial passive rights theories of the medieval period. Grotius' move sets the precedent for all modern codes centred around rights.[15] His theories and his contribution precipitated much controversy, the detail of which cannot be entered into here. Tuck notes, however, that the English civil war was played out between rival protagonists within the now-split tradition Grotius had helped to develop.[16] This conflict is the point at which economic, social and political rights became central to the Western liberal tradition.[17] The symbolic historical event here was the 'bungled, illegal, but breathtakingly daring trial of a king' – Charles I, in 1649.[18] After this event, an English monarch's rights ultimately had to function in the interests of the people, not the monarch.

One hundred and thirty years later, the voice of this new sovereign began to speak in the declarative language of rights. First, in Virginia on 12 June 1776; then, on 4 July 1776, came 'the unanimous Declaration of the thirteen united States of America'. The French followed fifteen years later with their National Assembly's 'Declaration on the Rights of Man and of Citizens', and two further declarations over the next six years. These documents encapsulate liberal democracy, the banner under which most political struggles of the nineteenth and twentieth centuries were fought.[19] This was not just a new way of promulgating a political and moral theory, nor was it merely an action plan to rid the nation of feudalism. Quintessentially, the Declaration was a 'whole philosophy of what it was to be a human being'.[20]

As such, its theorists – Hugo Grotius, Thomas Hobbes, John Locke, Jean Jacques Rousseau, and their lesser followers – were embarking upon something 'startlingly new'.[21] Knud Haakonssen points out the change by emphasising that 'few thinkers embraced, or even understood, the idea that moral agency, or person-hood, might consist in asserting claims against the rest of the surrounding world with no other guidance than one's own lights and that any common social world had to arise from accommodation of some sort among competing claims'. The predominant natural law theory, however, understood moral agency as submission to the natural law which imposed duties, from which rights (being the means to fulfil duties) were derived.[22]

It is the increasing influence of the former 'startlingly new' view which causes the story of natural rights in the eighteenth century to be one of scepticism by the intellectual elite towards the conventional foundations of an idea that was increasingly of political importance.[23] These foundations were still found for most in the strong tradition of natural law, which at the time of the Enlightenment was championed by the church, although it had pre-Christian antecedents as well. However, the acceptance of a full-blooded Christian theism as the proper foundation from which to pursue all scholarly endeavour was being rapidly eroded. Many, of course, maintained their Christian beliefs. But for many more, and for the elite culture at large, there was a shift towards deism, and that merely as an intellectual prop in the general architecture of Enlightenment thought. This had consequences for the concept of natural law and natural rights. Once they had been adopted from their pre-Christian Roman antecedents and become a part of the theological tradition, the matter of extricating them from that tradition was no small task. By this stage natural law and natural rights had become dependent on the full theological tradition. As the tradition became passé among the intellectual elites, who struggled to develop a sufficiently strong replacement, scepticism about the concepts themselves gradually mounted.

To illustrate, Locke, who in the late 1600s supplied much of the foundation for the liberal human rights tradition, based his theories of rights in his theology: humans were understood to be God's equal servants under the divine law. In agreement with Locke, Alexander Hamilton wrote in 1787 that the sacred rights of mankind (*sic*) were written by Divinity itself. But by this historical juncture, neither conservatives, nor socialists or utilitarians would accept the epistemological claims implied by Hamilton's words. It is then not surprising that, by the early twentieth century, there were few theoretical defences of 'the rights of man' being presented that operated from a natural law basis. 'Natural rights', in the eighteenth century, was an idea which had come too late to achieve philosophical respectability.[24]

The philosophes of the Enlightenment established themselves in a dilemma by both talking in natural law terms and yet claiming humanity as their highest tribunal: on the one hand, they fractured the logic of natural law with their new intellectual tools – epistemology, sociology, and history; on the other hand, they depended on the language of natural law in advancing social criticism and reform. The language of natural law and of the rights of men transferred easily into political tracts and eventually constitutions and bills of rights. But these in the end were only there for political effectiveness. This effectiveness was preferred to consistency, and the proclamations they used were made implausible by their own thought.[25]

Thus, the rights of man theories prevalent in the eighteenth century created a flourishing culture of rights-talk with no clear meaning.[26] Many people talked of rights, even the rights of women, but few understood what they were saying. This confusion was the consequence of the subversion of the dominant natural law paradigm by the development of genuine subjective rights theories – that is, theories in which rights were said to be basic to human persons by virtue of their humanity, rather than derivatively from the natural law. Thus, the subjective rights theories of, for example, Grotius and Hobbes were 'quelled' by a disbelief reinforced by powerful statements of natural law theory, such as that presented by Samuel Pufendorf. At the same time, such natural law theories were gradually losing their capacity to serve as the foundation for rights-talk precisely because the argumentative efficacy of such talk pointed in the direction of genuine subjective rights: the rhetorical claim that rights are basic or inalienable undermines the derivative approach of natural law theory. In addition, this period sees the internal weakening of the natural law tradition by an increasing tendency to stress the moral autonomy of the individual while, apparently paradoxically, depending on natural law as the basis for morals. All these changes are gradual and the exact point at which crucial paradigm shifts occurred is difficult to ascertain. But it is clear that a new way of thinking of rights was making philosophical inroads into the 'comfortable orderliness' of the conceptual structure of natural law–duty–right.[27]

Indeed, it is at this point in its history that the idea of natural rights becomes a politically efficacious rather than a philosophically satisfactory concept, a point which is marked by Rousseau. Till this point natural rights had been thought of, politically, as a way of correcting the occasionally errant behaviour of otherwise legitimate rulers. With Rousseau the social contract theory of natural right moves from being a historical account to being a utopian aspiration. Moreover, because in *The Social Contract* Rousseau sets out minimal conditions of political respectability that were of such a standard that no existing government could hope to satisfy them, his social contract theory of natural right became radical and revolutionary. The people could become sovereign – in the future, not in prehistory, as with Locke's social contract – and then they themselves could choose their own political arrangements. What is seen in the development of French revolutionary doctrine is that the ills of society are blamed on the failure to observe the rights of man.

This politicised and radicalised version of the rights of man came under critical attack from both conservatives and liberals. Edmund Burke, representing the conservatives, opposed the idea of such rights on the basis that they would lead to social upheaval. Burke was of the view that Rousseauesque rights of man led to anarchy because they gave free range to the whole 'train of disorderly appetites' – thus, the revolution over the channel was thought of not as a 'local French difficulty' but as a European civil war. Burke argues that rights should be thought of not in universal terms – the rights of man – but in particularist terms – the rights of *Englishmen*. That is, rights are understood by virtue of the laws and liberties of a commonwealth, and such a commonwealth was not constructed or put together by contract, but *grew* out of time immemorial. Burke therefore does away with the rationalism of a contract account of rights. By placing an emphasis on the commonweal, on custom and on the importance of the continuity of society from the past to the future he also undermines the individualism and radicalism of the rights of man.[28]

The liberal criticism is well represented by Bentham, who is infamous for declaring: '*Natural rights* is simple nonsense: natural and imprescriptable rights, rhetorical nonsense, – nonsense upon stilts'. They were 'unreal metaphysical phenomena'; they were unreal rights which stemmed from an unreal law: natural law. There was no natural law, because there was no divine lawgiver. Because of this, terms such as right and duty made no sense, whereas terms such as law, sanction and sovereign did, for these things actually exist. Thus Bentham presents his positivist and utilitarian critique of the notion of the rights of man: rights, abstracted from positive law, were nonsense. They were also 'mischievous': rights undermine the law, incite revolution, generate insecurity, lay the foundation for anarchy and, by appealing to selfish passions, undermine social solidarity. Manifestos such as that of the French thus deviate from reason and altruistic utility and do not lead to genuine liberty – the theme of Bentham's successor in the utilitarian tradition, J. S. Mill.[29]

Finally in this line of critiques of the rights of man came the Marxian critique. Here again the notion of universality is put to the test against historicism, with the view that it was a theory that had 'limited application in time and space', an application which had to be interpreted in the light of which political interests it was designed to defend. Hence, the rights of men were really only authentic in the society that discovered them, and, further, they only represented a certain outlook – that of 'bourgeois men', not 'all men'.[30] They reflected the wish of the entrepreneur to have a free hand in his (used advisedly) capitalist occupations, with little or no concern for the welfare of the masses who are exploited as grist for the economic mill. Rights to liberty, property, personal security – all these and others are rights oriented towards securing the success of the acquisitive individual. The form of rights contributes to this fault, being individualistic and abstract – and on both accounts committing us to 'an artificial and legalistic myopia' because of which we cannot see the real world with its inequalities and injustices. Rather, we have a view of the world mediated by 'rights', and as a consequence the wrongs that most need addressing in society are neglected. The Marxist critique thus faults the doctrine of the rights of man on grounds pertaining to historicity, individualism, economic equity and justice.[31]

The history of what we now call human rights, briefly and selectively retold here, is then the history of a doctrine subjected to severe philosophical, sociological and economic criticism. This explains why the philosophical exploration of the concept of human rights had been neglected, and by some quarters shunned – Bentham's 'nonsense upon stilts' – for some considerable time when the term gained international circulation to describe the tragic events of the Second World War. Suddenly, as we saw above, the term became politically active. Since the late 1940s 'human rights' has formed one of the centrepieces of international law and has become a mainstay of international politics.

Yet it remains the case that many of the same theoretical problems which caused the notion of rights to initially fall into disrepute and disuse before the twentieth century have not been satisfactorily resolved. Historical debates continue with respect to which theorists were significant, what effect their ideas had on the discourse and the extent to which their thought translated into popular culture. Philosophical and theological debates continue with respect to appropriate grounds for the justification of belief in universal human rights, natural law and other related matters. The gender discrimination of 'the rights of man' has not been rectified by merely using the more inclusive term, '*human* rights'. And political debates that extend beyond the boundaries of the West have arisen in the light of decolonisation, with important questions about racial, cultural and philosophical imperialism.

These difficulties appear unassailable in political and philosophical terms: it does not seem possible to construct a substantive meta-narrative that is able to satisfy the demands of our various traditions and at the same time be applicable universally. It appears that the human rights project embodies a fragmented nature, one that is politically efficacious but philosophically bankrupt. This appearance is maintained by the ongoing philosophical and political identification of human rights with the period in which modern theories of rights flourished and became central to the Western liberal political tradition: the Enlightenment. There is no radical homogeneity of thought during this period, and theories of rights as developed, modified and radicalised by Hobbes, Locke, Rousseau and others vary in approach and detail. There is, however, sufficient similarity in outlook among theorists of this era to justify the claim that the concept of human rights as it comes to the contemporary world through the Western liberal tradition was crucially shaped by the Enlightenment. Thus, what has been termed the 'Enlightenment project' must itself be probed in order to understand the contemporary problems of human rights theory.

The Enlightenment legacy and its problems

In general terms, the philosophical milieu of the Enlightenment may be characterised by identifying a range of dogmas regarding areas of human endeavour: liberalism and progressivism in the spheres of politics and reflection on politics; and empiricism, naturalism and materialism in philosophy and the sciences (in part due to the interpretation given to increasing scientific knowledge). The fundamental ontological category was seen to be Nature, and man's (*sic*) problems and unhappinesses resulted from ignorance of Nature. Knowledge of Nature (and hence of truth, *because* Nature was the fundamental ontological category) was obtainable through human thought and reason. Because of this, human thought and reason were sufficient resources to recreate man in the ideal image of moral systems determined by reason – as opposed to the church (and its God) being required to dictate the paths of 'right and wrong' or 'good and evil'. Indeed, the Enlightenment, or, as it is alternately called, the 'Age of Reason', was strongly antithetical to established religion, clericalism and all institutions based on monarchical or aristocratic principles.[32] It was thought that religion and supernatural beliefs caused states of mind which prevented adventurous thought and the discovery of knowledge which would lead to the fulfilment of the (assumed) fundamental aims of humankind: self-preservation and knowledge.

Instead of reference to the religion of the clerics as the means of determining the moral systems by which to live, the sufficiency of human reason was assumed. The ideological nature of this stance is often repressed or ignored – that is, there is an unwillingness to declare the assumptions on which this form of reason is founded, and a particular unwillingness to admit the legitimacy of thought based on different assumptions. While these foundations are often implicit, Gray identifies them explicitly in his account of the Enlightenment project, arguing that, despite the multiplicity of intellectual and political positions attributable to the time, there was a common thrust:

> The core project of the Enlightenment was the displacement of local, customary or traditional moralities, and of all forms of transcendental faith, by a critical or rational morality, which was projected as the basis of a universal civilisation. Whether it was conceived in utilitarian or contractarian, rights-based or duty-based terms, this morality would be secular and humanist, and it would set universal standards for the assessment of human institutions. The core project of the Enlightenment was the construction of such a critical morality, rationally binding on all human beings, and, as a corollary, the creation of a universal civilisation.[33]

The Enlightenment project and human rights

The universalist declarations on rights reflect this project: 'All human beings are born free and equal in dignity and rights' (UDHR). Here we can see the two-edged sword of the Enlightenment at work. On the one hand, there is an increasing awareness of difference and diversity, which gives rise to a questioning of authority-based political institutions and moral norms. On the other hand is an increasingly secularised construction: the universal civilisation that is the end product of the new final authority, the tribunal of humanity. Two corollaries to civilisation are the notion of *a universal history* for humanity, and the idea of *barbarism*.[34] Enlightenment historiography saw a universal history in which all peoples progressed to a state of civilisation from a state of barbarism, culminating in all civilisations becoming exemplars of the one model of 'civilisation'. Cultural difference is marginalised because of the belief that there is such a thing as 'generic humanity'. This philosophical anthropology is basic to Enlightenment thought, even more so than the belief in progress towards a universal civilisation, which was not held by all the philosophes (Hume, for example, did not hold out this hope). The parallels between the Enlightenment project and the project of an evangelising Christianity are quite clear. Indeed, it is from Christianity that the universalist aspirations of the project are derived, and these may be observed in the philosophical anthropology of a 'generic humanity'; that all people everywhere are the same with respect to the essential matters of being human: to will autonomously.

Natural rights therefore emerge out of the conflict between the critical rationalism of the Enlightenment project and the established Christian moral tradition of natural law. The transition from the idea of natural law to that of natural rights, while being parasitic on the language and morality of natural law, and using it as a plausibility structure, is a transition which is not in fact an evolutionary or 'natural' transition. It was, rather, a rupture caused by the rejection of basic philosophical assumptions. The attempt to preserve the language of natural law went against the philosophical developments of the day. Natural law, particularly as it had come to be understood within the Christian theological tradition, presupposed a lawgiver, a divinity who was the final court of appeal regarding the good.[35] By contrast, the moderns of the Enlightenment repudiated God and recognised only humanity as the highest tribunal. 'Natural rights' was a political doctrine used to challenge the then existing feudal hierarchies and notions of a transcendent plan. The result was the declarations, which took natural rights from a discourse about the natural law imposed by God and 'made them secular, rational, universal, individual, democratic and radical'.[36]

This philosophical project did not exist in a vacuum but had a symbiotic relationship with the sociological developments of the Enlightenment period. A case can be made for seeing social relations, 'human nature', 'human rights' and other such social artefacts as universal categories derived from a particular set of historical social circumstances, including class and ethnicity. 'Modern bourgeois social practice' had achieved revolutionary changes. These include the creation of the 'individual identity, free and mobile labour, money, the commodity and the market', all of these in turn based on an ordering of relations which depended on property, production and commodity exchange – ultimately, capitalist social relations. The crucial point to note, however, is that the formulations of these new social relations and notions of human nature and right were done from one point of view: that of the 'modern bourgeois', who operated with full and free access to these new social conditions. But these conditions were not universal and the population groups excluded from them 'remained beyond the Liberal field of vision'.[37]

It is then only the case that there are inherent human rights, by virtue of our human nature, if we accept as given the philosophical and sociological frameworks which justify such statements and which are represented by the Enlightenment project. It is only because of the uncritical acceptance of these frameworks that it is *self-evidently* the case that 'men are born, and always continue, free and equal in respect of their rights'.

Critique

The Rights of Man – human rights – developed as a means for critiquing the givens of a social order justified by metaphysical principles – divine rights, abstract essences, forms, ideas, substances – principles, which were, as Hobbes put it, 'repugnant to natural reason'. It is the irony of the idea that it was to become that for which its progenitors had such distaste: an ideology or meta-narrative simultaneously unaware of its character as such, and presenting itself as timeless and foundational. 'Human rights' thus became the very sort of metaphysical essence, noble lie or political myth that it originally emerged to critique. By becoming mythic in this way, human rights were made 'vulnerable to the critique of ideology; a critique inspired by the very project of the Enlightenment that human rights were meant to fulfil'.[38] And the ideology to be critiqued is that 'natural reason' of the 'rational autonomous man', the same supposed Truth that lies behind the same Enlightenment project: the 'truth of Man' which provides 'the Archimedean point, the decisive principle of reason'.[39]

Thus, the critical evaluation which had first led the Enlightenment to discard methods of knowledge that depended on anything but the autonomous reason of rational man – relegating superstition, revealed religion and other 'pre-modern' forms of knowledge to the museum of intellectual history – eventually turned to examine its own foundation. Once the critical gaze of Enlightenment rationality turned upon itself, it found that its own methods of knowing (rationalism and empiricism) were not able to secure a basis for its own ideals and morals. The aim was to retain the core of values which until now were founded in religion, but without God. As Montesquieu said, 'Even if there should be no God, we should always love justice ... though we might be freed from the yoke of religion, we should never be free from the yoke of equity ... justice is eternal and does not depend on human conventions'.[40] However, there is a hardly conscious assumption here that the content of justice will stay the same when we vary our religious and philosophical assumptions. But traditional social expressions of justice may well falter once they lose their raison d'être and thus become incomprehensible to a people.[41] It was Nietzsche who first penetrated this assumption, causing him to hold thinkers such as Montesquieu in contempt. Such thinkers wanted to maintain a content for terms such as 'justice', 'truth' and 'goodness' that came directly from and depended on the religion which they were so confidently and contentedly destroying. As Grant puts it for today's context, 'Justice as equality and fairness is that bit of Christian instinct which survives the death of God'.[42] Nietzsche, on the other hand, encapsulated his critique with this scene: 'The masses blink and say: "We are all equal. – Man is but man, before God – we are all equal." Before God! But now this God has died.'[43]

Not all have heard or agree with Nietzsche, and some continue the Enlightenment attempt to reach and understand truth, justice and goodness without the original religious foundations for the content of these concepts. Others argue that the rejection of these foundations undermines our understanding of the dignity of the individual, making notions such as liberty for all and equality under the law indefensible.[44] Yet others have eschewed the whole project of metaphysical justification and have turned against the need to suppose foundations of any sort, hence 'anti-foundationalism'.[45] This is also an ambivalent response, for much of the work based on this approach seems to undermine its own authority by insisting on the fluidity of all knowledge claims. When the ideologues of modernity extended their scepticism to the claim that no knowledge could be securely founded, they exacted a renunciation far stronger than the mere correction of long-cherished errors. In the end their accusation was that thought itself lacked power and integrity.

This assessment gained strength in part from the discrepancy between the universalist pretensions of Enlightenment knowledge and the actual results of the investigations made possible by the new critical rationalism of the Enlightenment as applied to the history and sociology of morals. Universality was expected. The unfaltering diversity of human norms and experiences was an unanticipated outcome, one with which many intellectual traditions continue to grapple.

It is not surprising that Enlightenment thought, placed against the historical background of a civilisation held together by the grand and universal narrative of Christianity, should produce a similar narrative with similar themes. The two major differences are the absence of God as the narrator, thus as the support for a realist faith; and an orientation towards the future centred around the capacity of 'man' to secure a means to the end of realising utopia on earth. With Enlightenment thought, then, the modern habit of xenophobia towards past cultures is commenced.[46] John Gray suggests that Enlightenment thinkers, inasmuch as they rejected Christianity, were mistaken in the attempt to construct a similar story, particularly one which was universal. In his work *Liberalism*, this is argued by looking at Kant, whose conclusions rest ('surreptitiously') on anthropological assumptions which have clear roots in 'the emaciated shadow of the immortal soul of Christian traditions'. Says Gray: 'Once Kant's metaphysic of the self is abandoned, there is nothing in his argument which favours liberal principles as uniquely appropriate for human beings'.[47]

Alasdair MacIntyre takes up the theme of the problems that have come to the Enlightenment project because of the continued fading of the 'emaciated shadow' of Christianity. MacIntyre argues that, although we continue to talk of moral judgements as being either true or false, why they are true or false has come to lack any clear answer. Indeed, he develops a historical argument, the main thesis of which is 'that moral judgments are linguistic survivals from the practices of classical theism which have lost the context provided by these practices'. In the context of classical theism, moral judgements had two particular characteristics: they were 'at once hypothetical and categorical in form'. Hypothetical because they took the form, 'You ought to do so-and-so if and since your *telos* is such and such' or, alternatively, 'You ought to do so-and-so: that is what God's law enjoins'. Categorical because they were seen to be an objective requirement, independent of the desires of the moral agents. When you take from moral judgements that by virtue of which they were hypothetical and that by virtue of which they were categorical, what they are becomes very difficult to understand. There is no longer any clear and undebatable meaning that can be ascribed to them: 'Such sentences become available as forms of expression for the emotivist self which lacking the guidance of the context in which they were originally at home has lost its linguistic as well as its practical way in the world'.[48]

This analysis suggests that the project to secure universal moral knowledge on the basis of Enlightenment thought failed because its own epistemological method was self-undermining. Given that the concept of human rights emerged in its modern form out of the Enlightenment, and given also that much thought about human rights attaches merit to the concept of human rights because of its Enlightenment credentials, the assertion that the universal basis of human rights and indeed of the whole Enlightenment project is unsustainable in intellectual terms has serious consequences.

Universalism doubtful

Human rights claims appear to suppose a common body of moral knowledge at the root of all cultures. It is this knowledge which grounds and constitutes human rights. This set of rights is then universally applicable because all cultures are supposed to have this common moral knowledge, which in many apologetics for human rights is claimed to be based on a universal natural law. These apologetics are often modelled in a neo-Kantian manner, with the claim that universal and necessary laws of morality are apperceived through the use of rationality, which rationality is the hallmark of what it means to be human. In contemporary political philosophy, the work of John Rawls is a clear example of this. Others argue that these assumptions ground instrumentalities such as the Universal Declaration on Human Rights. As we noted from Gray above, however, all such ideas of universality and rationality are dependent on a certain metaphysic of the self, which, as the empirical evidence shows, is not shared universally among the 'races of man' (sic).

The assumption of a universal reason which can be applied to determine human rights is itself one of many different ways of understanding what it means to be human, and what it means to think about this humanness. As was seen in chapter 1, for example, it is not possible for some people, such as those from certain Islamic traditions, to think about what it means to be human in the absence of what it means to be created by Allah and to be his obedient servant. The liberal methodology is to search for the universal truth in such an account and to discard the religious appearance. This, however, denies the legitimacy of a religious rationality (among others) and also denies the significance of behavioural outcomes understood as dependent upon such religious rationality, rather than on a secular universal truth uncoverable by what might be called cultural archaeology. As MacIntyre has famously argued, our differences and conflicts demand that we face the existence of rival conceptions of rationality – a claim some are still reluctant to accept.[49] This reluctance is demonstrated with surprising frequency in the literature on human rights, both popular and scholarly, where the prevailing view is often an unproblematised and confused pastiche of the natural law tradition, rights declarations, existential humanism and positivist state-centric international theory. What often appears is a smudged account of human rights as metaphysical entities, which inasmuch as they need a foundation for their inalienability and universality find it in our shared and common human dignity. Leaving aside the aforementioned problem of variegated understandings of what human dignity involves, there remains the problem that neither the concept of human dignity nor human rights, let alone their connection (with or without notions of duty for support), are self-evident realities.

It is in cross-cultural studies and similar encounters that the universalist aspiration of modernity is most questioned by diversity. Different ways of being in the world exhibit different forms of reason, challenging the assumption that the dominant, secular, modern, liberal form of reason is the only legitimate form. (This, it must be stressed, is not an argument for epistemological relativism. Nor does it rule out the possibility of concluding that some ways of being are better than others. It does suggest, however, that certain modern, secular and universalist pretensions to have ended the conversation may merely be a pause for breath.)

The concept of human rights is therefore in significant ways identified with the Enlightenment project, proving to be a useful tool in the attempt to articulate a critical morality, universal in its scope, secular and humanist in its content, and rationally binding. However, we have also seen that the secularist, rationalist, universalist, individualist, democratic and radical assumptions of the Enlightenment project are not shared by all, are questioned by alternative traditions of thought, and do not automatically find resonance in all modes of human being. Accepting this means probing the wider question of liberalism, the political philosophy which has sustained the notion of human rights since the Enlightenment.

Liberalism and human rights

Liberalism – the political ideology which grounds human rights in their contemporary form – is beset, according to Gray, 'with certain constitutive and incorrigible disabilities'. Consequently, the 'supposedly universal principles of liberal political morality dissolve into indeterminacy', revealing as they do the spuriousness of liberalism's 'universal humanity' and 'abstract person-hood'.[50] It is beyond the scope of this book to review comprehensively such critiques or the controversy they have provoked.[51] I shall, however, draw on them to briefly examine three significant liberal claims which relate to the argument presented thus far regarding the theorisation of universal human rights. These are, first, the idea of neutrality: that liberalism is a philosophy of the right, not of the good; in other words, that liberalism is procedural, not teleological. Thus conceived, it enables us to live together with our different conceptions of the good. Second is the conception of the individual self as an autonomously willing rational being, able to choose which version of the good life she or he wishes to pursue. Third is the conception of universal rationality itself: the belief that it is possible for reason to be universally authoritative on issues of morality and human institutions.

Neutrality

The idea of neutrality is the means by which liberal theory attempts to secure the consent of the wide range of people that will inevitably exist under any regime. The mechanism which allows for the existence of difference is *the idea of pursuing a conception of the good life.* It is argued by liberal theorists that, even though people have different conceptions of the good life, they nonetheless can appreciate that all people have a conception of the good life. This in turn is because all people are assumed to undertake their diverse ethical commitments in a common manner. Liberalism thus expounds a means for organising a society in which there are many diverse concepts of the good in a way which promotes tolerance between all members of such a society. Jose Ortega y Gasset expresses the beneficence and ingenuity of such a system, which, while being all-powerful, limits itself so that dissenters may have room to live: 'Liberalism … is the supreme form of generosity; it is the right which the majority concedes to minorities and hence it is the noblest cry that has ever resounded on this planet. It announces the determination to share existence with the enemy; more than that, with an enemy which is weak.'[52]

A liberal society is, therefore, a society in which the right is held to be prior to the good – that is, individuals have the right to hold whatever conception of the good they like, and individuals have the right to have their conception of the good tolerated by others with whom it is not shared. Public and civic administration is taken to consist in the procedural considerations needed for ensuring that autonomous individuals with diverse conceptions of the good can live together. Consequently, when members of the society meet in order to determine how the society should be organised, it is assumed that individuals will make decisions based on consideration of the right, rather than on consideration of any one conception (or several in combination) of the good. This would, after all, be unjust, as it imposes the good held by one person or group onto another person or group, which fails the test of tolerance and undermines the cohesiveness of such a society. Thus it is that consideration of the right becomes a matter of public debate – that is, consideration of the way in which society is organised to allow people to pursue, in their private lives, whichever conception of the good they feel appropriate.

The principle of the right and the good depends on dividing the world into public and private spheres. By relegating the good to the private sphere, society at large does not discriminate against individuals by supporting some visions of the good over others. This is the principle of liberal neutrality. As Ronald Dworkin puts it, state officials 'must be neutral on what might be called the question of the good life, or of what gives value to life'.[53] Joseph Raz further elaborates the way in which the idea of neutrality is used in modern liberal theory, distinguishing two principles. The first is that of 'neutral political concerns', which argues that states must help or hinder various 'life-plans' to the same degree. The second, 'the exclusion of ideals', argues that, while government action may help some life-plans over others, it should not act deliberately to help some over others. These respectively require neutrality in the consequences and in the justification of government policy.[54] In practice, however, political actors view the state as a tool for the advancement of their own private projects and are unlikely to be persuaded that this is inappropriate. The practice of politics suggests that the doctrine of neutrality, in either the consequences or justification of government action, is unattainable.[55]

This can be seen also at the theoretical level, as it is only the case that neutrality with respect to the good can be maintained *if* certain a priori limitations on the nature of such competing conceptions of the good are assumed. Any conception of the good is admissible if it conforms with a wider conception of persons and society, itself a liberal conception, being individualist, egalitarian, universalist and meliorist: individualist in that the moral primacy of the individual is asserted over claims advanced by any social collectivity; egalitarian because all persons are granted the same moral status, and moral worth is not a consideration in the relation between persona and political and legal institutions; universalist, as the human species as a whole is a moral unity, with cultural and historically specific forms of association being of secondary import only; meliorist inasmuch as it affirms that social organisations and institutions are capable of improvement and correction. It is these four features which give liberalism its identity and its unity.[56] Clearly, then, liberalism is not as neutral as some might claim. In this characterisation it is represented as more than a set of principles and institutions; it is a worldview or way of life which defines itself against its alternatives, alternatives which will find themselves fundamentally challenged if they stray onto 'liberal turf'.

Self

While liberalism advances the claim of neutrality, it nonetheless imposes a particular metaphysic of the self and society upon all. This obviously means that liberalism is only neutral among conceptions of the good life which accept such a conception of the self. Within the liberal conception of the self, it is fundamental that the person has the freedom to operationalise her individuality and autonomy by choosing the concrete conception of the good that she will follow in life. Human rights, then, as Robin Holt memorably puts it, are one way in which liberalism articulates 'the claim for autonomy, for self-rule, and the resultant political subjects end up like bottles on an apothecary's shelf; contained in neat and regimented equilibrium, none polluting the other and each fully identified and labelled as being free, capable and of intrinsic worth'.[57]

It is not evident to everyone, however, that we are all drifters, able to revoke every commitment, turn from any commonality with others at will. The portrait liberalism paints is of the unencumbered self, a self independent of and capable of choosing between all purposes and ends. While some social environments may allow for the existence of such socially disengaged individuals, most people find themselves embedded in relationships and circumstances which penetrate and define our very self-understanding:

> A vision of the self as antecedently individuated excludes any conception of the good which allows for or presupposes constitutive personal attachments to values, projects and communities; a society built with antecedently individuated selves in mind cannot provide a home for those whose conceptions of the good are built around such constitutive attachments and so founded upon a very different conception of the person ... A certain range of conceptions of the good will be unable to flourish in a truly liberal society because the individualist and asocial metaphysical foundations of liberal principles of justice generate an inability to perceive or acknowledge the varieties of human moral experience around which those conceptions of human good are crystallised and their true worth displayed.[58]

Within the Amish community, for example, communal solidarity is paramount, not individual choice. To educate and inform people such that they have the choice to leave is to undermine the meaning of being Amish. Instead, to the extent that its members are informed of their capacity to choose to leave, it becomes a liberal community with an Amish gloss. This may or may not be a good thing, but, whatever one judges about that, it is not the case that the community is still Amish. Clearly, liberalism is not at all neutral to different ways of life. Rather, the diversity of traditional and otherwise plural communities is replaced by a one-dimensional 'regime of individual choices'. Thus, in the liberal tradition individual free choice trumps the right of any community to collectively believe its truth claims. The community is prevented from fulfilling its role in shaping a people of character and virtue because the a priori legitimacy of individual choice championed by liberalism refuses the community any authority in its truth claims.[59]

The result of a liberal social order is the preservation of liberalism through the coercive means of the state at the expense of other forms of the good life. This seems to leave some liberals unperturbed. Rawls, for example, has a 'relatively sanguine view' of the manner in which various ways of life are destroyed by the liberal project.[60] According to Rawls, a conception of the good that is not able to flourish under liberal conditions shows by this that its value is not clear and that its passing is not necessarily to be regretted.[61] Once liberals are frank like this about liberalism's lack of neutrality they will also have to concede that there are a great many more people who will 'suffer under a liberal dispensation' than has usually been claimed to be the case.[62] This recognises that the demand for neutrality in public life is in fact a way of forcing people to participate on liberal terms, often with the consequence that they cannot be true to their own vision of civic community.

The unencumbered self, it appears, is a presupposition that is needed by the attempt to create a political philosophy which tries to operate on the principle of universal conceptions of justice or rights. However, Holt argues that 'to the extent that human rights conceives choice as constitutive of the development and *inner* commitment of some inner entity or foundational field they are incoherent. To have any substance life must have a hold of something, deep attachments to tradition coupled with equally deep revulsions ... If human rights are to function they must meld with the multifarious practices by which many people conceive integral aspects of their character; the very real and partial reasons for their bothering to exist in the world at all.'[63] By contrast, and as exemplified most famously by Rawls, the unencumbered self does not deal with people and their institutions as they are found in the world but tries to be agent-neutral and rid of all loyalties and conceptions of the good.

Rationality

Rawls contends that people who do not accept his political liberalism are unreasonable.[64] That is, one cannot be reasonable unless one accepts Rawls' understanding of society and shares his conception of the self. His view on both of these involves a divide between the public and the non-public, a distinction that is crucial to the Rawlsian definition of political reason and one that is clearly not accepted universally.[65] However, Rawls does not give us any independent reason as to why we should accept his 'morally driven and question begging definition'. In short, he, as much as anyone else, imposes his own comprehensive doctrine in his attempt to create a society neutral to different conceptions of the good.[66]

To think that this could be anything but the case is to make a mistake that Stanley Fish argues is common among liberals.[67] The mistake is to suggest that liberal neutrality is such that it makes no a priori substantive judgements whatsoever. His contention is that liberalism depends on the judgement that the public sphere must be quarantined from positions which owe their provenance to something other than the procedures of institutional liberalism. This is why Fish claims that liberalism is in essence antithetical, among other conceptions of the good, to religion. The substantive doctrine of liberal procedures for the public sphere is a continual pushing away, questioning and rebellion against orthodoxies, dogma and beliefs that are not open to consideration and re-evaluation. This is confirmed by George Grant's observation that in conflicts between religious voices and liberalism it is religion which is assumed to be at fault for moving from the private realm to the public.[68]

Liberalism developed in part as a response to intractable religious conflict. An irony exists here, however, which is brought out by Fish's contention that the substantive doctrine of liberalism is held in the same manner as are those other doctrines, such as religious ones, of which it disapproves. He argues that one cannot have rationality without faith – they are indissoluble. This argument is devastating to the liberal project, because the notion of a public sphere where people can discuss matters of civic concern, having left their comprehensive doctrinal systems at home, is dependent on the possibility of separating rationality and faith. The liberal account is one in which the operation of the faculty of reason is independent of any belief or worldview. This is the primacy of reason, that which allegedly enables it to adjudicate between competing perspectives and beliefs.

However, as Fish argues, this conception of reason is itself a belief, the recognition of which immediately destroys the primacy of reason so conceived: any conflict of interests must also be a conflict of conviction. A conflict of conviction cannot be resolved – that is, rationally arbitrated – because it is necessarily a conflict of rationalities: 'The belief whose prior assumption determines what will be heard as reasonable is not itself subject to the test of reasonableness. Reason's chain does not ratify it, but proceeds from it.'[69] He continues, 'The fact–value distinction, which allows theorists to bracket off a public sphere whose deliberations are procedural rather than substantive, is itself a substantive stipulation that has the effect of prejudging what will and will not be considered a fact'.[70] The acceptance of something as a fact depends on what counts as evidence; it is not possible for evidence to exist independently such that it is 'immediately perspicuous'. On the contrary, we can only see evidence if it falls within that category of things we allow as evidence – that is, it must pass muster with our basic presuppositions or essential axioms before being accepted as evidence. These presuppositions or axioms themselves are not open to question but are pre-assumed authorities.

Thus, potential new beliefs are only ever examined by us in the light of previous beliefs, rather than from a universal vantage point. This can be demonstrated by moving from the level of abstract Reason, to the level of the reasons given for any adjudication of positions. These reasons do not emerge from a universal all-seeing eye but, rather, from individuals who are shaped by institutions, education, culture, philosophical traditions, and so on. Reasons come from the realm of the particular, and thus any given reason cannot a priori and necessarily be a reason that has applicability for everyone. This does not mean that reasons cannot be given or that they cannot be used to settle disputes. It does mean, however, the recognition that the status of reasons as reasons depends on the functioning of a discourse in which particulars are already ordered by a set of distinctions: 'In short, what is and is not a reason will always be a matter of faith, that is, the assumptions that are bedrock within a discursive system which because it rests upon them cannot (without self-destructing) call them into question'.[71]

Liberalism's central tenet of the veracity of a universal reason which is 'above the fray' of politics, convictions and beliefs leads in the political sphere, as we have seen, to the attempt to establish a political system ordered on the basis of a political philosophy of the right – that is, 'an adjudicative mechanism that stands apart from any particular moral and political agenda'. However, as Fish says, liberalism has a 'very particular moral agenda ... privileging the individual over community, the cognitive over the affective, the abstract over the particular'. Fish argues that, playing 'by the very partisan means it claims to transcend', liberalism has claimed the moral high ground from the religious and partisan discourses that had held it for centuries.[72] The victory of liberalism is said to be different from the past victories of other ideologies, because through the operation of universal reason it surpasses difference. However, as Fish observes, because liberalism is not in fact different, because reason will always be particular, liberalism, paradoxically, does not exist.[73]

This paradox is expressed differently by Charles Larmore. He argues, as does Fish, that we can only find our rationality through particular traditions of reason, not by trying to ascend to a detached point of view, for 'when we try to rise above our historical situation, reason loses its substance and becomes mute'.[74] The paradox emerges, then, as a direct consequence of the attempt by liberal theorists, following the Enlightenment project, to provide a universal claim on reason for the principles of liberal society. The modern neo-Kantian expression of this is the attempt to create a pure philosophy of right (the early Rawls, for example, where the public good is procedural, not substantive or reflective of any particular good). However, as Fish has argued, along with others such as Raz and Isaiah Berlin, a political morality based purely on the right is not possible. A political system of right is at base dependent upon human interests, which are in turn defined by comprehensive doctrinal systems. It is these which are the discursive systems Fish refers to which order the particulars of our experience, and by which we resolve the disputes which arise over rights. Different views of what human interests we have are generated by different discursive systems, which in turn contain different accounts of human flourishing and well-being. It is these accounts of flourishing and well-being which determine the reasons and evidence which will be given in support of one right over another. Political rights can only ever emerge as institutional conclusions to a long process of reasoning and politicking through which some accounts gain public consent and institutional reality. Right is always an end or conclusion, not a foundation, for a public political morality.

Gray therefore argues that the traditional formulation of liberalism, where liberalism is seen as rationalist and universalist, 'runs aground' on the historical reality of value pluralism. Within liberal thought this pluralism has been avoided because of the philosophical anthropology of the Enlightenment, in which cultural difference was an incidental, transitional aspect of being human. The transition, in line with Enlightenment assumptions of progress, was towards liberal Enlightenment values, a hope which is still held out by such liberal fundamentalists today. However, the values of Enlightenment liberalism are not universal and nor is the aspiration towards them. As Eugene Kamenka says of human rights:

> The concept of human rights ... sees society as an association of individuals, as founded – logically or historically – on a contract between them, and it elevates the individual human person and his freedom and happiness to be the goal and end of all human association. In the vast majority of human societies, in time and space, until very recently such a view of human society would have been hotly contested; indeed, most cultures and languages would not have had the words in which to express it plausibly.[75]

It is quite clear, then, that both as a procedure for expressing values, and as a set of values – those implied by the procedure and those explicitly advanced as the content of the system – neither liberalism nor liberal rights are universal, either descriptively or normatively. Descriptively, for not all people at all times have held to such values, nor will they necessarily come to do so as Enlightenment or liberal historiography would suggest. Normatively, because of their inability to claim a universal hold on reason. Because of both these points, it cannot be expected that either liberalism or an account of human rights based on liberalism would accept the conclusions of these different rationalities with respect to the creation of norms and standards for behaviour. These different rationalities are, under the influence of the myth of liberal objectivism, put in a box allegedly, although we have seen, not actually, different from the rationality of liberalism. This process of categorisation means that from the liberal point of view, non-liberal ways of thinking about the good are not legitimate grounds for universals. The argument here, however, is that the liberal conclusion is only acceptable to liberals and is demonstrably not universal itself, because it too is substantive rather than merely procedural, and as such is only one of many human self-understandings. Gray makes what he claims is a commonplace observation strenuously avoided by liberals: that many different forms of government besides liberalism may contribute to authentic modes of human well-being. The observation is avoided, he argues, because it undermines liberalism's claim to universal authority as a 'political faith'.[76]

It is not tenable, then, that liberalism and its summary doctrine of human rights be thought capable of exerting a universal claim on reason such that, as a political philosophy and a comprehensive doctrine, it has universal moral and institutional application. Accepting this means human rights are necessarily demoted from a position of universal applicability or relevance to people in all times and all cultures. Even while liberal theorists ponder whether such a conclusion is tenable, its reality is apparent in the contemporary usage of the human rights discourse: the term 'human rights' is now used in both the West and the non-West to refer to substantive values which are not identical with those of traditional Western liberal rights. Third-world critics have long argued that conceptions of rights based on universal notions of 'freedom, equality, ownership and opportunity' ignore the 'historic specificities and community contexts that define human roles'. Such blindness is also argued to contribute to the further disenfranchisement of the powerless in society.[77] These voices and considerations point to a need to accept that the concept of human rights is firmly historical, with no claim to being an ahistorical 'view from nowhere' on the proper condition of the human person.

Universal human rights by other means

The theoretical problems relating to the claims made about human rights derive from the heritage that the human rights idea has in Enlightenment philosophy and anthropology and in the liberal tradition. These meta-narratives are historical products of a particular civilisational tradition, and their claims to simple universality are qualified by the realisation that they operate within a historical horizon. It is not possible – and some would say not desirable – for an account of human rights to be given which escapes the limitations placed by historical particularity. As Fish insisted, any justification of a position on the good life will draw on a set of reasons which, far from being the operation of a neutral and universal Reason, are no more than an account put together using a conglomeration of particular reasons. The attempt, then, to attain the universal in the sense referred to above is a misguided project, the recognition of which means that universal human rights, *understood as they have been* through various natural law, Enlightenment and liberal traditions, as a metaphysical entity which is participated in, or itself inheres in, all human beings everywhere – such human rights do not and cannot exist.

Some theorists, while concurring with this analysis, nevertheless seek to retain the notion of universality for human rights at a theoretical level by investing that universality in the physiological needs that we have as members of the human species. This argument, that human rights have as their basic foundation universal human needs, was initially presented as an argument for human rights by writers such as Henry Shue.[78] As Bryan Turner puts it, from this point of view the argument commences with 'the notion that through the human body one can lay some claims about a common existentialist environment for human beings'.[79] Turner's argument about the frailty of the ontological human person has various components. These encompass a broadly Hobbesian appreciation of our experience of life and also take into consideration the issues of technological development, social modernisation, pollution and chronic disease which are specifically modern phenomena.

The crucial next step in the argument is to move from what appears to be a valid universal ontology of frailty to human rights. Turner says, 'My aim is to derive the idea of human rights from the notion of ontological frailty'. More specifically, 'My argument is that we can, in the absence of natural law, avoid sociological relativism through a re-interpretation of philosophical anthropology to assert an ontology of rights in the claim that human frailty is a universal feature of human existence'.[80] It is, however, at precisely this point that the argument fails, and for much the same reasons as those already explored. What Turner fails to do is to explain by what mechanism universal human frailty and universal human precariousness translate into human rights. This is the crucial issue for any theory of human rights. Turner discusses the frailty of the human situation; he argues that we have a common ontology of need. What he does not demonstrate is how this can lead to rights claims that are anything other than positivist law claims. He writes, 'I have attempted to provide a minimalist understanding of human attributes in order to circumnavigate the traditional problem of cultural relativism', and it may be argued that, by indicating a common ontological frailty in humans, Turner has succeeded in showing that common minimal physical, social and environmental issues must be addressed for human being to be other than Hobbesian.

What Turner does not establish, however, is the relationship between such a need and the claim that having this need fulfilled has the status of a right. This appears to be a common mistake. Because it is assumed that needs should be met, because these needs are seen to be universal and because they can be made to correlate with certain formulations of rights, the two are juxtaposed. By this sleight of hand, a causal connection between needs and rights is often thought to be observed. Take, for example, Joseph Camilleri's statement: 'There is, then, an obvious correlation between the universality of human rights and that of human needs. The common universality is no coincidence.'[81] This may be so, but nor does the correlation establish a causal or philosophical link which turns universal needs into normative universal rights. To suggest that it does is to give us an instance of the naturalistic fallacy: the claim that we can derive propositions concerning how human beings ought to act solely from factual propositions about nature.[82] Which is to say that neither our knowledge of justice, nor of rights which may embody such justice, can be derived from facts about nature.[83]

The problem may be explicated in another way – that is, rather than arguing as above that Turner does not provide a mechanism for turning needs into rights, we may argue that he in fact *does* provide such a mechanism and that is by way of his normative stance with regard to human frailty. It is an underlying commitment to the value of the person which makes human frailty more than simply a fact of nature, but something to be fought against, in Turner's account. However, this stance depends on certain implicit (metaphysical and teleological) assumptions, which are not made obvious, about the value of human beings. 'People's needs, it is assumed, *should* be met. This imperative cannot be derived from the mere fact that unfed humans will die. The prescriptive force of the needs–rights argument comes from its acceptance of a normative position which comes from the Enlightenment and liberal traditions which have been critiqued above. Thus the needs–rights argument is also vulnerable to the same critique in that its moral imperative implicitly draws on the same sources. As we observed above, this critique is most strongly expressed by Nietzsche – our values are derived from religious and metaphysical frameworks which have been undermined: we are all equal before God; but we have killed God and we still like to have our rights and equality.[84]

In sum, needs per se are not morally prescriptive.[85] We only have morally significant needs in the context of a wider framework. People have need of subsistence living standards only because we have made certain teleological and axiological assumptions: that the human is purposed to live and develop his or her potential, and that ensuring this happens is a good.[86] Thus, we see that the attempt to avoid the big philosophical questions by taking a physiological approach that purports to reduce rights to material or naturalistic considerations only avoids the questions inasmuch as it ignores its own assumed answers to them, answers which in the end come from the very same philosophical tradition which has been critiqued in this chapter. The conclusion which this suggests is that we can only coherently talk about human rights when we are speaking within the parameters of a philosophical tradition that defines the human person and its relations to society, values, purposes and ends in a language which invests the term 'human rights' with meaning as a tool for regulating relationships. We have to concur, therefore, with MacIntyre when he insists that needs or any other considerations which we use in the development of social institutions can only be turned into *rights* when people corporately fashion institutions so to do: 'Lacking any such social form, the making of a claim to a right would be like presenting a cheque for payment in a social order that lacked the institution of money'.[87] MacIntyre continues:

> The best reason for asserting so bluntly that there are no such things as rights is indeed of precisely the same type as the best reason which we possess for asserting that there are no witches [or] ... unicorns: every attempt to give good reasons for believing that there *are* such rights has failed ... In the United Nations declarations on human rights of 1949 what has since become the normal U.N. practice of not giving good reasons for *any* assertions whatsoever is followed with great rigour. And the latest defender of such rights, Ronald Dworkin (*Taking Rights Seriously*, 1976) concedes that the existence of such rights cannot be demonstrated, but remarks on this point similarly that it does not follow from the fact that a statement cannot be demonstrated that it is not true (p. 81). Which is true, but equally could be used to defend claims about unicorns and witches. Natural or human rights then are fictions.[88]

That human rights as such are fictions, and are recognised as such, need not be seen as a call to do away with the political and legal machinery that has been put in place to secure the recognition of such rights in the political world. On the contrary, such machinery is the social institution that needs to be in place in order for people to claim rights.[89] What needs to be rethought is the nature of the rights that are being said to be claimed: natural or human rights *as such* (which MacIntyre so polemically dismisses), or a conceptual alternative which avoids the pitfalls of universalist claims in areas of ontology, epistemology, axiology and teleology – and yet is a useful tool in our moral discourses. This latter option is explored in the next chapter.

Conclusion

It is clear that, even while we want to affirm the necessity of norms and values for human community, particular moral norms cannot be said to be immediately perspicacious, self-evident, inalienable, universal and justifiable in the manner of Enlightenment thought and human rights declarations. Rather, they depend on continuing traditions and communities of thought and practice. This in turn suggests the need for a new approach to human rights theorisation which, rather than attempting a neutral, universal and rationalist justification of our political beliefs, attends to what Gray calls 'the project of the phenomenology of the forms of moral and political life we find among us'.[90] This would suggest theorising human rights through the way in which they are adopted by disparate political communities and moral, religious and philosophical traditions the world over.

CHAPTER 4

Human Rights as Incompletely Theorised Agreement

The need for there to be a reconceptualisation of the universality of human rights stems from the plurality of different approaches to questions of justice, morality and ethics. The language of human rights, in some instances, has failed to be sufficiently aware of such realities and has fallen into the trap of Western liberal triumphalism. The existing human rights discourse is often viewed as an unproblematic articulation of moral progress in the twentieth century, as allegedly demonstrated by near-universal state recognition of the UDHR and subsequent instrumentalities. This recognition, however, is often belied by state practice and is not representative of the values and traditions of non-state actors. As it stands, the human rights project exists as only one of a vast plurality of normative traditions. The issue for discussion is how the claim to universality should properly relate to this plurality.

The task of reconceptualisation can be divided into two parts. First, the plurality of human traditions and the local appropriation of the human rights discourse give rise to a multitude of different and sometimes antithetical philosophical, religious and ethical justifications for the human rights discourse. It is not possible to answer the questions 'what are human rights?' and 'why do we have human rights?' with a single account capable of gaining universal assent. This empirical reality suggests that the traditional philosophical approach to the discourse needs re-evaluation. Second, this plurality of justifications for human rights derived from the various human traditions gives rise in many cases to different and at times antithetical substantive values for embodiment in the human rights discourse. Thus, there is no simple universal agreement on what values should be designated rights, nor for whom. It is in this chapter that the first of these issues will be discussed: the question of differing justifications for human rights. The question of differing substantive values is taken up in the following chapter.

This chapter, then, starts with the recognition of a plurality of conceptions of justice, of the good and of the right. This contrasts with other paradigms in human rights theorisation: those of liberal foundationalism or anti-foundationalist Anglo-American postmodernism. Both of these options are found to be lacking with respect to the theorisation of a global discourse such as human rights. This is because they presuppose means for the explication of human rights which cannot garner universal support, even when the human rights values themselves are not in question. Theorists declare the need for a 'third way', while being resigned about its apparent non-existence.[1]

The irresolvability of this problem has come to exist because of the expectation that there must exist one universal theory of human rights that will command assent from everyone – that is, the project to understand the norms and values of human rights has been one that pushes us to greater and greater levels of abstraction in order to overcome our particularities and form agreement on basic principles. This is the model of Rawls' theory of justice, for example, and more widely stems from the English-speaking analytic philosophical tradition, which is animated by a need to view the world *sub species aeternitatis* (that is, in the species of eternity or, more commonly put, the Archimedean perspective or the 'God's eye view').[2]

Drawing on the work of legal theorist Cass Sunstein, I contend that attending to our uncommonly theorised common aspirations is a more fruitful task. The traditional liberal attempt to understand human rights involves the construction of completely theorised philosophies of justice; Sunstein advocates *incompletely theorised agreements*. His argument is that such incomplete theorisation is, at a practical and moral level, more suited to a world of diverse plurality than is the attempt to arrive at universally applicable complete theories. An exploration of Sunstein's model generates a resource able to further facilitate theoretical discussion among those who are committed to the values and aspirations of the existing human rights discourse.

This resource comes in the form of a suggestion about how the discourse might most satisfactorily be reconceptualised – namely, as an international political–legal *tool* developed through an international, discursive, political process agreed on the importance of justice and its expression in social and political institutions. This is not unrelated to the present human rights discourse, but nor is it identical. It is not identical because the current discourse is largely dominated by a set of moral and political interests propounded by Western concerns. And, more fundamentally, it is a discourse which is confused about its nature: is it legal, political, moral, metaphysical, institutional, state-centric, cosmopolitan or some combination?

An effective reconceptualisation of the human rights discourse would help to clarify the links between these domains and the discourse. While human rights will always be a moral issue, the correct domain is the legal and political. This is because it then allows there to be a multitude of specific, cultural, religious and philosophical foundations which may support the human rights discourse, itself clearly seen to be a set of political–legal institutions. This removes from the human rights discourse its dependence on any one metaphysical system, tradition or foundation. It also allows alternative accounts of what it means to be human to endorse an 'exigent standard', which becomes universal in that it is recognised as a valid move by the different human traditions.[3]

Human rights becomes less threatening if it is seen as a proposal for what it might be like for people of various cultures and backgrounds to live together, rather than being seen as a doctrine or ideology which is forced onto people in an authoritarian fashion. To the extent that the betterment of the human condition is a shared quest among humans of many cultural backgrounds, the concept of human rights can be used to serve as a universal cross-cultural tool for the facilitation of that quest. However, if this is to be the case, the way in which the concept of human rights will be useful is not as a philosophy of the nature of humankind as it comes to us from the Enlightenment, but, rather, as the political–legal instrument for enshrining a common set of values, which are supported locally by a multitude of different ethical, religious and cultural moral systems *where they are in agreement*. Thus, human rights becomes a political settlement about how we should behave towards one another.[4]

Cass Sunstein and incompletely theorised agreements

My proposal for the reconceptualisation of human rights involves the development of a theory which provides space for various groups to have their own independently justified morality, the overlaps between which comprise the support structure of international political and legal instrumentalities and human rights declarations. The outcome of such a reconceptualisation would be to allow various incommensurable moral systems to support human rights without needing to vie with each other as *the* universal or true or final appropriate foundation for human rights as such. This provides for a *politically* legitimate way of articulating and theorising human rights, such that the discourse is not undermined by the ongoing debates among elite philosophers using arcane and technical language much removed from the traditions and moral vocabularies of practitioners and 'ordinary citizens'. The theory is political, then, in that its concern is with how human rights can be made sense of by the diversely pluralistic moral systems that do exist and that to some lesser or greater extent have entered the human rights discourse; it is not concerned to establish whether or which of these traditions is the best or finally true explanation of human rights.[5] The work of Sunstein on 'incompletely theorized agreements' can serve as the basis for a further discussion of the proposed theoretical reconceptualisation of human rights.[6]

Justice and pluralism

'There is a familiar image of justice. She is a single figure. She is a goddess, emphatically not a human being. She is blindfolded. And she holds a scale.'[7] Far from being endorsed, this image is deconstructed by the real world. Justice is not a single figure: it is conceptualised variously and antithetically. Justice, inasmuch as it is done, is mediated by humans, not by gods. Human justice will always be partial, not blind. Further, the dispensers of justice have no scale, with its suggestion of a uniform gradation between pure justice and the basest injustice. 'Human goods are plural and diverse, and they cannot be ranked along any unitary scale without doing violence to our understanding of the qualitative differences among those very goods.'[8] Instead, the bringers of justice 'must operate in the face of a particular kind of social heterogeneity: sharp and often intractable disagreement on basic principle'.[9]

As a US legal theorist, Sunstein directs his work at the Anglo-American domestic legal system. The USA is a democracy and, as Sunstein says, 'Democracies – and law in democracies – must deal with people who very much disagree on the right as well as the good'.[10] Such people, he argues, often distrust abstractions or grand theories that purport to explain the proper function of society. Such people are not philosophers; in addition, while judges are not 'ordinary citizens', neither are *they* philosophers. Judges do not have the time for unhurried reflection on the grand principles behind each case; nor if they did would they be in agreement among themselves. Further, a commitment to mutual respect and reciprocity is likely to forestall attacks on one another's defining commitments unless these are essential for deciding a case. With this background Sunstein says, 'My particular interest here is ... incompletely theorized agreements on particular outcomes, accompanied by agreements on the narrow or low-level principles that account for them (given different fundamental views)':[11]

When people (and here we may speak of individual agents as well as of collective institutions) are uncertain about an abstraction – is equality more important than liberty? does free will exist? – they can move to a level of greater particularity. This phenomenon has an especially notable feature: it enlists silence, on certain basic questions, as a device for producing convergence despite disagreements, uncertainty, limits of time and capacity, and heterogeneity. Incompletely theorized agreements are a key to legal and political reasoning in particular and practical reason in general. They are an important source of social stability and an important way for people to demonstrate mutual respect.[12]

It should be noted in passing that the phenomenon of incomplete theorisation does not merely exist at the level of particular outcomes and associated low-level principles. A first alternative kind of incompletely theorised agreement is on general principles: 'People know that murder is wrong but they are divided on abortions. They favor racial equality, but they are divided on affirmative action.'[13] Here Sunstein says that agreements are incompletely theorised in that they are *incompletely specified*. This lack of specification is useful for allowing agreement on common aspirations while the practice of these aspirations remains ambiguous; social stability and flexibility are both preserved. Second, people may reach agreement on mid-level principles but fail to agree on both general theoretical terms and with respect to particular outcomes. So, for example, those who agree that it is not right for the government to discriminate on the basis of race may disagree on general theories of equality and may disagree about affirmative action.[14] In general, Sunstein's main concern is that while it is not possible, in any group of individuals or association of such groups, to reach full agreement on a general theory of the right and the good (let alone about which has primacy), it is possible to realise agreement at much lower levels of abstraction, about certain particularities.[15]

Sunstein holds that by elaborating incompletely theorised agreement he is, to start with, merely *describing* the way in which Anglo-American law, and within that particularly judge-made law, operates. This is to counter the claim of some legal theorists who hold that areas of the law's function do represent one or another of the grand theories: utilitarianism, Kantianism, and so on. Indeed, that the law *should* represent some such grand theory is the normative position which makes it 'customary to lament an outcome that has not been completely theorized, on the ground that any such outcome has been inadequately justified'.[16] Sunstein, however, wishes to advance an alternative normative position, which is that the incompletely theorised nature of these agreements is desirable, perhaps indispensable, for 'the distinctive morality of judging and perhaps the distinctive morality of politics in a pluralistic society'.[17] This is not to say that large abstract theories are unimportant. Sunstein's position, however, does represent the belief that human goods are irreducibly diverse and cannot be subsumed beneath a singular master value.[18]

Achieving moral decision making amid pluralism

Sunstein argues that people are able to come to agreement on issues of morality similarly, in that while they do not have theories which comprehensively account for all the judgements they make in life, they nonetheless make these judgements. A full account of why certain outcomes are good and right is not provided: 'What accounts for the outcome, in terms of a full-scale theory of the right or the good, is left unexplained'.[19] This lack of explanation is the 'silence' to which Sunstein refers, and is that which Sunstein sees as the most virtuous thing about incompletely theorised agreements. 'Silence – on something that may prove false, obtuse, or excessively contentious – can help minimise conflict, allow the present to learn from the future, and save a great deal of time and expense. What is said and resolved is no more important than what is left out.'[20] Given this, 'the virtues of incompletely theorized agreements extend as well to social life, to workplace and familial life, and even to democratic politics'.[21]

One of the ways in which we affirm the desirability of incompletely theorised agreements, Sunstein argues, is by our commitment to the ideal of the rule of law. In a judicial system the rule of law constrains, in advance, the results of judgements – that is, the rule of law ideal is set up in opposition to rule by individual persons making law by virtue of their unrestrained choices in the context of actual disputes. 'Insofar as the rule of law prevents this from happening, it tries to prevent people in particular cases from invoking their own theories of the right or the good so as to make decisions according to their own most fundamental judgments.'[22] Thus, the rule of law ideal here expressly prevents the application of individuals' 'deep ideas of the right or the good' if those individuals are occupying certain social roles. This is precisely because high-level views are hubristic or sectarian and will lead, in a pluralistic society, to greater disagreement and loss of legitimacy for the institution in question.

Sunstein thus emphasises the point that incompletely theorised agreements are 'well-suited' in a world where there is large-scale difference about significant and socially prominent issues. Incompletely theorised agreements, then, allow 'convergence on particular outcomes', despite radical difference at the level of theory or worldview. This advantage is not only highly important in a theoretical sense – whereby intellectuals and other thinkers can reach agreements on paper – but also in the day-to-day need for social stability between disputants over public and private matters.[23]

Several subsequent points are made on the same issue. These revolve around the way in which incompletely theorised agreements promote two of the goals of liberal society, enabling people to live together despite disagreement, and to so live with mutual respect. They do not, however, leave the door open to all views:

> It is not always disrespectful to disagree with someone in a fundamental way; on the contrary, such disagreements may sometimes reflect profound respect. When defining commitments are based on demonstrable errors of fact or logic, it is appropriate to contest them. So too, when those commitments are rooted in a rejection of the basic dignity of all human beings, or when it is necessary to undertake the contest to resolve a genuine problem.[24]

Similarly, for those who are appointed as arbiters in society on matters of controversy, and for those who have to accept such arbitrations, incompletely theorised agreements provide an important cushioning mechanism in that they effectively reduce the political costs of enduring disagreements. In the case of judges, for example: 'When the authoritative rationale for the result is disconnected from abstract theories of the good or the right, the losers can submit to legal obligations, even if reluctantly, without being forced to renounce their largest ideals'.[25]

Another significant merit of incompletely theorised agreement is that it facilitates moral evolution over time. The example used by Sunstein is the concept of equality, a concept which has gone through various developments and evolutions. This is particularly noticeable when we look at issue areas: gender, race, age, disability, sexual orientation, and so forth. For each one of these areas there have been changes such that the key assumptions have been modified, even reversed. Gender and race are the clearest examples: once, it was obvious that those of the opposite to dominant race and gender were to be subservient precisely because they vere not equal to the dominant. Now, such a position is morally untenable. *Completely* theorised agreements derive all particularities from total theories. If there is to be development in morality and ethics, the whole of the total theory will have to be renegotiated with every change in particular moral and ethical circumstances. If, however, incomplete theorisation is the way in which a society deals with moral and ethical issues, such developments are able to occur without having to shatter a 'rigid and calcified' theoretical structure at each juncture.[26]

Incompletely theorised agreements versus overlapping consensus

The final area of Sunstein's work on incompletely theorised agreements that concerns the broader thesis here regards the relation between his work and that of the political theorist John Rawls.[27] Sunstein argues that there is a relationship between Rawls' concept of 'overlapping consensus' and incompletely theorised agreements, in that 'the idea of an overlapping consensus, like the notion of incompletely theorized agreement, attempts to bring about stability and social agreement in the face of diverse "comprehensive views"'.[28]

'But', Sunstein goes on, 'the two ideas are far from the same'.[29] The two concepts might be united in their objective, but their means of achieving that are opposite. Whereas Sunstein, in the face of disagreement, would have us move towards particularity, hoping to find agreement there, Rawls would have us move in the opposite direction: towards abstraction.[30] Rawls tells us that the deeper the social conflict we are trying to resolve, the greater the level of abstraction that must be utilised with which to clearly view and resolve the roots of the problem.[31] Sunstein, however, thinks that people may well have difficulty with abstraction: 'A special goal of the incompletely theorized agreement on particulars is to obtain a consensus on a concrete outcome among people who do not want to decide questions in political philosophy. They may be uncertain about how to choose among forms of liberalism, or about whether to select liberalism or a certain alternative.'[32]

Rawls sets up his approach to political philosophy in such a way as to prevent people from having to make excursions afield into the areas of metaphysics and general philosophy in order to come to conclusions about how society should be ordered. It is precisely because there is no agreement on the philosophical or metaphysical basis for society that the attempt is made to avoid drawing on such a basis in developing a theory of justice. Thus, Rawls' approach is designed to be a political approach that 'leaves philosophy as it is'.[33] But this relation, between Rawls' political liberalism and philosophy generally, is the same relation that Sunstein wants to draw between those who have to make decisions about particularities in life, and Rawls' approach: these actors, lawyers, judges, legislators, citizens, do not want to have to go behind a 'veil of ignorance' and discuss political philosophy; rather, they want to be able to leave this field 'as it is'. The Rawlsian approach, Sunstein fears, may be too much to ask of the general citizen; it is a project that requires much work and a clear head. The Rawlsian strategy, says Sunstein, in a liberal society committed to pluralism and social harmony, 'may run up against confusion, limitations of time and capacity, and fears that political liberalism is itself too sectarian to serve as a defining political creed'. Sunstein steps back from saying that these obstacles are insurmountable; however, he opines that citizens – or at any rate, members of a liberal legal culture – are more concerned with seeking agreement on what to *do* rather than on 'exactly how to think'.

It is not possible, of course, to completely abandon the issues raised by Rawls' methodology of abstraction, because every particularity decided upon by an incompletely theorised agreement will be informed by some sense of political philosophy, some metaphysic, even if this is merely in a background manner and is not brought to the attention of those involved. Sunstein recognises this, and even sees it as necessary:

> Of course some background abstractions should limit the permissible set of incompletely theorized agreements. Otherwise there is no assurance that an incompletely theorized agreement is just, and we should design our legal and political systems so as to counteract the risk of unjust agreement. If we want to limit the category of incompletely theorized agreements, so as to ensure that they are defensible and not mere accident, we may have to move toward more ambitious ways of thinking. But if an incompletely theorized judgment does command agreement – and if one correct account of justice calls for it – nothing should be amiss.[34]

Sunstein's concern here is for justice, an issue which is at stake in every particularity, in every agreement, but one which cannot be defined simply with reference to that particularity or agreement: the degree of abstraction is forced to escalate when any attempt to understand justice is precipitated. So it should be noted that, just as Rawls is unable to escape philosophy and metaphysics, it may be as difficult for Sunstein to totally disengage those areas from which he wishes us to be released.

Indeed, at one level, Sunstein sees such a disengagement as undesirable. It is clear that he thinks it is not possible for judges to function consistently and continuously on the basis of an overarching legal theory. For example, he strongly rejects the approach of Ronald Dworkin, whose hypothetical judge, named (appropriately and instructively enough) Hercules, is obliged to render all pre-existing legal theory – both statutory and judge-made – into a coherent framework of large and abstract theories which are then applied to the particular case at hand. Sunstein says that law practitioners 'avoid such theorizing because it takes too much time and may be unnecessary; because it may go wrong insofar as it operates without close reference to actual cases; because it often prevents people from getting along at all; and because general theorizing can seem or be disrespectful insofar as it forces people to contend, unnecessarily, over their deepest and most defining moral commitments'.[35] While Dworkin conceptualises Hercules as exceptionally methodological, opening the hidden structure of ordinary judgements to study and critique and developing comprehensive theory, Sunstein argues that non-Herculean judges do not function in this manner. This, for two significant reasons: first, it is beyond their time and capacity, given the role they are called on to play; but, second, 'because of the distinctive morality of judging and ... politics in a pluralistic society'.[36] Thus, Sunstein holds, it is not possible for judges to be Herculean.

However, it is undesirable that judges operate on a completely ad hoc basis. Even incompletely theorised agreements depend on principles and reason, though they are 'low level'. They may also be incorrect and, if so, incompletely theorised agreement 'may be nothing to celebrate'. Or they may offer pockets of inconsistency in the law which are undesirable, and the existence of which should encourage us towards something wider and deeper than the incompletely theorised. Sunstein's summary account of these qualifications is expressed thus:

> In brief: Some cases cannot be decided *at all* without introducing a fair amount in the way of theory. Moreover, some cases cannot be decided *well* without introducing theory. If a good theory is available and if judges can be persuaded that the theory is good, there should be no taboo on its judicial acceptance. The claims on behalf of incompletely theorized agreements are presumptive rather than conclusive.[37]

To the extent that theory or abstraction is applicable in law, Sunstein sees it in close relationship with incompletely theorised agreements. He argues that, over time, an accumulation of such agreements and low-level principles may develop into a more ambitious theoretical structure through debates and concrete rulings: 'Eventually the contested can become uncontroversial as new categories emerge and harden through repeated encounters with particular cases'.[38] The theory that develops, however, will have done so on the basis of a relationship between incompletely theorised agreements, generalisations, clarifications and concrete cases. Thus, it is not top-down or highly theorised.

This is not to say that there is no room for highly theorised, general, ambitious theories in the public arena. It is to recognise, however, that the part of the public arena in which those theories play a role is more properly the *political* rather than the *judicial* sphere. The sweeping theories of human morality and polity are to be discussed and enacted by those whose public office situates them in the political arena. Those in the judiciary, by its very nature, are constrained to work with incompletely theorised agreements, unless they are a veritable Hercules: 'The argument on behalf of incompletely theorized agreements is therefore part of a theory of just institutions in general and deliberative democracy in particular, with a claim that fundamental principles are best developed politically rather than judicially'.[39]

There is, however, one significant exception to this presumption against high-level theorising which Sunstein insists on:

> In order for participants in law (or democracy) to accept that general claim, they must accept at least one general theory: the theory that I have attempted to defend. This is the theory that tells them to favor incompletely theorized

agreements. That theory probably cannot itself be accepted without reference to general theoretical considerations, and its acceptance or rejection should not be incompletely theorized. Many people claim that law should reflect a high-level theory of the right or the good, and they will not be satisfied with incompletely theorized agreements. The choice between the two approaches will turn on issues that are both high-level and quite controversial.[40]

This, then, is Sunstein's theory of incompletely theorised agreement. I consider it a theory that can be employed in the task of reconceptualising theories of human rights.

Appropriating Sunstein

While the analogue between the Anglo-American domestic legal scene and the human rights discourse is not exact, there is nonetheless a highly fruitful encounter to be had between Sunstein's account and human rights theorisation.

Justice, pluralism and human rights

Sunstein raises the issue of the relationship between justice and pluralism immediately and in a visually striking way by drawing to our attention the 'familiar image of justice': the depiction of a goddess, blindfolded and holding a scale. Here we have the Olympian standpoint from which justice may be done. In the real world, of course, all justice is mediated by human beings. Any point scored by an appeal to Reason is really a point scored under false pretensions of universality, for all Reason is ultimately the specific and particular reasons of individual humans, mediated through their institutional and constitutive histories.

So too with Justice within the human rights discourse. At the legal end, the attempt is made to reach the Olympian ideal through human rights declarations and international courts. These are said to have universal applicability and to be impartial – but they are the product of a specific time, place and political agenda. At the philosophical end of the human rights discourse, theorists have sought to devise accounts of the nature of human rights which are applicable to all people, even to those for whom the terms of these theories are unknown or antithetical to their stated beliefs. The human rights project, then, lends itself to the traditional iconography of justice. It is also subject to the same critiques.

It is precisely because of this that the human rights discourse is in difficulties today. In turn, this is why Sunstein's theory has appeal. For both, the goal is justice. But the theory of incompletely theorised agreement does not encounter the same structural difficulties as much thought on human rights because its overt starting-point is precisely a repudiation of a singular conception of justice, holding instead to a recognition that justice is conceived differently by different persons and groups, and that it is not possible to reduce these conceptions to one overriding master value. To quote again, 'human goods are plural and diverse, and they cannot be ranked along any unitary scale without doing violence to our understanding of the qualitative differences among those very goods'.[41] Similarly, the traditions which articulate these human goods are plural and diverse. This is not to say that they are without 'overlaps', to draw on Rawls' terminology. The attempt has been made by many different traditions to accommodate the discourse of human rights, to translate their values into human rights language and to articulate a foundation for human rights philosophy from within the traditions. On the one hand, this has led to dialogue and shared understandings of respective positions among the participants. It has not, on the other hand, led to universal assent as to what human rights are and how we know this. On the contrary, it has led to different ways of understanding what human rights are, with some areas of overlap.

A positive way of describing this project would be to assert that a neutral language – the human rights discourse – has been employed as a way of discussing the various conceptions of morality, social obligation, political arrangement, and so forth found across human associations. However, in the same way that there is no 'Justice' as signified by the blindfolded goddess, so there is no neutral language. And while many have eagerly attended to the task of translating their traditions into the human rights discourse, it is also the case that the discourse is alleged by others to have a distorting effect on their conceptions of self, society, moral obligation, political arrangement, and so on.

Inasmuch as this 'translation' is achieved at the level of theory or philosophy, the foundations that are articulated as the fertile ground for the human rights discourse in traditions which did not originate the discourse face the same problems which have been identified in the previous chapter with traditional Western ways of understanding human rights – that is, they are singular and perfectionist. It cannot be the case that the Hindu, the Muslim, the Christian, the agnostic and the atheist are all correct when they claim that we have human rights because of a theory which grounds human rights firmly in their various doctrinal traditions. Yet this is often the outcome of this root-and-branch adaptation of the human rights project. As Ann Elizabeth Mayer has pointed out, some Muslim theorists not only ground human rights in the Koran exclusively but claim that Islam invented the idea first.[42] The danger of the proliferation of such approaches to the human rights discourse is that it becomes the object of different discourses of power which seek to legitimise themselves by ownership of the discourse. And this is the danger of a universalist–perfectionist approach to human rights theorisation, which ignores pluralism and diversity in human goods.

Charles Taylor helps us to see the contrast, in his discussion of what 'an unforced world consensus on human rights might look like':

> Agreement on norms, yes; but a profound sense of difference, of unfamiliarity, in the ideals, the notions of human excellence, the rhetorical tropes and reference points by which these norms become objects of deep commitment for us. To the extent that we can only acknowledge agreement with people who share the whole package, and are moved by the same heroes, the consensus will either never come or must be forced.[43]

Such a forced perfectionist and universalist conception of human rights might be said to flow from a *completely* theorised agreement, as opposed to an incompletely theorised one. We noted, following Sunstein, that completely theorised agreements derive their particularities from total theories – that is, from complex and (as far as is practicable) complete systems of thought that set out an explanation of 'life, the universe and everything'.[44] In other words, a completely theorised agreement rests upon a fully adumbrated worldview. All particularities, including rights and obligations, derive from that worldview in the same way that mathematical particularities can be derived from starting axioms. A theory of rights that functions on the basis of a completely theorised agreement and aims at universality will find itself in crisis when those starting axioms or assumptions are challenged and disagreed with, or when it finds itself unable to take account of certain particularities. Such a crisis is inevitable, as it is not possible to assert without challenge that any given worldview is universal. This is a thumb-nail sketch of what has in fact happened with human rights, and of the need for them to be reconceptualised on the basis of incompletely, rather than completely, theorised agreement. A completely theorised account of human rights means that human rights cannot be accepted without the complete acceptance of that theory. An incompletely theorised account, however, leaves room for differences about final justifications.

As we saw, Sunstein is interested in 'incompletely theorized agreements on particular outcomes', with agreement also on associated 'low-level principles'. With respect to reconceptualising human rights, we can take these 'outcomes' and 'low-level principles' to be the sorts of minimal standards of behaviour that can be codified into bills of rights. The notable feature about such bills is that they are, in all-important (and legally functional) respects, a listing of certain ideals for behaviour. They do not incorporate justifications for such behaviours. The classic account of the differences between these levels was written by Jacques Maritain in 1947 for the Inaugural Address at the Second International Conference of Unesco:

I am fully convinced that my way of justifying the belief in the rights of man [*sic*] and the ideal of liberty, equality, fraternity, is the only one which is solidly based on truth. That does not prevent me from agreeing in these practical tenets with those who are convinced that their way of justifying them, entirely different from mine, or even opposed to mine in its theoretical dynamism, is likewise the only one that is based on truth. Assuming they both believe in the democratic charter, a Christian and a rationalist will nevertheless give justifications that are incompatible with each other, to which their souls, their minds and their blood are committed, and about these justifications they will fight. And God keep me from saying that it is not important to know which of the two is right! That is essentially important. They remain, however, in agreement on the practical affirmation of that charter, and they can formulate common principles of action.[45]

It is here that a second similarity can be drawn between human rights bills and Sunstein's incompletely theorised agreements: that the use of silence about certain issues is a device for producing convergence between people in the face of otherwise conflicting principles of justice or other sources of disagreement. It is for this reason that 'incompletely theorized agreements are a key to legal and political reasoning in particular and practical reason in general'.[46] Without such a device we have to start at first principles and work our way to agreement, with the inevitable consequence of stalemate and strife precipitated by the (quite reasonable) unwillingness of parties to forsake their different and contradictory arrays of assumptions about existence.

At this point the discussion about Southeast Asia with respect to conceptions of human rights becomes highly salient. Findings were made about people's understandings of the ontological, epistemological and substantive axiological nature of human rights. The strong conclusion from chapter 2 was that there was substantive pluralism about human rights, and that this pluralism derived from substantive pluralism about what we have been discussing as the good and the right. So, to draw on one of the rights issues discussed in that chapter, the notion of religious freedom as a human right, and indeed the determination of what religious freedom was, could not be separated from more primal affirmations about God, humans, the relations between the two, notions of human sociability that flow from this, and so forth. In Sunstein's terms, the model being described here is that of a completely theorised agreement because the general, universal, outcome with respect to religious freedom could not be understood nor accommodated without direct reference to the fundamental tenets of a particular worldview. In some cases, agreement on conclusions was observed, despite very different arguments with antithetical starting-points. In other cases, agreement existed at neither level. In short, the non-Muslim's argument for religious freedom rights will not convince the Muslim, and vice versa. Therefore, the attempt to articulate such arguments as universal is misguided. What this suggests is that *inasmuch as there can be agreement* on, for example, a universal right of religious freedom, the incompletely theorised approach is the model which should be adopted by which to theorise about such rights, as opposed to the widely attempted completely theorised model, which serves to entrench differences rather than to overcome them.

In this respect an apologetic for incompletely theorised agreement as a means for theorising human rights may follow the route Sunstein takes for incompletely theorised agreement within the Anglo-American domestic legal milieu. Sunstein holds that, in the first instance, he is merely *describing* the way in which the law works; it is the second step in his argument which then goes on to advocate this as a normatively desirable means. Similarly with the practice (though not the theorising) of human rights. As observed in the previous chapter, human rights have been appropriated the world over by governments, NGOs and other bodies, *despite* the lack of any clear understanding of what human rights are or why they are said to be had by individuals (and more latterly, groups). Sunstein argues that, within domestic law theory, it has been de rigueur to argue that the law's function is to represent one or the other of a number of contending grand theories – utilitarianism, Kantianism, and so on – and that incomplete theorisation in the law is therefore a matter of lament, because it leads to the conclusion that the judgements made by the law are inadequately justified – that is, justification is required to be by means of a universal theory which encompasses all done by the law. As we have seen, Sunstein rejects this as neither the way the law operates nor as a normatively appropriate response, given 'the distinctive morality of judging and perhaps the distinctive morality of politics in a pluralistic society'. I am suggesting that the same observations and conclusions are normative for the human rights discourse. It is clear that the near-global reach of the discourse occurred despite the non-existence of any single, authoritative grand theory of rights. This, with Sunstein, is the descriptive point. *The normative point is to argue that a single grand theory for understanding human rights is undesirable because of the distinctive pluralism of a global society.*

Sunstein does not argue, however, that grand theories should be avoided altogether, that they are unimportant. They play on a different stage, the stage of politics rather than of the judiciary. In politics one can appeal to grand theories, as explanative, as motivational, as normative. Because of the institutional limitations of the judiciary, however, only a Herculean judge could synthesise all the relevant material into a grand theory – similarly with human rights. Grand theories – Marxism, liberalism, Islam, Christianity, Kantianism, and so on – can be used within specific jurisdictions to justify specific lists of human rights and to garner political support and activism for them. However, the attempt to synthesise the various grounds that these traditions would variously provide in their particularist justifications of human rights is a Herculean attempt, unachievable even for a Hercules given the antithetical nature of some of the fundamental presuppositions involved. The alternative, incompletely theorised, approach has the additional advantage that, in the first instance, it need make no statement about the veracity of these grand theories. It is able to achieve a theoretical reconciliation of the concept of human rights without having to decide between Marxism and Islam, for example, inasmuch as there is agreement on certain norms. By contrast, any completely theorised account, or grand narrative, has to assert itself against its opponents for both political and philosophical allegiance. Such a completely theorised perfectionist account of human rights could never achieve universal acceptance. This is precisely the fate of human rights as traditionally conceived in the Western traditions.

Incompletely theorised outcomes and human rights

One of the particular virtues of incompletely theorised agreement as a theoretical tool for understanding human rights can be identified by looking at Sunstein's discussion of the rule of law and precedent, or the principle of *stare decisis*: the operation of precedent. In the case of the rule of law, Sunstein argued that it prevents people – judges, in this case – from arbitrarily applying their own ideas of the good and the right to the issues before them. Similarly, *stare decisis* means that a judge's decision making is done with reference to an existing body of determinative decisions. Which is to make the general point that, in the domestic legal sphere, incompletely theorised agreement is not – cannot be – arbitrary but proceeds on the basis of an established framework.

Accepting such a model as a reality for the theorisation of human rights makes achieving a satisfactory theoretical understanding more likely than other modes of theorisation. It removes the burden to find an abstract theory the philosophical moves within which are acceptable to all the variegated intellectual movements which, in some form or other, participate in the rights discourse. The task of human rights theory becomes much less abstract and considerably more related to the normative point of human rights. It is no longer necessary for theorists to attempt to produce a human rights theory on the model of Rawls' *A Theory of Justice*. Instead, theorists have two main tasks. One is to take account, historically, of the way in which the term 'human rights' has been popularised and employed in this century. The second task would be that of inter-tradition dialogue on specific human rights issues – religious freedom, economic development, and so on – in the continuing attempt to identify the outcomes which are to be incompletely theorised.

At the institutional level this process can be thought of as well under way, on the basis of the international human rights law section of the human rights discourse. This arena provides much fertile ground for the operation of incompletely theorised agreements, in a more directly analogous way to Sunstein's domestic legal setting. It is not my intention, and is beyond the scope of this book, to develop a long excursus into international law.[47] Suffice to point out that the UDHR and subsequent human rights instrumentalities, along with their legal and institutional infrastructure, provide a legal human rights forum which has been formally subscribed to by the vast majority of independent states. That this has happened, and that the norms set out in these instrumentalities have received assent by the international society of states, frame the ongoing development of this legal aspect of the human rights project in the incompletely theorised setting.[48] That the international human rights law discourse operates in an incompletely theorised mode can be seen in that the UDHR and subsequent instrumentalities *do not justify* the rights that they assert. They are merely declared.

This lack of justification, this mere assertion, has been seen by many critics as a severe shortcoming. However, if we are wanting to theorise human rights via incompletely theorised agreements, this result is the most satisfactory. *Inasmuch as there is agreement* and assent to articles in these legal instrumentalities (an assent which from a state-centric perspective may be near universal, but is not from other perspectives),[49] a lack of justification explicitly associated with the instrumentalities allows for assent based on different modes of justification[50] – in other words, an incompletely theorised agreement. The alternative, trying to compose a theory which makes sense of all that has been developed within international human rights law, is itself perhaps an impossible task. In addition, doing so in a way consented to by all parties involved would require one of Dworkin's Hercules.

Within the context of the human rights discourse, two of the points that Sunstein makes with respect to disagreement and the political cost thereof can also find application. Because incompletely theorised agreements are *agreements* about outcomes, correction, criticism and rebuke remain and are vibrant despite pluralism. Sunstein's account does not open the door to relativism. As will be discussed below, this is not an unproblematic area, but it remains the case that where there has been agreement about outcomes, and where conduct does not respect those outcomes, appropriate measures can be taken, as defined by the agreement or the wider forum of agreement development (such as the United Nations). However, and this is Sunstein's second point, the political cost of disagreement on a particular outcome is cushioned. The debate focuses around the acceptability of a particular outcome, rather than on the appropriateness of a particular justificatory account of the outcome.

This will not always be possible, but, inasmuch as the outcome exists as an intermediary step between disputing parties, conflict is cushioned.

Sunstein also argues that one of the particular strengths of the incompletely theorised approach is the manner in which it facilitates moral evolution over time. This has immediate application to the human rights discourse, as can be seen when one considers that it has not remained a static discourse. Since the UDHR, the United Nations has enacted various other instrumentalities and made various declarations, such as those about the right to development and the rights of children. These developments in international human rights law are often couched in the language of generational development: the first generation consisted of political and civil rights, the second of economic and cultural rights, the third of group rights,[51] and there are various proposals receiving attention about a fourth generation, the focus of which would be women's rights.[52] Those philosophers of human rights who have attempted to develop a comprehensive theory of human rights at any point in this generational development have been forced by the political recognition of a new generation of rights to expand their theories, or to repudiate the development.[53] The human rights literature is replete with debates about whether the next generation of rights could legitimately be so called, whether such rights ended by undermining the whole project of rights, and so forth.[54] Such concerns are understandable and, in many cases, have meant that one way of conceptualising human rights has had to be severely modified or abandoned, if congruence between the political realities of rights and their philosophical explication were to be maintained.

Given that the project of international human rights will inevitably continue in the ad hoc manner in which it has proceeded to date, it would be more advisable to develop a theory of rights that, as Sunstein puts it, is capable of accommodating changes in facts and values, rather than a 'rigid and calcified' theoretical structure incapable of such accommodation. This means that the theorisation of human rights must be premised on pluralism and an openness to political developments and redevelopments of the concept of human rights, rather than resting on an a priori apolitical and abstract theoretical construct. Van Ness agrees, saying with respect to the new generations of rights, 'In some respects the different generations of rights are in contradiction with one another, and debates rage about which should have priority. To my mind, this is a good thing. The debates are a lively, creative process, stimulated by a widening circle of concern about how best to protect human rights.'[55]

Incomplete theorisation, overlapping consensus and Hercules

To this point we have focused on the ways in which Sunstein's model relieves strains that exist in contemporary attempts to theorise human rights, strains that derive from the attempt to find a universally applicable and completely theorised account of human rights. I have proposed that this strain is relieved by allowing different routes to the one outcome. Sunstein, however, is not prepared to accept all routes nor all outcomes, and it is in relation to this issue that his stated position may need to be modified in order to fully make use of incomplete theorisation in the area of human rights. Sunstein's incompletely theorised agreement is a descriptive and normative account of legal reasoning within Anglo-American *liberal* democracies. At the same time, he appears more willing than Rawls to accept that many of the people who by virtue of accident of birth live in a liberal democracy do not necessarily take the doctrine of liberalism to be an accurate account of the human condition and proper social organisation. Sunstein argues that in a pluralistic society even Rawls' doctrine of political liberalism may be too sectarian a basis on which to establish social consensus. This problem increases in magnitude when the attempt is made to find consensus on human rights. As already shown, no one completely theorised doctrine will command universal assent.

It may be argued too that Sunstein imposes 'sectarian' constraints of his own. These constraints do not appear to be intrinsic to the notion of incompletely theorised agreement but are imposed as boundaries within which such agreements can be made. There appears here to exist a nascent conflict within his work around the issue of pluralism. On the one hand, he argues that human goods are plural and diverse, not capable of reduction to one another or measurement on a linear scale. On the other hand, he proceeds on the assumption that there is a theory of justice that acts as a framework for incompletely theorised agreement, that is agreed to a priori by all parties concerned. Sunstein here speaks in a partisan manner (as quoted above): 'Of course some background abstractions should limit the permissible set of incompletely theorized agreements. Otherwise there is no assurance that an incompletely theorized agreement is just, and we should design our legal and political systems so as to counteract the risk of unjust agreement.'[56]

The difficulty is that there simply is no agreement as to the nature of justice. Sunstein recognises this in the opening paragraphs of two of his writings on incompletely theorised agreement, where, as we have seen, he deconstructs the traditional image of the goddess Justice. If this deconstruction of justice is important within liberal democracies, it is even more important when thinking globally. As chapter 2 has shown, definitions and justifications of justice vary across different political, philosophical and religious traditions. This, of course, is precisely the trouble with human rights as such and is also why Sunstein's incompletely theorised agreement is attractive to the problem in the first instance. The risk is that the procedure of incompletely theorised agreement itself becomes unjust and exclusionary because it sets limits on the sorts of categories of agreement that are allowed to be made.

It is the case, however, that the incompletely theorised agreement methodology itself is not what is open to criticism here but, rather, Sunstein's own normative view of justice and, more generally, the wider context which delimits the space in which incompletely theorised agreement can operate. Unlike the theories of Rawls and Dworkin, for example, incompletely theorised agreement as such has the virtue of not predetermining outcomes. Rather, the outcomes are contingent upon the historical, cultural and political contexts in which incompletely theorised agreement operates.

By contrast, Rawls' liberalism or Dworkin's Herculean judge end by posing a singular, completely theorised and universal theory. In order to participate in the outcome of such theories, people and cultures must be translated into the completely theorised terms of the agreement. Those attachments – cultural, historical, religious – which cannot be so translated must be left outside and unaccounted for by the outcome. They move into a private realm which is to have no intercourse with the corresponding public realm. This is clearly the case in Rawls' theory, where individuals must proceed behind the veil of ignorance, forgetting who they are, in order to arrive at a just outcome. This model is based on a consensual mode of justification, the aim of which is agreement based on 'a singular standard of public reason'.[57] As we have already seen, however, such singular standards do not accommodate the diversity of modes of reasoning that exist. This, of course, is only a problem if one wants to claim universality for one's theory of justice or human rights.[58] Given that this is the claim of the human rights discourse, adopting Sunstein's approach with its rejection of such completely theorised conceptions of standards of reason points us in the direction of a proceduralism which is better placed to deal with pluralism.

Sunstein's approach allows for a procedural norm which does not recreate everything in its own image, thereby excluding certain conceptions of the good. Michael Walzer explains that this sort of proceduralism is desirable because it can both help us to allow for divergent outcomes – 'locat[ing] commonality on the way to difference' – and provide a mechanism for agreement – 'locat[ing] commonality at the end point of difference'.[59] Sunstein's work is thus a useful conceptual tool for theorising agreement between those conceptions of the good that are able to meet on common ground in respect to norms for ways of treating other humans – in a way which does not presuppose any particular conception or justification of the good but which, rather, celebrates the diversity of conceptions of the good (that is, Walzer's commonality at the end point of difference).

It appears that Sunstein and Walzer share in disagreement with modern modes of political philosophy in which abstraction from all local, social, historical and cultural particularity is thought to lead to some variant on the Olympian or Archimedean perspective, that perspective from which Truth and Justice can be perceived. This is the model pursued in the earlier Rawls in particular (with 'the veil of ignorance' and 'the original position'), and in Habermas' attempt to establish an 'ideal speech situation'. On the contrary, argues Walzer, 'different social goods ought to be distributed for different reasons, in accordance with different procedures, by different agents; and all these differences derive from different understandings of the social goods themselves – the inevitable product of historical and cultural particularism'.[60] His overall complaint against this mode of theorising is that the vision of universality employed runs against both democratic aspirations and social utility because it fails to rely on what any valid theory of justice must rely on: the meaning of goods in concrete and particular social settings.[61] Thus, it can be seen that the point of methodological agreement between Walzer and the way in which I intend to appropriate Sunstein's notion of incompletely theorised agreement is that both celebrate the particularity of social contexts and their meanings with respect to social goods as over against any Olympian or universalist standpoint. A model of human rights based on incompletely theorised agreements is therefore soundly based in the reality of many (historically, culturally, philosophically, religiously) differing conceptions of the good. This is precisely because, in incompletely theorised agreement, what is agreed on are the particularities, not the worldviews, which variously *justify* those particularities to different groups and persons.

Agreement on incompletely theorised outcomes

As we have noted, Sunstein's model of incompletely theorised agreements functions within the context of Anglo-American liberal democracies. While Sunstein stresses the diversity and pluralism of moral views within such democracies, he nonetheless establishes a normatively liberal safety net which delimits the arena within which incompletely theorised agreement can operate. In this context, there will more often than not be sufficient commonality for there to exist outcomes which can then be incompletely agreed. As noted above, this is one of the constitutive features of incompletely theorised agreements: they proceed from the existing discourse and build on it. They do not offer foundational justifications, complete theorisations or overarching abstractions.

It is in this that incompletely theorised agreements help make sense of the human rights discourse. The discourse already exists, comprising centuries of philosophical and religious speculation, and a half-century of institutional international law development. It is associated with the expansion of international society and the mechanisms of the late twenti-eth-century state. It is a discourse that has evaded every attempt at com-plete theorisation, either as a codification of the discourse as it presently stands or as a universally agreed proposal for how it should or might be re-theorised. There is, nonetheless, a certain normative structure to the discourse which provides the analogue for precedent or the principle of *stare decisis* referred to by Sunstein. In the same way that incompletely the-orised agreements in domestic legal contexts cannot proceed indepen-dently of the legal settings in which they function, nor can incompletely theorised agreement as a way of understanding what human rights should be proceed independently from the existing human rights discourse.

Thus, while there cannot be a human rights Hercules who is able to manipulate the existing discourse into a complete theory acceptable to all peoples everywhere, neither is it the case that theorising about human rights by the use of incompletely theorised agreement is in any sense arbi-trary. Sunstein argues that incompletely theorised agreements should not be ad hoc and nor should they operate in a fashion which produces incon-sistency within the law. This would be nothing to celebrate. Such out-comes would suggest that the agreements are too incomplete, are not taking sufficient note of precedent and the surrounding discourse. The existence of such cases is common within the human rights discourse and, indeed, they exemplify the problem of trying to approach the discourse with a preference for complete theorisation. Rights language is often used in politically charged environments, for example where political oppo-nents are using the discourse as an instrument in their cause. (This phe-nomenon has been examined in chapter 1 in the context of the Asian values debate.) Here, the discourse of human rights is being used by authoritarian governments in a manner which uses superficial plausibility to undermine the wider goals of the human rights discourse.

However, there are genuine cases where, precisely because human goods are plural and unable to be reduced to one master value, the inter-nally legitimate aims and objectives of religious and philosophical tradi-tions will be in conflict with one another inasmuch as they are translated into the human rights discourse and understood as rights. Can, then, universal recognition – using incompletely theorised agreement as a the-oretical foundation – mean that all people everywhere will agree on the particularities of behaviour that make up the standard corpus of human rights? The short answer is no.

The continuing problem

The continuing problem with relation to incompletely theorised agree-ment, for the purposes of this book, functions on two levels. There is the problem intrinsic to incompletely theorised agreement itself, which Sunstein identifies, and the corresponding problem which exists when the incompletely theorised agreement model is viewed as a possible resource in the task of theorising the human rights discourse. To revisit the first of these, Sunstein argues that, while the essence of the incompletely theorised agreement approach is the rejection of general, complete or abstract theories as the basis for the operation of the legal system within Anglo-American liberal democracies, there is one major exception. That exception is the general theory that posits the need for incompletely theorised agreements. Sunstein argues that the acceptance or rejection of this general theory should not itself be incompletely theorised. The issue turns on high and abstract theoretical considerations which are part of a broad theory of democratic government and institutions. The ongoing problem here is the basis on which one affirms this abstract theory of government and institutions.

When we turn to the project of re-theorising the human rights discourse with the aid of incompletely theorised agreement, the ongoing problem can be expressed in these terms: on what basis should one be persuaded that the particular outcomes known as human rights are appropriately located as objects for the practice of incompletely theorised agreement, and what is the rationale behind the attempt to persuade those who disagree on such outcomes, as are already established within the discourse, that it is the discourse which is authoritatively normative and not the objecting tradition?

The ongoing problem may be articulated in an alternative way. Which is to argue that the application of incompletely theorised agreement to the problem of human rights theorisation relieves the problems caused by antithetical justifications of sets of ethical practices which in all-important behavioural respects are identical. For example, a set of environmental rights may be variously justified as legitimate because commanded by God, necessary for utilitarian reasons, or intrinsic to the environment by virtue of its being. These three justifications in themselves privilege different fundamental values and may require additional beliefs and propositions which, because antithetical, cannot be synthesised into a complete theory amenable to universal assent. In such a situation, where outcomes are the same but paths to justification are different, incompletely theorised agreement is a useful means to re-theorise universal – in this case, environmental – rights.

However, an alternative scenario can be played out, also using environmental rights. Here we have an environmental movement that holds that the crucial factor is the preservation of the environment, with the recognition that, as John Gray has eloquently argued, what is good for the environment may not necessarily be what is good for humankind.[62]

On the other side may be the raft of adherents to different religions who are united in their common understanding that creation was designed for the dominion and stewardship of humans. The implication in this case is that humans are the pinnacle of creation and that the environment exists to serve and provide for humankind. In this situation there is no common agreement available on outcomes, even by the use of incompletely theorised agreement. The ongoing problem to be addressed is how this difference should be adjudicated. On what grounds, in both the philosophical and legal–political spheres, is one group's normative position to be dismissed?

What can be said at this point in the argument is that Sunstein's incompletely theorised agreement provides an invaluable tool for those functioning within the existing human rights discourse. It alleviates the crucial problem of repeated failures in the attempt to completely theorise human rights. And it provides a means for the further development of the discourse in a way which will continue to draw it together into a broadly consistent whole, capable of flexibility and development. An incompletely theorised agreement is inadequate, however, for the important question of dissent from the dominant human rights discourse, where there is considerable debate about the veracity of certain values which have been named rights.

Conclusion

The persistent claim of the human rights discourse is the claim to normative universality. By using Sunstein's work, I have attempted to develop a framework for the theorisation of human rights which is able to operate as the third way, which Michael Freeman has argued is needed in thought about human rights. The virtue of the Sunstein approach is that a universal outcome can be variously and particularly theorised, without the need for these theorisations to coincide. While the outcomes of necessity have to originate in one or another of the world's traditions, they can be appropriated by others and justified indigenously. This model works effectively for those who are already participants in the human rights discourse, or those for whom its behavioural norms are coincident.

As already discussed, however, there is not universal assent on what should be the content of the human rights discourse – that is, there is no universal agreement on outcomes, despite the option of incomplete theorisation. This signals the need for a more rigorous interrogation of the notion of universality and the role that it should play within the human rights discourse. It is with this observation that we are led back to Sunstein's concluding point: that such problems may force us to a level of higher abstraction, to the level of theory. Sunstein has been careful to argue that his claim for incompletely theorised agreement is presumptive, not conclusive, and, furthermore, that incompletely theorised agreement is a description of how the judiciary works. Inasmuch as the human rights discourse largely comprises the human rights international law discourse, there is a certain suitability for the translocation and operation of the concept. However, incompletely theorised agreement and its role in the judiciary are part of an overall theory of just institutions. The judiciary is only one sphere in such a theory; politics is another, and it is in this sphere that Sunstein sees abstract theories of the good and the right as properly operative. This sphere provides the forum in which such theories can legitimately fight for the allegiance of the demos.

This then raises a fundamental question about the way in which human rights have been theorised in the past, and with respect to the influence of a human rights *law* discourse of human rights. Which is to say, the deep assumption is that the human rights discourse should be modelled on the basis of a legal conceptual framework, whether that be an idea of the moral law or natural law, or, more practically and pervasively today, actual human rights law. The overtones here are of a fixed body of normative principles which merely need to be enacted once they have been recognised by right reason.

An alternative model is a political model of human rights, where disparate parties present their cases, argue their causes, discuss differences, and in the end a collective decision is made. When a decision is made by a judge, Sunstein argues, by virtue of incompletely theorised agreement, the outcome can be agreed. In the political arena, however, the decision will not be met with universal assent, except in rare cases. A model of human rights theorisation that is built around this paradigm better reflects the realities of difference in the world.

CHAPTER 5

The Return of Politics and Human Rights

The concern of the previous chapter was with the relationship between the human rights discourse and those understandings held across the human traditions about what constitutes just and emancipatory behaviour towards other people. The discussion revolved around the way in which the human rights discourse names behaviours commonly considered to be just and emancipatory, despite the radically different and even incommensurable reasons given for the rightness of these behaviours within the different human traditions.

Here the argument is taken a step further: to discuss the implications of diversity and intractable disagreement about what is meant by justice and emancipation. In doing so, the discussion does not attempt to define or ground the content of these concepts in a manner that will gain universal acceptance. This was the mistake of the Enlightenment and liberal projects. The discussion here proceeds on the assumption that the human rights discourse is about justice and emancipation, and that, while these terms may be defined diversely and even incommensurably between the human traditions, they are *not arbitrary*. In this way, the human rights discourse is recognised as an arena for the discussion, debate and institutionalisation of our various and sometimes antithetical conceptions of justice and emancipation. There is a need for an account of how this arena works and should properly be understood to work – a *political* account of the human rights discourse.

The ideas of a number of political theorists – Chantal Mouffe, John Gray, Seyla Benhabib, Stanley Hauerwas, John Rawls – are useful here. Mouffe's work is used as the principal resource in the discussion;[1] the others serve to add support, vary emphasis, expand application and act as foils. The main theme is introduced through Mouffe's notion of the 'political': that which in our interactions is based around power relations, struggle, conflict, antagonism and difference. It is the recognition that all our theoretical terms – equality, liberty, justice – have multiple tradition-dependent interpretations and are vigorously contested. Furthermore, it is to acknowledge the relationship between that which is thought to be properly 'political', the traditions of thought which define it as such and the influence of these traditions in any given social structure. It is to see that, in the absence of an Archimedean point, there can be no neutrality: reason will always proceed in a particularist fashion. This does not reduce rationality to brute force but, rather, demands that the *particularity* of reason be taken seriously even as it strives for *common* understandings. Thus, Mouffe argues for a new kind of articulation between the universal and the particular, an articulation which I suggest makes possible an intelligible account of *universal* human rights. In the political model of human rights developed below, the articulation between particularism and universalism is mediated by an examination of the universal *and* discursive tradition-dependent nature of justice. It is by examining the discursive and constitutive nature of justice, and the role that human rights can play as a language for expressing what is involved in the moral choices we make about whether to treat other persons justly or not, that universality and particularity may be reconciled.

It is crucial to recognise that, despite diversity and even incommensurability, *justice is not arbitrary*. Similarly, despite great differences across traditions and local situations, the values of human rights theory and praxis are not arbitrary either: theory and praxis both strive for the doing of justice, for emancipation from those ways of being which constrict proper human existence. All these terms – theory, praxis, constriction, emancipation, justice – are variously defined. These definitions are rarely synonymous across traditions. But at the meta-level they can be identified together as a language which seeks to articulate the ideal conditions for *being* as humans, given their fundamental assumptions about what constitutes such being. Thus, despite its necessarily political and discursive nature, it is not possible for the human rights discourse to arbitrarily comprise any values at all – such as those which would support injustice. It is for this reason that the position of Asian authoritarianism, examined earlier, fails.

A political account, therefore, explicates the human rights discourse so that the universal and particular aspects of multiple accounts of justice and emancipation can be articulated together, in a fashion which reinforces commonality of purpose and respects difference of understanding and application within the normative framework of the discourse.

Returning politics to human rights thought

The context in which I shall apply Mouffe's account of the political is that explored in chapter 2: that, despite the claims of much of the literature, there is widespread and fundamental substantive disagreement on the values which are said to be enshrined as human rights. This disagreement is masked by both methodological assumptions, which privilege agreement on certain values and use these as the model for the others, and philosophical assumptions, which generate the expectation and hope of common agreement. With respect to the former, widespread agreement that economic subsistence and freedom from torture are basic norms that all people accept is used to fortify the philosophical assumptions about the universalism of other values. These values are then built up as elaborate bills of rights which allegedly cover the gamut of human experience and are said to apply to all peoples everywhere.

However, the widespread agreement propounded by many human rights advocates does not exist beyond those very basic values of economic subsistence and freedom from torture and cruelty. Indeed, even these are problematic because of definitional issues. Practices, such as female circumcision, which are condemned in one culture as cruel are not so condemned in another and are even sought illegally by the alleged victims of cruelty when the practice is proscribed.[2] The particular issues explored were the rights of women generally, abortion, homosexuality and freedom of religion. Substantive agreement on these issues was not to be found among the interviewees who participated in the research, in the secondary literature on these issues pertaining to the region, or globally. Clearly, the list of issues involved may be multiplied, as indeed the values which have been nominated as human rights have multiplied during the last fifty years. Charles Taylor is correct when he says:

> All this must lead to differences of practice, of the detailed schedule of rights, or at least of the priority of them ... The demands of a world consensus [on human rights] will often include our squaring these differences in practical contexts, our accommodating, or coming to some compromise version that both sides can live with. These negotiations will be inordinately difficult, unless each side can come to some more fine-grained understanding of what moves the other.[3]

Taylor goes on to say that such a consensus cannot occur without mutual respect; in general he is hopeful that this can be achieved, although he remarks that this hope might find its basis in his optimistic outlook on life. He goes further than some in his recognition of the differences and difficulties that the human rights discourse faces because of such fundamental disagreements.

The question still remains of what is to be done when the accommodating, compromise and negotiation that a world consensus requires cannot be achieved. Chris Brown appears less optimistic than Taylor: 'Nothing in the recent history of human rights protection gives reason for believing that a meaningful consensus on human rights – as opposed

to a willingness to subscribe to unspecific norms which do not, in practice, affect state behaviour – actually exists'.[4] This is also Gray's point:
'The real agenda for political thought – ignored by the new liberals and
by their communitarian critics – is given by the conflicting claims of communities, just as the agenda for ethics is the conflict among duties and
among goods and evils'.[5]

It is by appropriating Mouffe's thought that Taylor's consensus can be
brought together with Gray's awareness of intractable difference in a way
which preserves rather than undermines the project of universal human
rights.

The antagonism of human rights values

Mouffe argues that relations of power, authority and antagonism exist in
societies and that the liberal idea of a transparent society, reconciled with
itself about its values and institutions through the objective use of universal reason, is harmful to democracy, liberty and equality. Ignoring,
covering over or disguising conflict by the imposition of a doctrine said
to be universally agreed to and arrived at rationally *is* exclusionary, even
as it is a pretender to pluralism. The doctrine of universal human rights
has impressive global support, and yet it is rarely questioned in the way
that Mouffe's critique of liberalism suggests is important.

The doctrine of human rights is built upon unproblematised assumptions of universality, individualism and rationality, assumptions which
Mouffe critiques as plural, discursively created and intransigently dependent on power relations. The classical account of human rights is that
they are self-evident and universally true. What such an account fails to
bring to people's attention is that the claim 'I have a right to x' is an assertion of power or authority which may not be warranted. The right of the
rich to own slaves, of men to dominate 'their' women, of women to ter-
minate the life of the foetus, of the church to deny women that right, and
so on – these are all 'rights' that have been arrived at through the establishment and hegemony of a certain set of social practices and values. It
is the case that each of the 'rights' or values just listed has been socially
questioned and in many such instances the present 'right' is quite the
opposite of what was previously the case. The point is that it is the very
language of 'universal human rights' that hides from us that these values
are contested, not universally held and often maintained by and for the
advantage of the powerful and authoritative in society. They are rights or
can only become rights with the evolution of the social practices which
support the hegemony of those values, such practices being the result of
either imposition or dissent in a range of social environments – that is,
they are dependently related to power and authority.

Many of the sorts of rights that Western liberals have traditionally claimed for all people are not recognised by intellectuals, NGO workers, political activists or politicians living and working within traditions other than that of Western liberalism. Yet, internationally, it is still the agenda of Western liberals which controls the human rights discourse. This is not in any conspiratorial sense, but in that it is these values which are hegemonic within the human rights discourse and which are continued because of the social practices of the human rights elite (crucially, an elite that is not accountable to the people whose rights it would ensure, comprising as it does NGO workers, intellectuals, bureaucrats, and so forth). It is of concern that the human rights discourse itself becomes a form of domination and control because it unrepresentatively enforces one account of the good life, ignoring pluralism. Emancipation to the liberal agenda is not the desire of all people everywhere and the liberal claim to know how best to organise society for 'human flourishing' easily reduces to an ideology of control and power.

Mouffe argues that it is in the move beyond the universalism of the Enlightenment and liberal projects that genuine liberty and equality are further protected. This is the recognition that claims to universality disavow specificity and particularity: universalism claims applicability to everyone and by so doing eliminates the significance of any aspect of a person's identity that cannot be found in every other person. Hence, the irrelevance of specific religious claims, gender identities, ethnic histories, and so on for the person as commonly conceived in recent contractualist liberal political theory. In reclaiming specificity and particularity, the significance of difference and the identification with particularist traditions and identities are recognised. Such a theoretical move, if successfully integrated into the theory and praxis of the human rights discourse, may prevent the ideological reification of the discourse and help to ensure its emancipatory nature.

It is at this point, though, that we need to hear Mouffe, because of the political nature of such a proposal – that is, the fundamental existence of antagonism and power relations in the proposal. 'The new rights that are being claimed today are the expression of differences whose importance is only now being asserted, and they are no longer rights that can be universalised.'[6] If we operate on the presumptions of the unitary individual self, the foundationalist liberal project with its 'veils of ignorance', its universalism and rationalism, the task of mapping out a set of universal rights which when adhered to properly by all social actors would ensure a just plural society is imaginable – for some, achievable. This vision is denied by Mouffe's contentions that (a) there is no unitary self, and that (b) we must, by way of recognising the political, encourage the development of the new set of specific and particularist rights according to difference. In exploring why this is so, we can see that the same issue is represented by the self conceptualised as an entity that can hold or be beholden to many possible subject positions, and the societal existence of difference, antagonism and competing values.

A man may be a husband, a father, an employee, a landowner, a religious worker, a homosexual, and terminally ill, simultaneously. These may be a limited sample of a wider set of 'subject positions' which serve to constitute the man's identity. Mouffe argues that there is no necessary relation between these subject positions, and that there is therefore no definitive identity that can be established for the man in question. At any point in social relations any one of these subject positions may become politicised, with the possible reshaping of priorities and rearticulation of self-conceptions, perhaps ending with consequences quite different – even antithetical – to those possible with the politicisation of other subject positions. This may particularly be the case if subject positions are held in tension with one another; where, for example, a man's sexual preference causes conflict with his constitutive religious beliefs, or his role as an employee causes conflict with his family responsibilities or property holdings. Within the individual there exist conflict and antagonism, the constant angst of holding all this together as that which is 'I'.

This experience of the self is replicated within society, and Mouffe draws attention to it in her characterisation of the change that is required within the human rights discourse as it expands to include till now unrecognised social movements seeking justice. Society, conceptualised as a homogenous entity, is analogous to the unitary self. A society recognised as diverse – multicultural, multi-religious, and so on – to the extent that it is diverse, finds itself in the situation of the decentred self: it comprises different sorts of people, and different sorts of groups of people, who have different and at times antithetical ideas about what human life is for and how it should be shaped, individually and corporately – that is, in the private *and* public arenas. It is here that we see the limitations of the liberal vision, for it cannot facilitate conflicting accounts of the public arena, only conflicting accounts of the private and personal good. It is for these reasons that the growth of the existing set of rights to include those pertaining to the new social movements will not be a smooth journey of inclusion but will be riven by controversy, antagonism, conflict. For these new particularist rights represent ideas of the public order which are not aspired to or agreed with by all those involved in the public order. The achievement of these rights is the end of a struggle between groups in society. It is not a process of social institutions being made to conform to an agreed theory of justice by rational actors but, rather, one group having mastered the arts of political persuasion so as to see their cause through, as against those who wish to retard such social change.

An illustration of how Mouffe's argument applies on the international scene is provided by Shih Chih-yu. Shih argues that human rights are not natural and universally guaranteed, but that they are 'psycho-cultural derivatives of wo/men's quest for collective identities. In other words, human rights are historically constructed notions that without question mean different things in different contexts for different people.' He argues that the traditional notion of human rights assumes that people everywhere have the same set of identical needs. This is obviously not the case, as attested by Mouffe's discussion of the new social movements.

What Shih then goes on to discuss is the way in which the human rights discourse has been used to guide political action between China and Taiwan, and how in this case the understanding of human rights is observed to be a function of identity: the 'Republic of China (or Taiwan) has attempted to change its human rights practices from those sympathetic with national security arguments to those in line with so-called "universal" understandings of human rights'. He interprets 'these changes not as convergence toward universal standards but as a reflection of identity politics in Taiwan, one that used to present itself in affective terms but does so now in intellectual and cognitive terms'.[7] Because of the particular political context in Taiwan, the notion of universal human rights is being used to protect certain interests and to discriminate against others. Shih says in conclusion that 'political acts that objectify certain human beings as the targets of human rights protection and others as irrelevant have come to be identified by the current KMT regime as central dimensions of an emerging indigenous image'. He argues that the affective need for identity in Taiwanese politics leads to a politics of difference where the creation of boundaries becomes pre-eminent, as opposed to the refining of self-understanding: 'This boundary-creating mentality further compels local human rights policies to attend only to the human rights of the in-group, and to conceive of those of the out-group as inconsequential'.[8] The result is that an ostensibly emancipatory human rights policy discriminates against certain categories of people and deprives them of *their* human rights.[9]

This outcome plainly exemplifies the political nature of the human rights discourse: that the way in which one group – be it an interest group, a new social movement or a state – conceptualises human rights and identifies itself with the discourse may be in conflict with the way in which this is done by another. Further, one or other of these groups may have entrenched political influence or power, may court public opinion more effectively, may have greater resources for communicating its message – and so may win out over the other. Even where, in principle, the rights being claimed by the different and competing groups are not antithetical (which will not always be the case), the needs, aims and ends of the groups in question lead to a political struggle. As Mouffe argues, once we deny the unitary self and extend the discourse of rights to particularist groups within society – and then, if we add from Shih the recognition of the play between identity politics and the human rights discourse – it becomes clear that the universal practice of human rights observation is not, *pace* much contemporary liberal theorising, going to be a calm collective convergence on a singular set of behavioural norms. Rather, it is going to be a political contest formed by the question of competing understandings of the practice of justice. This account is succinctly articulated by Gray:

> The most basic assumption of Rawlsian liberalism, which is that the task of political philosophy is to specify once and for all a set of basic rights and liberties that are immune from the vagaries of political conflict, denies the deepest truth of modern pluralism. This is that, since we hold to a diversity of conceptions of the good life, we have no alternative to a Hobbesian *modus vivendi*. Our liberties cannot be fixed once for all – least of all by a philosopher – precisely because the *political* task is to reach a practical agreement on them that is bound to shift with circumstances.[10]

This understanding of both the political process and Mouffe's theoretical analysis is confirmed by the discussions in chapter 3. There we saw that the values which were to be identified as rights values were derived not from the universal rationality ascribed to the unitary subject, but according to a process of contextual reasoning which derived its content from the tradition out of which it operated. Thus, the conclusions which were arrived at about the acceptability or otherwise of standard liberal rights – rights to freedom of expression, to religious freedom, to sexual preference, women's rights, and so on – differed depending from which 'subject position' the people in question were operating.

With respect to religious freedom, for example, highly articulate, well-educated, female academics can argue that it is not legitimate for a Muslim to think that she or he can just leave her or his religion at whim (or even upon long reflection). What is at stake here is not merely a matter of a different conception of the private good, but a matter of public concern. In Malaysia it is an issue of great political import, as cross religious–ethnic marriage laws insist that those changing religion must be converting *to* Islam, not away from, with attendant punitive consequences. The rights which should be accorded to the subject conceptualised as a religious subject are not the same as those for whom other subject positions have become politicised – thus, those who do not wish to convert to Islam on marriage to a Muslim believer may articulate a different set of particularist rights which (if sufficiently resourced) they will go into the public political arena to defend: the right to mixed religious marriage, premised perhaps on a belief in the equal standing of all religious traditions. It is not possible in this debate to settle the issue neutrally, rationally arbitrated according to universal principles of justice. This rationality, as such, does not exist. (It is in this sense that Mouffe terms 'politics' an indicator of the limits of rationality.) As Gray says, 'There is no overarching theory or principle by which such conflicts can be arbitrated'.[11] Instead, the outcome has to be a *political* decision one way or the other – the need for this act of decision being for Mouffe fundamental to the return of politics.

A decision means winners and losers in the first instance – an 'us' and a 'them' – and it means, in the longer term, response, reaction, persuasion, continued debate, antagonism, conflict; perhaps the revision or reversal of decisions, depending on who among the protagonists persuades the larger number of people (if it is a democratic process) or the significant authorities in society (if societal organisation is less democratic). Nikhil Aziz highlights these concerns, in respect to third-generation rights: 'If we ask the question, and we must vis-à-vis collective rights, as to who determines the collective, then we must also raise the issue, when we talk about internationally accepted human rights, of who is doing the accepting [of these rights] and how'.[12] For those who work with human rights in the field, the political nature of the concept is beyond dispute.

The recognition of antagonism, the decentred self, the necessity of decision, and the discursive nature of universality, rationality and individualism may be taken together as suggestive of a reading of human rights which does not leave them vulnerable to the critique of previous chapters. It involves moving the location of human rights. In much of the literature, human rights are conceptualised as being, as it were, 'above the fray' – that, inasmuch as achieving the political recognition of rights was concerned, this was an issue of forcing people who wilfully disregarded justice and sought their own aggrandisement and power to see what was 'right' and submit to justice, the natural law, reason, human rights. By contrast, what I am suggesting is that human rights should also be moved into the arena of politics – the contestable, the antagonistic, the 'us' and 'them' relations.

This move recognises that the concept of human rights and the surrounding discourse are the evolving product of a given historical tradition. The political nature of the human rights tradition can be observed by the way in which the tradition has been named, and by the evolution of the content of that tradition. The tradition we now call human rights derived from the natural law and natural rights tradition. Subsequently it was called the rights of man, or the rights of men and of citizens. It is now routine for commentators to point out that Jefferson, in his declaration of the rights of man, excluded blacks, women and slaves. The distinction between citizen and human is a fundamental one, signalling a seismic shift in the nature of political community. Similarly, the last fifty years have seen an increasing number of different rights recognised by the United Nations, as different interest groups have done the relevant politicking within the UN human rights machinery. The rights that result have undoubtedly been formulated and (to the extent that they are) implemented by a *political* entity: the United Nations is not the Archimedean point of liberal political philosophy.

What needs to be recognised is that all human rights have the status of the more recent and controversial generations of rights elaborated by the United Nations. The original declarations (as quoted in chapter 3) – the French, the American and the United Nations – were devised as a consequence of politics, by political actors, and they were contested in the public arena by those who had disquietude about the rights of man project. The human rights discourse is dynamic, evolving and changing. The internal debate and contradiction are part of that which stimulates a creative expansion of the discourse. It is as a consequence of a false philosophical method that human rights have ever been seen as other than political, in this sense.

A counter-argument is that this political conception of human rights gives some legitimacy to the activities and rationales of governments and other holders of power and authority that justify their ill treatment of peoples by recourse to different cultural understandings of human rights, such as those investigated in chapter 1. However, this is not the case. Any such legitimacy is only prima facie and is not sustainable beyond the point of cursory acquaintance with the arguments. To return politics to the discourse of human rights does not mean that any claim about the nature of human rights is acceptable; nor does it mean an end to rationalism, universalism and individualism in the articulation of the nature of human rights. Rather, as Mouffe stresses, it recognises that these are arrived at discursively – that is, they are not the product of an abstract, objective universal Reason, but of reasoning particular to the resources of the different human traditions.

This does not imply any form of arbitrariness or irrationalism, nor does it legitimise brute force or a 'might is right' mentality in the attempt to persuade others of the veracity of any given tradition's account. What it does imply is a recognition of different forms of rationality, different traditions of understanding human association and behavioural norms, and it opens the human rights discourse to input from these different streams of thought. The criteria for what is finally adopted into the discourse are determined by the state of the discourse at any one point in time, conceptualised as a set of living shared practices, combined with those ideas and ways of life that can be absorbed through interaction, discussion, living together, and so forth. The discourse functions in this regard as another of the human traditions. Its growth, change and development are regulated by the interaction of its composition in the past with its present circumstances. This provides a profoundly and prescriptively normative framework for development but one which is also open to reinterpretation and change, evidenced by issues such as slavery and women's rights. Thus, the criteria for what may or may not be accepted into the discourse of human rights are not determined by trying to get to the universal rules or reasons that are thought to be behind our moral perceptions. Rather, they are determined by the norms and ongoing practices of the existing discourse and the 'analogical comparison of cases' across traditions.[13] It is precisely this which prevents the political nature of the discourse from being arbitrary. The political is the recognition that reason is discursive and tradition-dependent; it is *not* the acceptance of majoritarianism or force as the sole criterion for determining what is right. The content of the human rights discourse, no matter how contested, cannot be arbitrary, because it depends on the interaction of the human traditions, themselves not arbitrary, within an evolved and evolving framework of prescriptive norms, the discourse, which is also not arbitrary.

In this context, Jeffrey Stout's work on historicism and relativism is particularly constructive. He asks, in the course of a discussion of 'rational adjudication' between competing options, whether the fact that '[rationalist] rules neutral with respect to any disagreement whatsoever are wild geese often chased but never found' means 'that the decision to take one side or another in a disagreement beyond "rational adjudication" is arbitrary?' His answer is a firm historicist 'no':

> To say that such a decision would be arbitrary is to give far too much weight to the notion of neutral rules. In understanding or judging the rationality of a choice, we need to know *whose* choice we are considering and the epistemic *situation* of this choice. Once the relevant details have been filled in, the sense of the arbitrariness will subside. 'Neutral' rules distract attention from the very details a situated agent would find most compelling.[14]

This would suggest that, when a thorough contextual examination of differing views on human rights is completed, although differences may still remain, they will rightly be judged non-arbitrary. Moreover, it is in the examination of context and local situations that the way of justice in individual conflicts will be found. This, in contrast to setting conceptual abstractions against each other. As Stout also argues, differences are rightly differences between people, not between abstract conceptual schemes. A liberal anthropologist and a nomadic tribeswoman in personal relationship with one another can come to see eye to eye in a way that static conceptual abstractions articulating their respective world-views cannot. Similarly, relativism is only a haunt to human rights for as long as the theoretical justification of human rights seeks to identify a foundationalist conceptual scheme to be used as the measuring rod against other such (but mistaken) schemes.[15]

The non-arbitrary normative orientation of any right within the discourse will be about justice and emancipation, even when some parties dispute whether the right in question is just and, indeed, whether an understanding of justice that gives rise to such a right is just. Two examples may be drawn from the earlier chapters to illustrate. The first is the issue of abortion. There are very strong arguments for and against the use of abortion and its legitimacy as a right. The key point is that the discussion is held within a normative framework of justice and emancipation. For some parties, the right to abortion is a matter of justice for women; for others, the concern is with justice for the foetus. The outcome of the debate depends on the way in which justice is defined, the entities to which it is thought relevant and how it is applied. The definitions, relevance and application differ between the human traditions (and even within them), but the debate is obviously facilitated by a non-arbitrary framework: that of claims to justice.

Second, the move by authoritarian Southeast Asian governments to justify their rule in the name of culture is disallowed. As discussed earlier, the traditions drawn on by the governing elites exemplify their non-arbitrary nature. In order for them to act as legitimating forces they have to be abstracted from the practices of the people for whom the tradition is alive, and turned into propositions which can be manipulated to serve the altogether different social practices of authoritarianism. As Hauerwas comments, the witness of our forms of life 'is one of the most determinative forms of rationality'.[16] In cases such as these, the non-arbitrary nature of witness is quite clear, and the 'analogical comparison of cases' evinces a definite normative judgement against the possibility of including the authoritarian behaviour of Southeast Asian political elites within the human rights discourse as a legitimate interpretation of the discourse.

Raimond Gaita argues powerfully that the ways in which we live and work together form the language we use, that our concepts are conditioned by our ways of living. This stands against the belief that 'rational inquiry' is not to be conditioned by any way of living, that it is objective and transcendent. Gaita argues, using Stanley Cavell's formulation, that 'the denial that our concepts are constituted by and can only be mastered in the living of certain kinds of life is … philosophy's longstanding and deeply motivated "denial of the human"'. (The attempt, it might be said, to understand love rationally without giving oneself to others, the attempt to understand religion without being religious.) Thus, Gaita speaks of concepts such as rights and obligations being directly linked with certain forms of living – that there is a fundamental link between a language of love and its expression in behaviour and human relationships. This, as with Hauerwas, is what Gaita calls 'the nature of witness'.[17]

The point of application to the matter at hand – Southeast Asian authoritarianism in the name of cultural values – is this: there is a relationship of witness between our forms of life and the words and concepts we use to discuss our living. This relationship is not arbitrary and, because it has application across large numbers of people, it cannot be limited by self-appointed authoritative spokespeople. It is because words and concepts relate to the ways of life of communities that outsiders or political operators cannot simply and arbitrarily redefine the terms for their own benefit. The reality of lived words and concepts in the experience and responses of the community acts to prevent this. Such action is not always easy; it may often be costly of human life when a community stands against those would-be rulers and definers of community. This too is the role of witness: authenticity, integrity and commitment to the truth.

The witness we make to our forms of life, however, will also be a witness to our differences. In the same way that authoritarian imposition will not change the forms of life and love of a community, so, too, these forms – the human traditions – cannot be assimilated to each other. The modernist Islam of some in Malaysia is well able to stand as a form of life which critiques and subverts the authoritarianism of Mahathir's government. However, this modernist Islam is not the same as Western liberalism, no matter how much they may be in conversation with each other. These two human traditions cannot be reduced either to one another or to some underlying set of universalist values. Thus, we may again turn to the idea of the political.

An understanding of the political, given these considerations, suggests that it has the strength of recognising the antagonisms between the different human traditions and of facilitating a non-arbitrary conversation between them – that is, the real differences that exist between and within traditions are recognised and thus open to positive facilitation, rather than being smothered by an ostensive consensus on societal values. In Mouffe's writing these strengths are discussed in relation to democracy. She argues that democracy is hindered when there is too much consensus as well as too little. Similarly, too much consensus about human rights in the past has marginalised women, blacks and slaves, among others. In the present, the whole range of new social movements is challenging the existing consensus on human rights to extend and particularise these rights to a greater number of marginalised social groups. This phenomenon is significant as an indication that the human rights discourse can be further broadened to take into consideration the voices of traditions onto which it has been grafted: the Islamic, the Buddhist, the Confucian, the indigenous, and so forth.

To this point, it appears overwhelmingly the case that this expansion of the human rights discourse has been under the sway of – to adopt from Mouffe – too *much* consensus. This is finely explained by Holt:

> Human rights as certainties can and often do function as 'veils of ornamental deceit' which obscure the numerous different ways of solving problems of self-expression and control, many of which lie in the hands of indigenous peoples as opposed to the lofty tenets of international declarations. The genealogy ... of human rights is characterised by flux and continual emergence, it is dia-logic, yet most codes of human behaviour seem to remain solid, impersonal. This transcendental illusion which has concepts like human rights as invari-ant appendages to some inner, human core assumes an intellectual authority best exemplified by the uni-dimensional political utopias of Skinner (*Walden Two*) and More (*Utopia*) – a disturbingly uncontested non-agonal human con-sensus in which language feels somewhat redundant; where everything has been said before and the only quality required is that one much feared by Mill, the ape-like virtue of imitation.[18]

This 'imitation' is perhaps evident in the quest to find, within the various non-Western traditions, the rights outlined by Western liberalism. The non-Western traditions are forced to justify their own traditions in the rights language of the dominant Western tradition. According to this argument, even when the values themselves are consonant, the very act of having to translate them into the rights discourse of some form of Western liberalism in order to give them a certain validity is to cramp or even stop the expression of the tradition itself through the expectation of consensus on values and their form of articulation.

Rather than looking at lists and bills of rights as the final pronounce-ment on the values of a society, or of international society, it should be recognised that, as those values themselves are in a constant state of con-test, antagonism and ambiguity, so, too, the bills or lists of rights should exist more as prompts to discussions about our values and identities rather than as final accounts. It is one of the strongest arguments against having a domestic bill of rights, in the English common law tradition, that the rights which one generation sees as indisputable are seen by another to be insufficient, discriminatory, undesirable or actively destructive of society – the American right to bear arms often being cited as a clear example of the latter. That rights can be ambiguous in this man-ner is a good thing, for an awareness of the fragility of the things we hold most precious is a sure sign that there will be efforts taken to protect them. This is Mouffe's argument about democracy: it is not inevitable in human evolution, it is fragile and must not be taken for granted.[19] Simi-larly, I am arguing that taking human rights for granted as a settled account of what it means to be human is, in fact, more likely to endanger the rights of some humans than if the human rights discourse is recognised to be intransigently political, with the concomitant and continuous debate about the discourse that such a recognition should generate: 'The debates are a lively, creative process, stimulated by a widening circle of concern about how best to protect human rights'.[20] Further, Seyla Benhabib suggests that fairness and integrity in moral norms and values can only be arrived at through a process of 'practical argumentation', where all participants have equal opportunity to initiate, continue and give content to the debate.[21]

An alternative way of exploring this point is to consider Mouffe's statement that no social agent should be able to claim any mastery of the foundations of society. This again is said in the context of her critique of the methodology of modern political philosophy. Given the foundational place that rights occupy in much political thought, this statement has quite profound implications for the received wisdom that the functioning of society is dependent upon a set of stable fundamental premises about human relations between one another conceptualised as rights. Mouffe's own discussion of the rise of new social movements, and my suggestion that this also be applied to the interaction between the various Western and other political traditions, demonstrate the way in which these rights, as foundational to society's operations, are not so amenable to mastery. It is not, after all, possible to develop a theory of the foundations of society which will satisfy all members of society, *pace* Rawls. The liberal desire for a conflict-free society is a noble one, but, as Mouffe reminds us, it ignores the ontological reality of conflict in human relations. Neither a theory of justice nor an account of human rights can succeed, therefore, if it is premised on the notion of a unitary or singular outcome for questions concerning the just organisation of society, derived by foundationalist methodology. The paradigm of Enlightenment certainty is not an appropriate one for meeting the challenge of global justice.[22] How, then, should we defend and justify any question of what constitutes just social behaviour and organisation?

Justifying human rights values by social practices

Ethical knowledge is dependent on the cultural and historical conditions of a given community; it is open to the reasonable and the plausible, not just the 'rational'; indeed, it recognises multiple forms of rationality. However, Mouffe argues, 'to assert that one cannot provide an ultimate rational foundation for any given system of values does not imply that one considers all views to be equal'.[23] In other words, the non-existence of an Archimedean standpoint by which to determine ethical values does not reduce all ethical judgements and decisions to the arbitrary.[24] Thus, the values which are to be identified as human rights values are neither foundationally ascertained and universally perceptible, nor are they arbitrary or irrational. Hauerwas' comments on such a position in relation to theological and religious claims are significant for the present discussion, not least because many of the non-liberal voices wishing to enter the human rights debate draw on religious traditions:

> Antifoundationalism is not the same as irrationalism. 'The issue is not whether there are universal norms of reasonableness, but whether these can be formulated in some neutral, framework-independent language.' All that is called into question is the idea of a foundational discipline that can determine the standards of rationality within fields or even between fields. Reasonableness, as Aristotle maintained, is more like a skill than a universal principle. Rationality resides not in the mind but in intelligible practices which we must learn. Religious and theological claims are thus not immune to challenge, though they may be, like many other activities, not susceptible to definitive refutation or confirmation; they can nevertheless be tested and argued about. For finally, 'intelligibility comes from skill, not theory, and credibility comes from good performance, not adherence to independently formulated criteria'.[25]

Thus, the determination of which values should inhabit the human rights discourse emerges not out of foundationalist liberal philosophy, but out of a certain way of living together with other people, a certain mode of human behaviour, certain social practices and skills. This was the way in which the human rights discourse initially developed; it is through this process of shared living that human rights evolved from the limited rights of man and citizens to the vast array of rights that presently exist. This historical reality might suggest that the political philosopher's quest to rationally derive certain rights from fundamental axioms is indeed guided by an inappropriate methodology.

The task cannot be, as Rawls thought it was, to justify a universal and definitive trans-historical account of just societal arrangements.[26] Stout argues that this approach to justification is bound to end in frustration:

> Justifications are answers to why-questions of a certain sort. As such, they are dependent on context for three reasons: first, because conversational context determines the question to which a justification counts as an answer and thus the sort of information being requested; second, because conversational context determines a justification's audience; and third, because a justification's success can be appraised only in relation to the epistemic context of its audience, including its relevant reasons for doubting and the propositions its members are justified in believing.

Stout makes the very salient point which many appear to have ignored in their attempts to explicate human rights: 'Whatever a justification's intended audience may be, its actual audience cannot extend beyond the class of people who understand the vocabulary in which it is cast and who have mastered the patterns of reasoning required to follow it'.[27] Rawls appeals in his justification of *The Law of Peoples* to a liberal sensibility. He uses a liberal vocabulary, he reasons in the manner of liberal philosophers, he operates on the basis of liberal assumptions – one of the consequences of which is that he aims at universally applicable conclusions. This sort of philosophy will only be well received by liberals. Other audiences will find it strange and only distantly related to their understandings of the world.

In the first instance, this reasoning suggests that different justifications will be necessary for different audiences – a point which takes us back to the discussion in chapter 2. However, the critique bites deeper than merely suggesting that the terms of explanation should be different for different audiences, because, as Stout notes above, people's epistemic contexts are different, as are their ontologies and teleologies. No one justification has the capacity to embrace the various and antithetical starting assumptions held by members of the world community. There will never be one single authoritative account of justice; correlatively, there will never be one single standard by which prospective human rights values can be judged.

The liberalisms that seek such a standard 'foster a legalist and constitutionalist mirage, in which the delusive certainty of legal principles is preferred to the contingencies and compromises of political practice, where a settlement among communities and ways of life, always temporary, can alone be found. This primacy of the political sphere ... is an insuperable objection to ... all standard forms of liberal thought.'[28] Rather, the question is to be formulated by the way in which our shared practices of life (political and otherwise) embody certain values, and by so doing demonstrate that these values are constitutive of what we mean by justice – constitutive, not foundational. Thus, when Mouffe argues that modern politics is the struggle for order around certain 'nodal points', she says that this order will only ever be partial and precarious because of antagonism between different forces. These forces include discourses of justice which with their various interpretations of liberty and equality legitimate different forms of community, identity and politics.[29] For Gray, 'the end of politics is not the construction of institutions that are universally rationally authoritative. It is the pursuit of a *modus vivendi* among cultures and communities. Because ways of life are always changing, the terms of peaceful coexistence among them are permanently unfixed. For that reason the end of politics is always unfinished.'[30]

Again, however, the process of politics is not arbitrary. It happens within the context of a certain set of institutions which in modern democracies, in particular, foster a certain type of social intercourse which at least in intent is inimical to the subjection of groups or individuals to violence. So, there exist procedural restraints which are capable of reducing violence and establishing transparent discussion. Second, those who engage in politics operate out of traditions and approaches which are themselves, internally, not arbitrary, and usually, in practice, are able to communicate with other such traditions around them. While it is impossible, therefore, to establish a final grounding for the values which may or may not be included by a society in a list of human rights, the decision which determines the list is not arbitrary. Further, such a decision is renegotiable, depending on whether certain social forces have managed to gain hegemony such that their account of human rights values becomes the commonsense account. If and when it does, changes are made, as is evident throughout democracies in the West today, and elsewhere, as well as through history.

By taking this as the empirical as well as the theoretical account of how human rights are determined, the initial problem of different conflicting accounts of what human rights are becomes a part of the solution. This happens as a consequence of no longer seeking for a foundationalist interpretation of justice which is then parcelled into human rights. Instead, what is desired remains justice (expressed in part through the human rights discourse), but with the recognition that such a notion is discursively produced and that therefore, in order to ensure justice, it is important to allow the different accounts of justice to persuasively and dialogically contend with one another for allegiance. Justice is not defined from a neutral standpoint:

> It is neutrality that destroys dialogue, for the power of political talk lies in its creativity, its variety, its openness and flexibility, its inventiveness, its capacity for discovery, its subtlety and complexity, its potential for empathetic and affective expression – in other words, in its deeply paradoxical, some would say dialectical, character.[31]

It is, then, the maintenance of this debate which prevents society from stalling at the location of one interpretation of justice, and by so doing disenfranchising those who disagree. This account assumes the wisdom of Mouffe's principle that too much consensus is a bad thing. It also operates with Mouffe's account of power and decision: a society's political process is constituted by those who hold the authority to make decisions about issues. Decisions will be made about human rights values, even perhaps with the intent to disenfranchise when, say, the office-holder's views conflict with those of a radical social movement. This is the nature of the political: it is of necessity based on acts of exclusion and inclusion. The consequence of these processes is a rolling hegemony of different artic-

ulations of justice, of human rights values, which take their turn at being
the common sense of a society; which are open to debate; which are contentious but are also just to the extent that they are revisable through the
return of the political. Even when one disagrees with the 'liberal myth
of rights', it can still serve as a significant vehicle for the realisation of
agendas held by social movements.[32]

The application of Mouffe's return of politics thesis to the human
rights discourse has the consequence that the issue of different accounts
of what human rights values might be is not resolved by a rational arbi-
tration between accounts from a philosophically attained Archimedean
standpoint. This cannot be so, because the recognition of the political is
the recognition of the limits of rationality: that it is discursive and tradition-dependent, better represented as a skill which one uses within traditions than as a universal principle which judges between them.[33] To
demand that reason be able to provide a foundation or to serve as an
objective mediator is to ask something of which it is not capable. This
does not mean we discount reason and settle our difference by recourse
to power, force and a 'might is right' ethic. On the contrary, it suggests
that a wrong conception of the role of rationality in settling our differences *itself* employs a 'might is right' ethic by falsely claiming that reason
does in fact have the power to settle these differences and that this, 'X',
is the answer you must thereby live with (and that any dissent is a consequence of a false or mistaken use of reason). Reason may be applied
more 'rationally' once its limits and false claims are acknowledged.

Consequently, our differences are settled inasmuch as one or more of
the variously rational accounts of the meaning of human rights, in synergy, become the shared life practices of a community. In such a community the interpretation of justice is the subject of ongoing debate,
discussion, decision, revision – in short, justice is a fundamental issue of
politics. The answer to the question of which account of human rights is
legitimate is the account which holds hegemony within a context of continual challenge, contention, change, antagonism. This model ensures
the possibility of justice actually being done, for it does not close down
debate nor hold to the myth of a neutral or rational consensus, but maintains order in the same way that a juggler does: by keeping the balls
moving and in the air.

The return of politics and universalism

The political model of human rights better reflects the realities of the
world in which we live; it has more explanatory power than the traditional
law-based model. The law-based model, in its normative framework, draws
on the traditions of the natural law or the moral law, and in its positive law

framework – for example, domestic and international human rights law – is usually depicted as operating on the assumption that it is transferring that normative law into a positive law structure, which is then operated by a state or inter-state body. In short, the law-based model traditionally operates on the assumption of the existence of a fixed set of normative principles which can be enacted into positive law once they have been recognised by right reason.[34] Following from this, it is thought that agreement on these values will emerge in the development of a consensus at the international level. Thus, human rights can be thought to be universal because of this international consensus.[35] However, this consensus is highly qualified – as is signalled by such appellations as 'almost', 'at least in word', 'widely' accepted, 'more or less', 'aspirational commitment', and so forth. It is hard to avoid the conclusion that the consensus argument is 'both empirically and logically weak'.[36]

It is not possible to arrive at consensus in a way that will receive unanimous assent from the various religious, political and philosophical traditions of the world. There cannot be *one* agreed theory of justice when there is so much dissent as to what justice entails. In the above I have described a way of theorising human rights which provides a mechanism for understanding what we mean by human rights in the context of difference and without the guarantee of a knowable fixed moral law.

Reconceptualising universalism

By way of counter-argument it may be contended that such a political account of human rights does indeed make sense of human rights and pluralism, but that it does not make sense of *universal* human rights and pluralism; that the resolution offered undermines the claim to *universality* which has been behind human rights and which is the source of much of the moral persuasion of the human rights discourse. Such an objection has in mind an account of universalism which might be called 'simple universalism', whereby x is universal if and only if x is recognised (either positively or negatively, that is, in the observance or in the breach) to be normative for all peoples at all times. Such an 'x' has not existed: that is the implication of the foregoing critiques. Thus, if universality is applied to human rights in such a way that the singular rights must attain the status of x above if they are to be considered universal, then there is obviously no future in the adjective 'universal' for human rights; it will only ever be the case that a certain 'we' recognises the content of the human right in question. Thinkers from almost every area of scholarship have responded to the futility of covering over the complexity, heterogeneity and difference of humanity with some rigid uniformity.[37] Perhaps human rights thought resists this recognition so strongly precisely because of the regular appellation of 'universal' to particularist values.

Such recognition does not, however, end the discussion on universality. According to Andrew Linklater, 'it is not universalism as such which should be at issue in contemporary debates about ethics and difference but one specific form in which it is supposed that individual reason can discover an Archimedean moral standpoint that transcends the distortions and limitations of time and place'.[38] Giving up this universalism does not lead us into what Mouffe has called 'apocalyptical postmodernism', where all is characterised by 'drift, dissemination, and the uncontrollable play of significations'.[39] On the contrary, such a nihilistic response only demonstrates a continued captivity to foundationalism.[40] Given this, I wish to argue for a sense in which human rights are universal – an understanding of universalism, however, which is not totalisingly uniform, and yet which enables us to confidently avoid the sort of relativism that is often thought to be the only available alternative.

The human rights discourse represents something that is universal in all human beings: that we all are moral agents and that, as such, we need to judge human behaviour in moral terms. This is to see human rights as a contemporary language through which to express an aspect of being human which is universal, namely the capacity for moral judgement and choice, the moral sense which we all have, even if (as is the case) the content of that moral sense is not the same between you and me and others. Moral obligations, the construction of systems of understanding human behaviour in moral terms, thought about the content of morality, ethics, righteous living – these are universal characteristics of what it means to be a human person. It is true that moral obligation is conceived of in multitudinous and antithetical ways; it is true that systems of understanding moral obligation are diverse and even contradictory in regard to their epistemology, axiology, teleology and ontology; it is true also that not only most systems for understanding morality, but also most individuals within a given system (at least after the advent of modernity) will differ about the content of morality. This gives us a fluid and diverse content for the category 'morality', denying any one moral system's bid for universal acclaim. What cannot be denied is that, regardless of the moral system they identify with, persons are universally and constitutively moral, universally and constitutively creatures that make moral choices. By virtue of being persons with identities, we all make choices about the good, the valuable, what ought to be done, what ought to be endorsed or opposed.[41]

Human rights can therefore be argued to be universal in the sense that the discourse of human rights exemplifies something universal about being human, that we need to make moral choices about how we are to behave towards one another, that these choices (however they are additionally understood) are normative and binding (through whatever mechanism: this is one of the factors people will differ on), and as such their observance should be encouraged in the strongest possible manner.

It is seeing the human rights discourse as such a language of moral engagement that prevents our difference and plurality leading to a nihilistic relativism. The discourse must be able to offer identity and presence, as well as recognise difference and absence. The actual content of the discourse is an open, although not arbitrary, question: both practically and theoretically the content of the discourse is subject to the political. Human rights understood as a discursive response to the moral faculty of human being, however, can be understood in universalist terms, because to be human is to have to make moral choices.

The term 'concrete universality' has been used to indicate that human phenomena that occur interculturally (such as moral decision making) will not do so in an ahistorical or abstract form but will be 'clothed in the conceptual garments of particular cultures'. Here, the discernment of concrete universals comes from 'analogical comparison and contrast' and captures 'the phenomenon of structurally similar experiences constructed in different cultural idioms'. The universal is seen to exist in and through concrete differences.[42]

Such an account of universalism, as applied to human rights, can be elaborated by analogy to Mouffe's radical democratic politics, where liberty and equality are the core values.[43] In the same way that moral decision making is constitutive of being a human person, so liberty and equality are the constitutive principles of a liberal democratic regime. But there are many different interpretations of equality and liberty, and of how these should be applied in social relations and institutions. It is the character of modern democratic politics to prevent any one interpretation from being finally fixed, an outcome which would preclude the possibility of change. On the contrary, within the constitutive principles of liberty and equality, any number of interpretations vie with each other, constantly changing the social order. Thus, in the context of Mouffe's radical liberal democracy, equality and liberty are universal, but they are also particular, and that particularity is the consequence of the continual process of interpretation of equality and liberty – that is, of the political.

There is a similarity of approach between Mouffe and Ken Booth's politics of emancipation, which he terms the 'preferred discourse for human rights'. When Booth talks about an 'emancipatory politics' of human rights, he refers to a politics of becoming – not an ahistorical and timeless state of being – a politics which is not static, but which is contextual, open and flexible. He speaks of emancipation as a philosophical anchorage. Knowing what emancipation means does not rest on foundationalist groundings (as with many Western liberal accounts of freedom, equality or rights), but is developed intersubjectively, contextually and historically. It is not therefore relativistic, however, because it is guided by non-arbitrary particularist claims of emancipation (even though these may well differ or even conflict in detail due to their context). As with the terms 'justice', 'liberty' and 'equality', the answer to the question 'what is emancipation?' is both easy and difficult. It is easy because it clearly draws on the idea of resistance to human wrongs. It is difficult because we do not know what it will always look like in specific struggles. Emancipation, as Booth's preferred discourse for human rights, is then both universal and particular.[44]

So, too, human rights exhibit both universal and particular characteristics. They are universal by virtue of being an expression of the universal human capacity for moral judgements about behaviour to other persons, one's self and one's environment; they are particular in that the exact content of the human rights discourse will take its form as a consequence of an ongoing political process at local, regional, international and global levels, through the human traditions and existing or yet to be established institutions. These might be seen at their best to be a constantly renegotiated account of those things which are most necessary for protecting and enhancing that which is humane in humankind.[45] It is this political process which creates a genuine universalism. The dynamic nature of human rights, on this reading, is what enables the discourse to claim universality. The crucial requirement for this to be so, however, is that the discourse must be open to debate, critique, and expansion from diverse sources and traditions. In practice this rarely happens because it challenges the Western liberal dominance of the world system.[46]

This is to argue for a very different sort of universality than that which is usually presumed in discussions of human rights. The standard paradigm for universality provided by the context of liberal political thought is of a proposition about human behaviour that, because given assent by the proper use of right reason, has applicability to and normative force over all human persons. As we have seen, Mouffe rejects this form of rationality because it closes public debate and reifies one historically contextual account. Such a rationalist defence of liberalism makes the same mistake as do theorists of totalitarianism: 'it rejects democratic indeterminacy and identifies the universal with a given particular':

> Modern democratic politics, linked as it is to the declaration of human rights, does indeed imply a reference to universality. But this universality is conceived as a horizon that can never be reached. Every pretension to occupy the place of the universal, to fix its final meaning through rationality, must be rejected. The content of the universal must remain indeterminate since it is this indeterminacy that is the condition of existence of democratic politics.[47]

There is a relationship between this and what Benhabib calls 'interactive universalism', a universalism where difference is regarded as the starting-point for reflection and action which, in turn, aims for the development of moral attitudes and the achievement of political trans-formation. This is the ongoing struggle of people who are concrete embodied selves seeking a point of view acceptable to all – recognising that any such achievement cannot be legislated by Reason and will be contingent.

To reiterate, that the universal is indeterminate does not make it either arbitrary or relative. In the context of Mouffe's work, the universal is that indeterminate space constituted by the relations between certain institutions and interpretations of the meaning of equality and liberty. Similarly with human rights, the universal is found in the relation between the constitutive need for human beings to make just moral deci-sions, interpretations of the meaning of justice and the existence of the human rights discourse and concomitant institutions. The form univer-salism takes is the responsibility for engagement with others in open dia-logue on those issues which affect our welfare – regardless of nation, class, creed, gender, race, ethnicity, or other characteristics. The crucial point about such engagement, however, is to recognise difference and not assume it will lead to a rationalistic consensus.

Universalism, politics and extending the 'we'

What is universal about human rights is that they exemplify the universal need for human beings to make moral decisions based on their under-standings of justice. It is to ignore the realities of pluralism to hope that such a universalism will end in exactly the same content for human rights prevailing everywhere. However, it is here that we can pick up a second sense in which human rights retain their universalism. Not only is it uni-versally the case that people are moral creatures making moral decisions, but also that moral decisions made within a discourse of justice are either directly or indirectly evangelical – that is, they seek to enlarge the com-pass in which justice (however variously this may be understood) is done. Human rights are universal in this second sense, then, in that they seek to expand the compass of their practical and normative application such that, given time and good will, they do become descriptively universal. It is this future horizon that is the hope of the human rights project.

While often neglected, politics is fundamental at this juncture as well. Two examples illustrate this contention. First, An-Na'im suggests that the current international human rights regime 'is the best possible candi-date for the proposed universality of human rights' and that a deliberate strategy of internal discourse and cross-cultural dialogue will broaden the consensus that exists on the current international regime. As the con-tent of the regime is accepted within various cultures, it will be socially enacted and adopted so that eventually a 'jointly constructed cultural foundation ... will progressively diminish the aforementioned apparent paradox of the organic link between rights and culture on the one hand, and the reality and permanence of global cultural diversity on the other'.[48] Second, Camilleri argues that, if the human rights discourse is to be universal, it must 'necessarily engage and give voice to all major civilisations, cultures and ethical traditions. Cultural difference and universality merge when human rights discourse is understood as a dynamic process of continuous dialogue, which seeks to identify and cultivate the universal within each culture.'[49]

What is missing from such accounts is conflict, antagonism and unresolvable substantive difference: the political. These accounts appear to assume that there will not be sustained, reasonable and diverse objections to various of the values notionally dubbed 'human rights'. The attempt to embrace cultural difference has paradoxically led to its neglect. So, while the inclusive sentiment about all cultures and traditions has become very popular in writing on human rights, and rightly so, what is usually left out is Mouffe's insistence that there will nonetheless always be difference and with it, exclusivity. On the one hand, we have Rorty's concern to include people within 'our group'. On the other hand, to think that we can avoid forming groups based around differences is to be utopian. And similarly, not all of the values which different cultures conceive as universal may coincide; a simple attempt to encourage a focus on what people perceive as universal may thus encourage conflict, not prevent it.

The human rights project, then, may be pictured as a map (not just geographic, but, for example, economic or philosophical as well) on which centres of human rights awareness are identified, and from each of which emanate concentric circles which indicate the attempt to spread the human rights culture over that centre's immediate area of influence. But there may be substantive differences in the accounts of human rights given at each of these localities, and these differences will become antagonistic at the point where the concentric circles from one locality overlap with those from another. It is here that the stuff of politics occurs, an outcome which cannot be avoided. As each locality extends its influence by enlarging the group known as 'we', the potential for conflict with 'them' grows more manifest. Within the context of a liberal democracy Mouffe has argued that it is the institutions of such a democracy which allow for the political to be 'domesticated', for difference, conflict and antagonism to be channelled such that they become beneficial to the community rather than harmful. In the absence of such parallel institutions at the global level, I am arguing that it is only by negotiating our differences that we can prevent our genuine and legitimate differences from degenerating into conflict.

What are the criteria for such negotiations? It may be said that with the present theories, where universals are appealed to, at least there is a recognised standard by which people may be judged. If that is relativised by being made discursive and political, to what does one have recourse when the accused violators of human rights appeal to their own standards?

It is in confronting this series of questions that the approach being suggested here is not new, but merely describes more properly what presently happens with the human rights discourse as it stands. For to argue that recognising the discursive nature of justice opens the possibility that dominating discourses and political actors might enforce their hegemony is to fail to recognise that such is the case now, and that it cannot be any other way. There are dominant paradigms in human rights thought, liberalism being the one most critiqued throughout this book. There are dominant actors, most of whom are associated with the United Nations and NGOs (such as Amnesty International). These do not hesitate to enforce their theoretical foundations and moral positions as they have opportunity. Thus, the way in which the discourse functions *is* political. Dominant actors will of course seek to reinforce their hegemony.

This may be seen as a vicious circle which is sanctioned by a political account of the human rights discourse. But the reverse is the case, for it is only by there being widespread awareness that this is how the discourse works that hegemony can be questioned and issues of justice related to the role of dominant theories and actors raised. The key, therefore, is to see that the circle, by being recognised as such, moves from being a vicious circle to being a virtuous circle. If the hegemony of a particular set of dominating ideas and institutions is thought to represent the Archimedean point that provides us with universal norms, those disenfranchised by that set of ideas have no recourse to justice, for justice has already been defined against them. It is only by recognising that justice is discursive and political that justice can be done, that a vicious situation can be made potentially virtuous. Such an account may be seen to leave little room for rationality. However, given the account of rationality discussed above, it also becomes just another tool of power or force if it is not recognised to be tradition-dependent. Reason is thus given its real purchase among all parties when it is recognised that it cannot legitimately be absolutised by any one group.

Does such discursiveness lead to relativism? The answer here is a clear, historicist, no – because, to repeat the point made above, while justice is recognised to be discursive, it is not arbitrary. It is this, fundamentally, which ensures that the political circle of the human rights discourse is virtuous, not vicious. The discourse of human rights is a discourse about justice. The contributors to the discourse come from traditions which have criteria for judging just behaviour. The issue is not whether any behaviour at all can be described as just, but is one of different criteria. Differences in ways of being and behaving exist: what is crucial to understand is that their self-descriptions and their descriptions by others are not arbitrary. It is this which allows the negotiations of these differences to proceed in 'good faith'.

Theory and practice: strategies for pursuing justice

In what ways, then, can the negotiation of our differences proceed – in good faith – in relation to the issue of human rights in Southeast Asia? Such negotiation is a complex business, and to be successful must happen at a range of different levels. It is clearly beyond the scope of this book to survey and assess the variety of different projects which may be assigned to this agenda. The present work is designed to help open up a space in the discourse of human rights for the serious discussion of such matters by critiquing those assumptions and forms of the discourse which appear to have prematurely set the agenda in concrete – in particular, Western liberal forms of concrete. The task of grounding the human rights discourse in the various human traditions, and of spelling out the relations between those traditions and international human rights law, local, state and regional human rights regimes, enforcement mechanisms and procedures – the task of both pursuing the project that Taylor wrote of as an 'unforced consensus on human rights' where there is agreement on norms but 'a profound sense of difference ... in the ... reference points by which these norms become objects of deep commitment for us',[50] as well as adding the political dimension of ongoing dialogue about unresolved differences – this task is an ongoing project which must be tackled in as many different ways as there are reference points by which it may be secured.

Nonetheless, it is important to indicate the manner in which the philosophical discussion which has occupied much of this work may find application in the region where we began: Southeast Asia. I suggest that there are three levels (to nominate only the most obvious) at which particular strategies may be undertaken to facilitate and spread the understanding of the human rights discourse explored above. The first is the individual level, where discussion and genuine 'good faith' relationships between individuals may function to extend appreciation for, if not agreement with, the different ways in which ideas of justice are interpreted. Second, there is the level where scholarly accounts of the various human traditions are brought into conversation with one another in the task of ascertaining the extent of their normative agreement and disagreement. A third level is that at which existing state and legal regimes are studied and contrasted. The manner in which states go about the business of enacting and implementing the regulations which govern society is at issue, both with respect to normative structure and institutional framework.

Three recent studies demonstrate the different ways in which non-arbitrary but diverse and differentiated conceptions of justice may find practical application. Each of these studies may be seen to function as exemplars of the different levels identified above. Daniel Bell's fictional dialogue *East Meets West* shows the way in which conversation and personal engagement can alter the basis on which we think and act. William Theodore de Bary's *Asian Values and Human Rights* is a fine example of the way in which the resources of a – in this case, cultural/philosophical – tradition can be employed to contribute to the discussion. Anthony Woodiwiss' *Globalisation, Human Rights and Labour Law in Pacific Asia* is a particularly salient examination of the relationship between specific socio-cultural characteristics and labour law regimes. Each of these books represents a different approach and operates on a number of different levels. For our present purposes I will demonstrate only the way in which each of these different approaches may be seen to contribute to my overall argument – that the human rights discourse needs to own its political nature in order for it to be an effective tool in the pursuit of justice in a globalised world.

East Meets West is the second of Bell's dialogues in which fictional characters discuss issues that can be located in the crossover area between philosophy and politics.[51] As well as being engaging to read (no mean feat), Bell argues that 'this form vividly illustrates the need for cross-cultural social critics concerned with practical effect to actually understand and engage in respectful dialogue with members of other cultures'.[52] The three conversations in the book are between Sam Demo, who represents a fictitious American government organisation called the National Endowment for Human Rights and Democracy (NEHRD), and a number of characters representing different Asian viewpoints on democracy and human rights. One, Joseph Lo, is a businessman and a human rights activist. Another is a Chinese professor of political philosophy, Professor Wang. And then – where Bell's material is at its most documentary – there is a conversation between Demo and the fictional Lee Kuan Yew, much of which is drawn from actual interviews and other publications by, with or about the real Lee.

The intention behind Bell's book is to promote genuine engagement between Western views on human rights and democracy, and those from other places – specifically, in this case, Asia. Bell is concerned at the lack of willingness to learn from others; repeatedly throughout the book the theme of being open to how things are done differently in different places comes through. This is brought out most clearly in those instances where Sam Demo is forced to confront the suggestion by his interlocutors that he is only really interested, as it were, in discussing his own views about Asia with Asians, that there is no openness in his approach to changing his mind, to learning from the local situation. Demo's Asian interlocutors, especially Lo, challenge him with regard to his conception of dialogue. They want him to take them seriously, to treat them as equals, to acknowledge that by having a dialogue they might both move to new positions. Demo does seem to recognise – after considerable persuasion – that his prescriptions for human rights and democracy in Asia need to be tempered by local knowledge. As Bell says in the introduction, 'The ultimate aim is to argue for the need to take into account the meanings and priorities East Asians typically attach to a set of political standards that have been largely shaped by the Western experience'.[53]

On the one hand, there will always be difference between the human traditions on a large range of issues. Bell, in the context of the human rights and democracy debates, indicates a number of areas: 'criminal law, family law, women's rights, social and economic rights, the rights of indigenous people and the attempt to universalise Western-style democratic practices'.[54] On the other hand, the same traditions provide the resources for decision making to be premised on a genuine concern for justice, rather than merely as a consequence of authoritarianism. Bell's book shows a practical dialogue about the nature of justice – a dialogue that is realistic about our differences but one which is capable of moving us closer together in agreement about the practice of justice.

One of my consistent themes has been the importance of the role of the human traditions in relation to determining the content of the human rights discourse. The traditions which provide the foundations for the way in which the human rights discourse has been formulated and has functioned in the past have been those of the European Enlightenment and, in direct descent from this, modern European liberalism. Moreover, this dependence on Enlightenment thought and liberalism has been the Achilles heel of the human rights discourse. Specifically, it is the conception of universalism arising out of these which, in practice, undermines the claims of the human rights discourse to be universal.

The remedy is a human rights discourse that seeks to ground itself not only in European liberalism but also in the variety of human traditions. The challenge is that the various human traditions do not all privilege the same values or share the same assumptions about the nature of reality. While there may often be overlap, epistemologically, ontologically, axiologically and teleologically there are crucial differences, about which there can be no a priori assumption of possible harmonisation. However, the extent of difference and agreement, the possibilities for consensus, co-operation and co-belligerence – these cannot be found without the availability of in-depth scholarly and (as much as is practicable) objective readings of the human traditions, readings which endeavour to do justice to both the human rights discourse as it stands and the various human traditions by critically exposing them one to another. This is what we have in the work of de Bary.

His *Asian Values and Human Rights* is subtitled *A Confucian Communitarian Perspective*, thereby directing our attention to one of the human traditions that has often featured in debates about so-called Asian values. Many articles have been written suggesting links between Confucianism and the meteoric rise and rise of the East Asian economies, suggesting that the shade of the late-lamented (by some) Protestant work ethic had found a new region to haunt. Confucianism and economic success were also linked with notions of authoritarianism, consensualism, and so on (see chapter 1). Confucianism was enlisted by the Singaporean elite as the tradition which provides the justification for its form of soft-authoritarian social governance (with democratic characteristics). I recite these instances as a reminder that Confucianism has long been instrumentalised by parties who, at a remove, are seen to have a stake in the possibilities it offers for political and economic legitimisation.

By contrast, de Bary's book is one which allows the tradition to speak for itself. It is beyond my competence to directly engage his scholarship on Confucianism. My intention in bringing his work to the attention of the reader is rather to point to the role that works such as de Bary's can play in the debate over human rights and Asian values. His work serves as a needed corrective to much of what is said within Southeast Asia on the part of ruling elites about their relation to Confucianism. As noted above, political elites use appeals to tradition as a blunt tool for persuading the masses of their legitimacy. The work of a scholar like de Bary is, however, nuanced, softly spoken, differentiated, historically informed and philosophically astute.

De Bary manages to tread that line between cultural differences and human commonalities. By doing so he manages to avoid the pitfalls into which many studies of this genre fall. Claims are made (caricatured here for ease of identification) that human rights are a Western idea suitable only for Westerners; or that the Western idea of human rights is the gospel that must be brought to all and sundry, regardless of their own cultural identification; or that the non-Western cultural tradition under examination thought of human rights first; or that the existence of some consonant values in different traditions means the existence of a common core of human rights; or, finally, that there are no real differences between the ideas expressed by Western liberalism and those of others of the human traditions.

I would suggest that de Bary's approach should serve as a model for all those who wish to bring genuine engagement between non-Western traditions and the Western-originating discourse on human rights. The way de Bary proceeds is instructive: his express intention is to take us beyond the somewhat superficial task of noting consonant values – select quotations from the *Analects* of Confucius – to examine issues of continuity and change in the development of the Confucian tradition. He correctly argues that Confucianism is not static or monolithic: it is an 'often conflicted ... gradually maturing ... tradition'.[55] He takes us to specific parts of that tradition, both historically and socially (looking, for example, at the specific cases of community schools (*she-xue*) and community compacts (*xiang yue*)) and explores, as in the latter case, the efforts of 'Confucians to strengthen community life and build consensual fiduciary institutions'.[56] In the end, de Bary manages to leave us sympathetically persuaded by his contention that 'a constitutional order supportive of some liberal democratic values and human rights, though not at all an assured prospect on Confucian grounds or Chinese calculations alone, nevertheless was not an idea totally foreign to Confucian thinking nor out of line with the growing critique of dynastic rule'.[57] For those whose support for the human rights project is predicated on the project's commitment to authenticity and genuine engagement, it is this form of considered, yet committed, reflection (rather than the bombast of polemic) that is most likely to generate hope.

Woodiwiss' book is, the author tells us, a report on a thought experiment conducted in the field of sociology regarding the claim that the patriarchalism of Pacific Asia can serve as a basis for an alternative human rights regime. Woodiwiss is qualifiedly optimistic that such a claim can be supported. While he admits to having undertaken this experiment against his better judgement – aware that the motives of many who question Western human rights are far from pure – he argues that the degree of cultural difference from the West means that, even were one to eliminate all such dubious motivations and have only morally commendable intentions, the end result would still be far removed from Western arrangements. Moreover, he suggests that a positive reading of globalisation gives the North an opportunity to learn from the South. Like Bell, he does not accept the idea that it is the North's job to bring the gospel of democracy and human rights to the South, thereby bringing liberation and civilisation. On the contrary, both North and South struggle to live up to the moral norms of their traditions and, in the process of coming to exist in 'a single global space', the process of globalisation, each can learn from the other in their pursuit of righteousness – right living.

Woodiwiss' thought experiment, then, is to suggest that the human rights project should be revived on a more equal civilisational basis, an experiment which is made more possible because of its coincidence with the end of the Cold War and the consequent 'eruption' within world affairs of a force in addition to the liberalism and socialism of the Cold

War. That third force is patriarchalism 'in all its diverse forms'.[58] Woodiwiss argues that this eruption of patriarchalism has seen many of the human traditions, often in the form of their associated 'reinvented traditions', come to play a significant role on the world stage – or, at the very least, has come to see these traditional bodies of thought gain a 'global presence … unthinkable even five years ago'.[59] In addition, he argues that the global centre of gravity, at least in economic terms, is shifting from the North Atlantic to the North Pacific. This, he claims, adds to the urgency – if we wish to understand the 'fate of the human rights discourse' – of fully investigating, in a sustained, serious and open manner (that is, to repeat, a posture which leaves 'us' open to learning and changing 'our' positions as a consequence of genuine engagement with 'others'), the manner and extent of the possibilities for a cross-cultural reconstruction of the discourse of human rights.

To this end, Woodiwiss' study has three express goals:

(1) to advance our theoretical understanding of transnational sociality and the consequent porosity of national boundaries in general, as well as of the varying legal forms that enforceable human rights may take in particular;

(2) to contribute to our substantive understanding of the interrelationships between transnational processes, economic and social development, and variations in the form of, and the level of respect afforded to, human rights in the theoretically and politically critical Pacific–Asia region;

(3) to contribute to the construction of a non-Eurocentric basis upon which increased efforts may be made to enhance respect for human rights in the wider world in addition to Pacific Asia.

In the movement towards these goals, Woodiwiss identifies a form of patriarchalism – 'enforceable benevolence' – the expression of which he analyses by looking at the sub-set of human rights dedicated to labour law and industrial justice, as they are found to be practised in Pacific Asia. The Philippines, Hong Kong, Malaysia and Singapore serve as case studies and receive intensive and detailed analysis. He argues that the question of whether 'enforceable benevolence' provides 'a plausible template for effective labour and human rights regimes throughout Pacific Asia' is answered 'in a largely positive manner' by the outcomes of his case studies.[60] 'Enforceable benevolence' will lead to a distinctive expression of the human rights discourse, but not one which is totally dissimilar to the outcomes of liberal versions of the discourse. One gets the impression of a family likeness that will be in play. There will be distinctive differences, as well as many similarities.

Woodiwiss' contribution to the debate is rich, erudite, detailed and sophisticated in its capacity to link theory with the examination of case studies. I have reviewed it here because of its quality as a work which engages the different human traditions in an attempt to work together on a specific range of human rights, not just at the level of theory but also at that of practice: the implementation of industrial justice in diverse societies, using conceptual and legal tools drawn from a range of traditions and melded together as part of the human rights discourse.

When theorists of human rights go beyond the comforting rhetoric of universalism to look at specific human rights and their relation to the various human traditions and modes of state practice around the world, it becomes evident that much work remains before it will be possible to sustain widespread cross-sectional support for large numbers of those claims which are called human rights. More studies are needed which take specific rights or sets of rights and review them in the manner that Woodiwiss has done, in order to provide a clear and realistic picture of the degree of engagement that exists with the human rights discourse, and the extent to which the discourse can be grounded in diverse modes of practice. Woodiwiss concluded, in his specific study, that the tradition of 'enforceable benevolence' could be interpreted as a foundation for those human rights relating to labour law. It is my suspicion – aside from the disagreement some might have with Woodiwiss – that such positive outcomes will not always be forthcoming. This outcome can only reinforce the need for the manner of discourse which I have defended.

Conclusion

In much of the literature that has developed in discussion of the concept of human rights, there is a tacit belief that the content of human rights is unproblematic, that there is indeed widespread (even universal) acknowledgement of and agreement with these rights. There are two main contributing factors to such a view: one is the law-based model for understanding human rights. This model seeks to explain the international and domestic bills of rights adopted around the world as a positive law manifestation of those rights which exist in the moral or natural law, and which are self-evident to our moral intuitions and understood by those who have engaged in sufficient rational reflection on the matter. The second factor follows on from this, being the influences of Enlightenment thought, liberalism and contemporary analytic political philosophy, with their universalist, rationalist and individualist assumptions about politics and the self. This approach also, and in a related way, suggests that the hope of agreement on certain principles of political association (included in which are human rights) is achievable. Both these factors have been criticised for their inability to satisfactorily deal with the vast and diverse plurality of human traditions of thought; particularly, they offer no satisfactory mechanism for dealing with substantial and intransigent difference on the question of how best we should behave towards one another across the gamut of human existence.

Mouffe's political philosophy has been used here as a model by which to make sense of the two principal realities of the human rights discourse as its stands today: first, the claim to universality; and second, the intractable disputes about the content of the supposed rights. Mouffe offers an interpretation of liberal democracy in which it is the conflict and antagonism of difference, domesticated by the social institutions of a democracy, which operate to insure the continued life of genuine democracy. The same can be argued for human rights: it is the very debate about what the content of human rights should be which operates to ensure that they are observed. It is through the mechanisms of contest, protest, debate, persuasion, that voices other than the dominant one are heard and, through being heard, are more likely to be provided the space they need in which to be, if not agreed with, at least respected. This, then, is a political model of human rights, one which preserves and makes sense of both universalism and particularism by virtue of its preparedness to articulate difference, rather than legislate similitude.

Conclusion

Going beyond the politics of Asian values

The starting-point for this book was the political and theoretical issues that were raised by the so-called Asian values debate of the mid to late 1990s. As we saw, this debate was largely precipitated by the government leaders of countries from the Southeast Asian region who desired to legitimise their practices of 'good governance' in the eyes of the international community. A close examination of the positions held by the main protagonists in this debate demonstrates that the arguments used to support their claims about a set of alternative Asian values are not tenable. These arguments were advanced on cultural, economic, and state sovereignty grounds, and on their own terms are shown to be fallacious.

The debate has, however, served a useful purpose in that it raised an important question about the universality of ethical values, such as those enshrined in international human rights documents. Unfortunately, the question has not received the attention it deserves, partly because it has been dismissed on the grounds that those raising the question were clearly doing so for their own political advantage and not out of any genuine concern for the diverse human traditions lived throughout the region.

The first part of this book is offered as a contribution to the Asian values literature. Most of the literature on the debate either focuses on the contentious claims made by the region's governing elites, or it argues for the legitimacy of Western liberal values, often expressed in human rights or democratic theory terms, as a tool for the region's people to use towards their own emancipation. Rarely seen is consideration of the possibility that the people of the region find neither of these two options fully satisfactory: that, while many reject the authoritarian rule of contemporary elites, they also find the alternative that Western activists and academic commentators advocate wanting in significant respects.

So it is, for example, that many in the region view Western secular liberalism as inadequate because it is *secular* and, as such, has no place for their constitutive religious self-understandings. Similarly, the standard Western account of human rights is often critiqued because it privileges values which groups in the region do not find acceptable. Indeed, the very act of having to translate consonant values from their various indigenous discourses into the discourse of liberal rights may be interpreted as a response to pressure from neo-imperialistic political forces. Values are only acceptable to international political forces if they can be successfully translated into some variant of the rapidly globalising liberalism (economic and political). However, it is an open question as to whether such translation is adequate to the original human tradition. The a priori expectation that liberalism and the rights discourse can serve as a neutral universal language in which dialogue will lead to consensus prejudges the outcome and cramps, distorts and, for some, terminates the expression of their cultural traditions. In addition, it is often forgotten by many Western observers that the distortions of translation also work in the reverse direction. Thus, the discourse of rights can be co-opted at the local political level in a purely utilitarian manner. Local political and ideological agendas often take precedence over the grand talk of universal values; the latter may find itself abused for political advantage or juxtaposed with antithetical ideological views by the necessities of local politics in a manner which discredits the ostensible aims of the human rights discourse.[1]

These questions are not in any way confined to the Asian region; indeed, they are at the centre of many of the debates within the traditions of Western political philosophy. The Asian values debate, however, operates as a significant reminder of these issues. The diversity to which it attests and the significance of this for the theorisation of the human rights discourse have not received sufficient attention from political theorists and philosophers in the fifty years since the discourse commenced its rapid climb to global efficacy.

It is, then, the contribution of the latter part of the book to suggest possible ways of developing a model which makes room for difference while maintaining an intelligible sense of universality for the concept of human rights. This suggestion has been developed in two stages, which correspond to the two observations made in chapter 2's exploration of different approaches to the human rights discourse within the region. The first observation was that often people from diverse human traditions find that they have values and ethical principles in common, despite antithetical views about the foundation of morality, the existence of God, the ontological nature of humankind, and the purpose and meaning of life. Differing philosophical and religious traditions are found to commonly support certain values, even though there could not be agreement among adherents to these different traditions as to why such values were supported or what gave them significance. This common agreement despite difference has often been celebrated as a suitable foundation upon which a global ethic such as universal human rights can be established. The second observation suggested, however, that as often as there is agreement about values and ethical principles, there is conflict. This is only surprising to those who accept a view of the world which, because of its a priori philosophical assumptions about nature, reason or intrinsic humanity, expects all human traditions to converge on a singular set of universal values.

By contrast, I argue that the diverse and antithetical assumptions which ground the various human traditions are determinative of the conclusions that are developed about how humans should relate to one another. Thus, the fundamentally different understandings of what it means to be human that are displayed across the human traditions translate into different patterns of and expectations about human behaviour which cannot be reduced to one universal code. What such reflection teaches is that there is commonality and difference in our shared humanity. Thus, simultaneously, there is hope for common ground and yet the likelihood of intractable difference in the project of establishing a universal ethic.

The project of human rights has been traditionally understood as the attempt to enshrine a universalist ethic. Remarkable achievements have been accomplished in the name of this project in the second half of the twentieth century. When the project is observed from an international law- and state-oriented viewpoint, the progress that has been made has often been sufficient to suggest to commentators that, indeed, a universal ethic is imminent.[2] The human rights discourse does have global reach and has served as the motivational drive behind much relief, development, educational and emancipatory work. As we have seen, though, the global language of human rights also fragments into many local dialects, some of which find communication with each other difficult. In some places the human rights language is not spoken at all; other forms of expression mediate people's moral self-understandings.

Such realities have rarely been taken into account in the way that the human rights discourse has been theorised. It has well been said that the human rights movement is a movement in search of a theory[3] – that the philosophers have been striving to catch up with political developments. Human rights theorists have operated on the assumption that it is possible, on the basis of autonomous reason, to come to universal conclusions about the content of an ethic such as human rights. The foundational role played by this assumption has, however, engendered vigorous critique. Much of the theory it has supported has proceeded as if the assumption had the veracity which Descartes attributed to his 'clear and distinct ideas', forgetting that assumptions along with other ideas and modes of reasoning have histories and are contingent upon the intellectual, social and political milieu out of which they emerge. The attempt to ground human rights in a comprehensive or completely theorised manner is the attempt to find a justification for human rights which will be applicable to, normatively binding upon, everybody. However, such all-encompassing theorisation founders on the reef of pluralism. Such an approach fails to recognise that the various human traditions have different ways of reasoning, that their base assumptions and presuppositions are different, and that therefore their forms of reasoning and the 'evidence' they appropriate will be different, with the common result of intractable difference.[4]

At issue is the historical, contextual and tradition-dependent nature of rationality – an understanding of rationality which has often been absent in twentieth-century political philosophy, influenced as it has been by the ahistoricism of English-speaking analytic philosophy.[5] Reason, as such, does not exist; what does exist is a multitude of particularistic reasons which are applied depending on the milieu of the time. Thus it is that Locke could ground human rights in arguments from the divine author of life – doing so for everybody; whereas Dworkin must appeal to a variant of secularism for his public theology of rights – again, on everybody's behalf.[6] Locke's 'everybody' found Locke's reasons persuasive, as indeed the 'everybody' Dworkin has in mind is likely to accept his reasons. What is clear is that the respective reasons would fail were they placed in each other's historical period. Most followers of Western intellectual history would be happy to so aver. What they are less happy to aver, particularly if they are part of the Dworkinian everybody, is that in our contemporary setting the same situation pertains. The reasons adduced by contemporary practitioners of secularist liberalism are *rightly* not found persuasive by everybody, for they do not rightly engage with the contexts in and traditions from which all people reason. Some liberals, such as Rawls, have reluctantly and tentatively acknowledged this.[7] It is, however, an issue that often is not acknowledged either by practitioners or by theorists of human rights. Once the point is conceded, the question then becomes whether it is possible to reconcile our partial agreements and intractable differences about human rights values with the political reality of a discourse which trades on, and finds its political and moral legitimacy and efficacy in, its claim to universality.

This book is an attempt to address this – the key question confronting the human rights discourse – in a way which furthers the discussion and highlights some of the major issues. The predominant way in which human rights have been theorised has prevented the discussion from being held in such a way that it is of use to those with philosophical questions *and* to those who work on the ground where the tensions between theory and practice are most profound. In what follows I will highlight those ideas which are of fundamental importance for furthering the discussion. These ideas may raise significant questions from both philosophers and practitioners within the discourse. I do not claim to be able to answer such questions; I do suggest, however, that the discourse can only be constructively furthered if they are on the table.

My argument has both affirmed and questioned the notion of universal human rights. The affirmation comes in the claim that all persons are agents who make non-arbitrary moral decisions about how to treat other persons. It is universally the case that people live on this basis. The questioning proceeds on two grounds. The first is the observation that, while all people make moral decisions, they make different and often incommensurable decisions in ways which suggest that only very few substantive moral values might be universal. The second ground for questioning universality is a critique of the philosophical framework by which such universality gains its legitimisation within the (increasingly contested) canon of Western political thought.

There are two approaches to how we might think about the agreements and differences that exist within the human rights discourse: incomplete theorisation, and a political model of human rights. The former finds ready application in contexts where there is significant agreement on outcomes but not in how one justifies these outcomes; the latter deals with the more fundamental problem of difference at the level of both outcomes and justification. At a deeper level, these two approaches suggest a different way of thinking about human rights than that which has classically been the case. It is this different way of thinking which is the key to preventing the discourse of human rights from stagnating around the old polarities: relativism versus universalism, individualism versus communitarianism, economic rights versus political rights, and so on.

The following is therefore an attempt to suggest a range of intellectual tools and approaches which will profit the debates within the human rights discourse. As such, it seeks to provoke discussion, disagreement and doubt in the hope of furthering our capacity to release justice among the marginalised and oppressed.

A different way of thinking

Name dropping is an unfortunate habit but, for identifying where the human rights discourse has come from and where I think it may most profitably go, it serves very usefully. The first list of names includes people such as Rawls, Dworkin, Ackerman, Nozick, Nagel, Larmore and

Donnelly. These figures may be taken (more or less unfairly) to be indebted to various aspects of the Enlightenment project and to a foundationalist liberal approach to theorising human rights. Rawls' name appears at the head of this list and he (in both his earlier and later incarnations) epitomises the nature of the approach against which I define the different way of thinking.

The second list is different and quite eclectic: Mouffe, Gray, MacIntyre, Rorty, Taylor, Fish, Wittgenstein, Stout, Beiner, Hauerwas, Gaita, Grant. These authors come from a diverse array of positions and have much disagreement with one another. Moreover, few of them are known as human rights theorists. Indeed, some have written in a manner highly sceptical of the supposed benefits of the human rights idea, as either a philosophical, ethical, theological, legal or political term – MacIntyre, for example, famously places them in the same category as witches and unicorns.[8] However, selectively appropriated, their work provides a range of resources for those seeking to overcome the limitations of the received liberal way of theorising and otherwise participating within the discourse.

The standard liberal or 'Western' ways of thinking about the human rights discourse are inadequate. I propose a series of concepts, taken from these authors, which are crucial to the successful thinking and living of this discourse.[9] The human rights discourse, rethought through these concepts, has great potential for synergy with local ways of being which it traditionally does not have. So rethought, the discourse can make more sense to those who wish to adopt it as a language of morals and politics co-extensive with their own local environment and tradition, while at the same time facilitating their engagement with the global community. The human rights discourse may thus be regarded as an entry point into the global community for the marginalised and oppressed. The danger is that such a point of entry can be counter-productive if it simultaneously destroys local self-understandings – if it redefines those whom it seeks to help in precisely the terms which those people were seeking to avoid by appropriating the human rights discourse. The received tradition of human rights thought does precisely this because of its dependence on assumptions and concepts derived from the European Enlightenment and liberal political philosophy. I suggest that incorporation of the following into the discourse will enable human rights to more authentically attain its stated aims of care for the marginalised and oppressed.

Narrative thinking

The first set of concepts which animate the suggested new way of thinking are captured by the words 'story', 'narrative' and 'tradition'. At one level this book can be read as a series of stories: about human rights, about Asian values, about the arguments between political theorists and philosophers, and so on. This may be understood as the attempt to dispel the stories in order to replace them with the objective fact of the matter. However, this was the mistake of liberalism: it tried to replace all stories and traditions with a rationalist epistemological method which could apprehend the truth about the world, including our moral behaviour towards one another, without the need for stories – with their implication of an authoritative story-teller. Liberalism, ironically, was the story that told us we did not need stories in order to live as free and rational beings.[10] It is in recognising this irony and recanting the liberal mistake that we can give a methodological account of how to think about the human rights discourse which does not disenfranchise those communities who have never doubted the importance of their traditions, narratives and stories, as did the liberal tradition.

The first step, then, in thinking the discourse differently is to think it *through* the stories, narratives and traditions that define us as individuals and communities, rather than trying to avoid them. Avoiding the stories that define our identities means that whatever we are protecting with the human rights discourse will always be something that is slightly different from and out of touch with those things we value most. The issue here is how to use the discourse of human rights as a means for telling our local stories to a larger audience. This gives rise to the tension between the discourse as a universally substantive language of morals and the discourse as a formal structure for the preservation of the rights of individuals and local communities, cultures and traditions to being and self-expression. For some of the ways of being and self-expression valued by the latter do not coincide with the former as traditionally received.

Ambiguities exist because our stories, traditions and narratives tell of what is bad about us, as well as of what is good. Stories can be told which disenfranchise and exclude. Telling such stories to a global audience may work against the goals of justice, doing no service to the ends of the human rights discourse. This, however, presupposes that we can determine which stories are desirable and which are not. The capacity to so determine, though, is questioned by the recognition that we *only* have our stories. The argument may be made that when we take the rationalist approach we are able to develop objectively neutral rules. These in turn stand as guidelines for judging which stories have appropriate morals, and which are subversive of justice and social order. (See chapter 3 for my critique of the rationalist position.)

The question of judgement is central to the issues of this book. How do we judge whether the behaviours advocated by one narrative and critiqued by another should become values enshrined in the human rights discourse? Does not the critique of objectivity, neutral values and universalism undermine our capacity to say with any confidence that there are certain things which simply should not be done?

The witness of social contexts

A second set of concepts informs the way in which we could deal with this question: contextualism, witness and social practices. I agree strongly with Stout that the lack of neutral rules does not lead to relativism.[11] The fear of arbitrary outcomes is dispelled by paying attention to those things which situated agents think important in their situations. It remains the case that agents in analogous but different situations may make different and even incommensurable decisions, but this is not the same as the making of arbitrary decisions. By taking seriously the different ways in which justice is contextualised, by focusing on the surrounding web of motivations, reasons, emotions, actions, justifications and traditions, the spectre of unbridled relativism disappears and genuine conversation about the relationships between substantive behaviours and their normative identification with justice can begin. To express the issue differently, it is not clear that apparent incommensurability automatically means that one decision being correct, the other is necessarily incorrect. It is common enough that the one action in two different situations does not retain the same moral significance. Thus, we need to pay attention to the context in which agents are acting, the social practices which obtain, and the way in which these together give witness to the legitimacy of a particular narrative.

This is why we can say with complete confidence that many of the arguments put forward by authoritarian leaders in Southeast Asia with respect to Asian values can be discounted. There is a relationship between the way we live in our societies and the words and concepts we use to discuss our living. Because these are used across and throughout our societies, they cannot be arbitrarily redefined by self-appointed cultural police without encountering strong resistance. The reality of what words and concepts actually mean in the lives of everyday people acts to prevent this. Of course, such redefining agents may have very powerful institutional and coercive support. The point is not that they cannot force change, but that change will be noticed and resisted because ways of living and speaking are not arbitrary.[12]

Stanley Cavell has said that philosophy denies the human when it tries to abstract our concepts from our forms of living.[13] In order not to undermine what it ostensibly protects, the human rights discourse must be intimately bound together with the ways in which we live, with our social practices. This is why it is important for the discourse to be open to reinterpretation by stories other than liberalism, because it claims relevance to societies other than those which are liberal Western societies. This relevance, however, can only be maintained if the discourse can touch the practices – good and bad – of the 'little people',[14] wherever they might be. For this touching to take place, one of two processes must happen: either the discourse must be converted to the ways of life of such people, or they must be converted by the discourse. But the latter option undermines the claims made by the discourse to be a protector of the marginalised and oppressed.

Again, however, we have talk of the 'good and bad' that may exist in other people's stories. The fear is that, by saying we only have each other's stories to go on, we lose all criteria for judging between stories. But this fear fails to take account of how stories relate to our identities and the way we live. Our identities, formed by our stories, are not accessories that can be changed at will. Even radical identity changes are not arbitrary but part of our storied character. The problem may be that we have a long-ingrained habit of thinking that our stories and narratives must derive from or be codified into abstract conceptual schemes.[15] In the liberal tradition, it is only when our stories and ways of life can be so schematised, and in the process removed from how we actually live, that we can then assess – against a rationally objective standpoint or procedure – whether our lives are moral and ethical. Hence the liberal academic discipline of 'applied ethics', where objectively ascertained neutral rules are applied to the real stuff of life.[16]

Once such a methodology is accepted – the abstraction of our stories into conceptual schemes, which by definition are removed from the contexts and narratives of how we live, the decisions we make, and the consequences of these – it becomes easier to see how the absence of an objective standard could lead to fears about relativism. Ways of life, with all their practical consequences, are de-storied and turned into propositional credos which give no indication of what happens to people when their lives are based around such beliefs. Relativism implies that, because there is no way of objectively judging between these credos, because there is no Archimedean standpoint, we should then be able to live by any of the credos on offer.

Such an approach *does* deny the human, for it fails to count as significant that, while there is no objective way of judging between credos, they do nonetheless affect people in different ways – and the situated effects of these credos, the ways in which they change our lives when adopted, offer a human and contextual site for differentiating between possible ways of living. Stories and narratives are, it turns out, more useful for determining how to live than propositional credos or lists of neutral rules. Stories tell us of the consequences of adopting ways of living. We can say, on the basis of hearing a story, whether we do or do not want to be like such and such a person, live such and such a life. As Stout argues, neutral rules, abstract conceptual schemes, and the like, do not provide us with the details, the contexts, which are necessary for making the everyday decisions of life.[17]

People meeting together and telling their stories to each other can be engaged and changed in ways that are anathema to lists of propositional statements about beliefs. Credos are static and impersonal conceptual abstractions. Theorising the human rights discourse on the basis of such abstractions may lead to a coherent theoretical model for the discipline. Fundamentally, however, human rights are about people, not conceptual abstractions. It is stories about how people have been treated that have generated the power of the discourse, not credos as such.[18] And it is when the discourse is reduced to credos and to theorising their coherence that it loses its rationale. Human rights must be theorised in a way that privileges the stories and lived experiences of individuals and peoples. It is as these stories are personally engaged with, reflected upon and lived out by becoming part of our lives that we are most likely to find the resources to respect others. This personal engagement might be thought of as a process of witness.[19]

Enhancing relationships

This leads us to look at the relative place of human relationships in theorising about human rights. As we saw, the human rights movement in this century arose in response to the abhorrent way in which many people were treated during the Second World War. In Germany in particular, Jews, people of other minority religions, the ill, and the otherwise vulnerable found themselves victims of horrific practices. Human rights became the language in which this sort of behaviour was denounced. It was a language that placed priority on preventing abuse and cruelty, a language which sought to provide a framework in which human behaviour and relationships could be enhanced.

The articulation of these goals for human relationships in the universalist terms of a rights discourse seems, however, to have been unfortunate, given the state of the disciplines which would subsequently take up the theorisation of human rights. Universalism is fundamental for our understanding of justice. However, it may come in different forms, and the form which has come to pervade the theorisation of human rights appears in some significant degree to have shifted the focus of theorisation. The concern is that the point of human rights theorisation becomes that of establishing a philosophical system in which universalism becomes the end goal – not universalism in the service of enhancing human relationships, but universalism as such. Thus, much contemporary theorisation of the human rights discourse has focused more on the need to massage the diverse array of human values into some systematic and internally coherent theory of public values, than on the ways in which we can better help people behave towards one another. Not that a theory of public values can be dispensed with, but, when theory becomes irrelevant to the real world it purports to theorise, it undermines its initial goal.

Many critics of liberal theory claim this to be the case, their work being the provenance of the critique of liberal rationalist ways of theorising human rights discussed above. In cameo form: liberal universalism becomes the *telos* of theorisation, and is successful in its goals, for those who agree with liberal presuppositions. However, the pre-eminence of such universalism within the discourse does not enhance human relationships, and cannot, for it fails to take non-liberal positions and realities seriously. Thus it is that, as Gray scathingly points out, we get 'political philosophy' that bears no relationship to the lived experience of people or polities, but which does build beautiful castles of universal agreement in the air of liberal presuppositions.[20] Human relationships can only be enhanced when there is first a commitment to understand each other on each other's terms. Certain dominant forms of liberal universalism fail to do this. The possibility of the human rights discourse being for the enhancement of human relationships is thus undermined for as long as liberal universalism is thought to be *the* correct theoretical framework for the theorisation of the discourse.

A misplaced understanding of the concept of universality as it relates to human values is at fault here. The expectation that all people everywhere will or can agree on certain values – with the attendant theorisation that must go on in order to overcome the obvious fact that we do not – takes our attention away from the opportunities for theorising our differences so that our relationships are not harmed by the application of false expectations or demands for agreement. This contrast can be illustrated with examples from the existing human rights discourse. On the one hand, there is the provision for the enhancement of human relationships in that rights of religious freedom are proclaimed – these determine that I cannot force my religion on you – and, as such, champion difference. However, inasmuch as the discourse (in its received form) requires theorisation about freedom of religion to be undertaken upon a non-religious, secular, liberal basis in order to be accepted by society, it undermines its own claim to respect freedom of religion: someone whose self-identity is constituted by religious beliefs cannot think through his or her public or private life without reference to his or her religious assumptions.[21]

Thus, while ostensibly enhancing the lives of all humans, a human rights discourse which depends on this kind of substantive universality undermines some valid forms of being, which in turn impoverishes the ways in which people relate to one another. There are numerous examples of this in the history of the rights discourse. Women, slaves, blacks and children are only the most obvious exceptions to the universality of human rights, historically and into our own period. Consistently, people in these categories have been excluded from recognition as rights-bearers by those who campaigned for universal rights.[22] The question then is how do we reconceptualise universality so that its focus and effect are enhancing to human relationships – so that substantive universalisms do not undermine the capacity of individuals and groups representative of all forms of human life from having enhanced relationships? While insisting on one form of substantive universality may undermine and abuse actual human relationships (as has been the repeated experience of those, such as Aboriginal Australians, who live under various forms of imperialism), it is nonetheless the case that some agreement and commonality must obtain in order to establish either the criteria for what constitutes 'improvement' or 'enhancement' in human relationships or for discussing the ways we understand changing behaviour as non-arbitrary. A fourth set of concepts may help to make this vexing question more answerable.

Particularist universalism; performative reason

These concepts pertain to how we think about the nature of reason and the relationship between reason and universalism. The form of universalism usually claimed by proponents of human rights is consequent upon Enlightenment assumptions about the competence of Reason to be objective, to establish neutral rules and independent criteria, to search out and tell an account of the universal history of humanity. Reason had access to the Truth and because of this was able to promise a final reconciliation of all things at the end of modernity.[23] It is not hard to see these assumptions reflected in the search for lists of values or rights that should be affirmed substantively by all people everywhere. These lists of underlying values and rights were held to be more determinative than the surface ways in which people lived their lives consequent upon their own cultures, traditions, religions and local ways of doing, being and understanding. All these must come under the philosopher's gaze, there to be assessed against the canon of Reason. Diversity and pluralism are allowed, providing they function as window dressings, adding colour and spice. They are not permitted if found to contravene the standards and criteria of Reason.

The main line of criticism here is that Enlightenment and liberal Reason are not and cannot be objective, value free or neutral. The fear that appears to bother many is that this recognition will lead to epistemological anarchy, to what Mouffe calls 'apocalyptical postmodernism' – where anything goes, where there are no standards, no criteria of any sort, where relativism is stark, final and nihilisitic.[24] This only seems to be the case, however, if one is still caught in Enlightenment presuppositions about the nature of Reason: say, when one replaces Reason's substantive content with epistemological anarchism instead of foundationalist liberalism. The mistake here is to identify reason with a particular substantive content, philosophical canon or religious account. When one makes this mistake, assumes this identification, then the universalism which one derives on the basis of that reason will be a universalism which accepts as legitimate only those behaviours and norms which measure up to its substantive content, and which can be justified or explained according to the canon of its tradition. The sense in which universalism operates here is that 'Reason tells us these values are objectively True; we must ensure all people live according to them'. This was the civilising mission of modernity and aptly describes the substantive universalist model of human rights theorisation.[25]

What of reason and universalism if one tries to extricate oneself from the substantive models for reason given by Enlightenment thinkers? Reason is not substantive, universal, objective or capable of supplying us with an Archimedean point for surveying the cosmos and determining right and wrong. Rather, it is particularistic, local, dependent on assumptions and presuppositions which themselves cannot be 'objectively' tested. Reason can be used and applied more 'rationally' once these limitations are taken into consideration. Reason, thus, is better seen as a skill than as a substantive principle. Reason cannot tell us *what* to think, in substantive terms, but is a tool that we use to sort our thinking. Our reasonableness depends on how well we perform the skill of reason; it depends on our capacity for good performative thinking in the context of our particularities.

What then of universality? Under the Enlightenment model of objective Reason, substantive universalism was an obvious corollary. However, if reason is a skill through the good performance of which we make ourselves intelligible in diverse and plural particularistic settings, then universalism describes a motivation, orientation or objective for the performance of that skill, rather than being properly descriptive of substantive content.[26] Universalism, on this argument, may be more properly defined as the practice of enhanced relationships, rather than as a list of propositions to which all give approval. It is with this suggestion that we see the talk of universal human rights as another way of expressing our desire to enhance the nature of human relationships across the plurality and difference of our ways of being, self-understandings, cultures, traditions, and so on. The discussion of 'universalism' as the 'practice of enhancing relationships' must engage us directly with all the particularities of human experience in order to have any purchase. In other words, it places the truth of universalism in the domain of human relationships, communities and the stuff of real politics, rather than in the domain of abstract theoretical reflection or mind games the presuppositions behind which deprive participants of their particularistic relational identities. This truth, as Campbell argues, is a truth which principally occurs through action, a truth that is achieved in being 'true to' those with whom we relate, in the context of our specific locations in the historically situated human traditions.[27]

It is for these reasons that I have tried to think of universalism not as substantive content but as what motivates the need for the substantive content we advocate based on our own particularisms, the human traditions to which we differently give our allegiance. We need the raw materials of our traditions in order to establish enhanced relationships with others; this cannot be done in some objective space that exists 'behind' how we live now. Relationships are particularistic; they are built around shared interactions, practices and beliefs. To establish enhanced relationships we must draw on what is universal in human traditions: notions of justice, right living, moral behaviour towards others, proper conduct, and so forth. Some of these practices coincide in substantive content, some are complementary but different, some antithetical. What we cannot do is to assess their 'universalisability' by attempting to get 'behind' the human traditions to some neutral theoretical standpoint. As Hauerwas argues, this form of ethical reductionism tries to provide for reason and the self a unity which can only arise from what I have termed 'relationship enhancing practices'.[28] To claim that a propositional (or theoretical) account of any one of the human traditions can provide this unity, can be substantively universal (as liberalism claims for itself), is to claim that reason (as skill) can become Reason (as objective Truth) and is in the end to cast a role for reason which it cannot play.

Defining justice

It may be said that everyone knows the nature of justice. It may be replied that the thrust of my argument has it that no one actually knows. In the end we are thrown simultaneously in the direction of how we live – for none of us can live as if we do not know the nature of justice – and of epistemological habits that suggest the need for the way we live to be objectively validated and defensible. The only 'objective' validation and defence that we have available to us come in the form of social practices, of the skill of reason given good performance in history, of witness amid relationships.

Justice is not a platonic Form or Idea; rather, it is the consequence of enhancing human relationships through non-arbitrary decisions about behaviour and actions. Justice, it might be said (*pace* Rawls), is not fairness but faithfulness[29] – and faithfulness is something which must be practised by and between individuals and communities. In order for faithfulness to exist, it must be practised, embodied in relationships. Faithfulness, too, according to Campbell, is the key to understanding truth. He argues that in English as in many other natural languages the word 'truth' evolved from older words meaning 'good faith', words with implications of reliability, trust, constancy, steadfastness, fidelity and loyalty. Campbell says, 'Faithfulness ... involves our commitments and actions, our being open, honest, and steadfast. In so far as we apply the concept of truth to ourselves – to our thought, our speech, our actions – it consists in our being dependable and trustworthy, in our acting faithfully in our situations.'[30]

Thinking about human rights, justice, universality, reason, and truth through the concept of faithful action provides a possible avenue for the reconceptualisation of the human rights discourse which retains its connection to enhancing human relationships at both the practical and theoretical levels. Faithfulness may be seen as the underlying commitment that is needed in order for the composite model of human rights theorisation presented above to have purchase. Both incompletely theorised agreement and the political model of human rights assume that the differences and conflicts between people and traditions in their discussions of human rights are differences which arise in good faith, that arise in the context of seeking to enhance human relationships. The Truth and Reason of the Enlightenment undermined the hope of justice by reducing it to the scope of one ideology. However, truth seen as faithfulness – and reason seen as the skill we need in order to enact faithfulness – these together may return the thinking about justice, in philosophy and the human sciences, to that which witnesses to the power of ideas to enhance the lives of the marginalised and oppressed.

Notes

1 The Asian Values Discourse

1 Edward Friedman, 'What Asia Will or Won't Stand For', 87.
2 Stewart, 'Mahathir's Allies Go West'.
3 Camroux, 'State Responses to Islamic Resurgence in Malaysia', 858.
4 Christie, 'Regime Security and Human Rights in Southeast Asia', 215. It may be argued that such statements were made in an environment where racial tensions were running rife and there was widespread concern about conflict and further violence. On the other hand, Mahathir's consistent practice and statements suggest that in his view democracy should serve to legitimise the agenda of the government, rather than that agenda being formed in response to a democratic polity.
5 Mahathir bin Mohamad, speech at summit-level meeting on 'Cooperation for Development', 3.
6 Khoo Boo Teik, *Paradoxes of Mahathirism*, 275–6.
7 Mahathir, quoted in Bob Reece, 'Crimes for Democracy', *Far Eastern Economic Review*, 18 September 1969, 688, quoted in Khoo, *Paradoxes of Mahathirism*, 261.
8 Mahathir bin Mohamad, 'Keynote Address', 9.
9 Although Anwar's own political circumstances have undergone a drastic reversal, with his sacking and fall from favour with Mahathir, there is no indication that his personal commitment to the Asian Renaissance agenda has changed. Moreover, his popularity among the middle class and political class has arguably increased as a consequence of Mahathir's moves to disenfranchise him. Anwar's changed position, then, does not invalidate the assessment of his contribution to the Asian values debate, or its ongoing influence; see his *The Asian Renaissance*.
10 Anwar Ibrahim, speech at International Conference on the Philippine Revolution and Beyond, 2.
11 Morris, 'Interview: Anwar on Currency Woes, Elders and Asian Values', p. 3 of printout.
12 Anwar Ibrahim, 'Asian Renaissance and the Reconstruction of Civilisation', 1, 4.
13 Chandra Muzaffar, 'From Human Rights to Human Dignity', 8.

174

14 Camroux, 'State Responses to Islamic Resurgence in Malaysia', 857–8.
15 Mahathir and Ishihara, *The Voice of Asia*, quoted in Thio Li-ann, 'Asian Values and Human Rights', 5.
16 Anwar Ibrahim, speech at conference on Islam in Southeast Asia, 2.
17 Anwar, *The Asian Renaissance*, 124.
18 *Time Australia*, 'I'm Not a King. I'm Just Like You', 53.
19 Cohen, 'Man of Many Parts', 21.
20 Speech by President Suharto at 1992 NAM Summit, 8.
21 Ibid., 8–9.
22 Ali Alatas, statement to Second World Conference on Human Rights, 2–3.
23 Ibid., 4.
24 Ibid.
25 Radio National, 'Doing Human Rights in Asia'.
26 Ibid.
27 Ibid.
28 Juwono Sudarsono, 'Human Rights: An Indonesian View', 1.
29 Juwono Sudarsono, 'The Diplomatic Scam called Human Rights', 2.
30 Ali Alatas, keynote address, Indonesia–Canada Colloquium on Human Rights.
31 Kishore Mahbubani, 'The West and the Rest', 1. See also his *Can Asians Think?*
32 Fareed Zakaria, 'Culture is Destiny', 112.
33 Mahbubani, 'The West and the Rest', 8.
34 Ibid., 9.
35 Para. 41, Shared Values White Paper (Cmd 1 of 1991) (Singapore National Printers), in Thio, 'Asian Values and Human Rights', 15.
36 Bilahari Kausikan, 'Asia's Different Standard', 37–8.
37 Bilahari Kausikan, 'Governance That Works', 26–7.
38 *Straits Times*, 'The Democracy Debate – SM', quoted in Christie, 'Human Rights Agendas and Southeast Asia', 11.
39 Roy, 'Singapore, China, and the "Soft Authoritarian" Challenge', 231.
40 Hsiung, *Human Rights in East Asia*, 5–11.
41 Roy, 'Singapore, China, and the "Soft Authoritarian" Challenge', 232.
42 'Chinese Culture outside China Changing with the Generations', *Sunday Times*, 11 August 1991, 21, quoted in Roy, 'Singapore, China, and the "Soft Authoritarian" Challenge', 232.
43 Kraar, 'A Blunt Talk with Singapore's Lee Kuan Yew', p. 4 of printout.
44 Roy, 'Singapore, China, and the "Soft Authoritarian" Challenge', 234.
45 Ibid.
46 Bilahari Kausikan, 'Governance That Works'.
47 Ibid., 31.
48 Ibid., 32.
49 Wilkinson, 'Culture, Ethnicity and Human Rights', in Wilkinson (ed.), *Culture, Ethnicity and Human Rights in International Relations*, 14.
50 Walker, 'The Concept of Culture in the Theory of International Relations', 6.
51 Zechenter, 'In the Name of Culture', 334.
52 Lawson, 'Democracy and the Problem of Cultural Relativism', 252.
53 Thio, 'Asian Values and Human Rights', 20.
54 Walker, *One World, Many Worlds*, 49.
55 Thio, 'Asian Values and Human Rights', 21.

56 See, for example, Lawson, 'Occidentalising Democracy', 7–9. Lawson is a strong critic of monolithic constructions such as 'The West', 'The East', or 'Asia'. While, as is here discussed, Asia is a vast and highly heterogeneous area, the use of 'The West' as an identification term does have significantly more legitimacy because of the thousand-year-long cultural ordering principle that was Christendom, which even in its fragmentation in recent centuries ensures an internal cultural continuity absent from Asia. See Ingleson, 'The Asian Values Debate', 229–30; Masakazu Yamazaki, 'Asia, a Civilisation in the Making', 109. In the Introduction to his *Europe: A History*, Davies interrogates 'a dozen or so variants' of what is meant by Western civilisation. Gress focuses more on what Davies called the 'Allied Scheme of History' in his *From Plato to Nato: The Idea of the West and Its Opponents* – note that the title is meant to be ironic. See also O'Hagan, Conceptions of the West in International Relations Thought.

57 Lawson, 'Occidentalising Democracy', 8. See also Robison, 'Introduction', 305.

58 Birch, 'Constructing Asian Values', 181.

59 Rodan, 'Civil Society and Other Political Possibilities in Southeast Asia', 166.

60 See de Bary, *Asian Values and Human Rights*.

61 Mohamed El Sayed Said, 'Islam and Human Rights', 7. It is at this point that the argument becomes very complex, for Said's statement assumes some principles or criteria for discerning these intrinsic themes and tendencies which will be accepted by those who live out these traditions, academic experts and outside observers. Developing such criteria is a profoundly political task. The argument of chapter 5, focused on the human rights discourse, can equally be developed with regard to this issue – what may be called 'cultural guardianship'. Said's position may indicate a foundationalist methodology predicated on a normative assumption that favours 'liberal' values. It is not clear, however, whether this argument remains legitimate when used by those predisposed to authoritarianism who wish to mine the tradition for supportive resources.

62 Rodan, 'The Internationalisation of Ideological Conflict', 337.

63 Robison, 'The Politics of "Asian Values"', 322.

64 Ghai, 'Human Rights and Governance', 10.

65 Ingleson, 'The Asian Values Debate', 233.

66 Robison, 'Indonesia: Tensions in State and Regime', 42–3.

67 Bourchier, 'Indonesianising Indonesia', 212.

68 Sajoo, *Pluralism in 'Old Societies and New States'*, section entitled 'The Rukunegara and Beyond in Malaysia', 43–54.

69 See also Clammer, 'Deconstructing Values', 36.

70 Bourchier, 'Indonesianising Indonesia', 209.

71 Steadman, *The Myth of Asia*, 44. Quoted in Rodan, 'The Internationalisation of Ideological Conflict', 330.

72 Rodan, 'The Internationalisation of Ideological Conflict', 333.

73 Friedman, 'Asia as a Fount of Universal Human Rights', 58–9.

74 Robison, 'The Politics of "Asian Values"', 321.

75 Ibid.

76 Rodan, 'The Internationalisation of Ideological Conflict', 338. As opposed to Huntington, *The Clash of Civilisations and the Remaking of World Order*.

77 Ghai, 'Human Rights and Governance', 13.

78 Friedman, 'What Asia Will or Won't Stand For', 111.

79 Christie, 'Regime Security and Human Rights in Southeast Asia', 209.
80 Thio, 'Asian Values and Human Rights', 19.
81 Sidney Jones, 'The Impact of Asian Economic Growth on Human Rights', 4.
82 Christie, 'Regime Security and Human Rights in Southeast Asia', 210.
83 Jones, 'The Impact of Asian Economic Growth', 4; Thio, 'Asian Values and Human Rights', 19.
84 Ng, 'Why Asia Needs Democracy', 22.
85 Jones, 'The Impact of Asian Economic Growth', 5.
86 Freeman, 'Human Rights: Asia and the West', 16.
87 *Economist*, 'Why Voting Is Good for You', quoted in Jones, 'The Impact of Asian Economic Growth', 6.
88 Sen, *Human Rights and Asian Values*, 13.
89 Aryeh Neier, 'Asia's Unacceptable Standard', 43.
90 Eric Jones, 'Asia's Fate', 23.
91 The following closely follows Sidney Jones, 'The Impact of Asian Economic Growth', 6ff.
92 Ibid., 6.
93 Lev, 'Human Rights NGOs in Indonesia and Malaysia', 146.
94 Crouch, 'Indonesia's "Strong" State', 112.
95 Kayoko Tsumori, seminar, Department of Political and Social Change, Research School of Pacific and Asian Studies, Australian National University, Canberra, 18 September 1998.
96 Rodan, 'Preserving the One-Party State in Contemporary Singapore', 78. See also Rodan, *Singapore Changes Guard*.
97 Crouch, 'Malaysia: Neither Authoritarian nor Democratic', 141.
98 Jones, 'The Impact of Asian Economic Growth', 11.
99 Joseph Chan, 'An Alternative View', 40.
100 Liddle, 'The Islamic Turn in Indonesia', 614.
101 Jones, 'The Impact of Asian Economic Growth', 15.
102 Inoue Tatsuo, 'Liberal Democracy and Asian Orientalism', 30.
103 Caballero-Anthony, 'Human Rights, Economic Change and Political Development', 49.
104 See Dauvergne, *Weak and Strong States in Asia–Pacific Societies*.
105 Ibid.
106 Ghai, 'Asian Perspectives on Human Rights', 62.
107 Van Ness, 'Introduction', in Van Ness (ed.), *Debating Human Rights*, 12.
108 Onuma Yasuaki, 'Toward an Intercivilizational Approach to Human Rights', 104.
109 Sen, 'Thinking about Human Rights and Asian Values', 2.
110 Chan, 'An Alternative View', 36.
111 Ghai, 'Human Rights and Governance', 8.
112 Onuma Yasuaki, 'Toward an Intercivilizational Approach to Human Rights', 105.
113 Bell, 'The East Asian Challenge to Human Rights', 651. See also his *East Meets West*.
114 Woodiwiss, *Globalisation, Human Rights and Labour Law in Pacific Asia*, 12. See also Lev, 'Introduction', xiv.
115 Lev, 'Human Rights NGOs in Indonesia and Malaysia', 158.
116 Ghai, 'Asian Perspectives on Human Rights', 63.
117 Nikhil Aziz, 'The Human Rights Debate in an Era of Globalisation', 16.
118 Kahn, 'Malaysian Modern or Anti-Anti Asian Values', 29.

119 Chua Beng-Huat, 'Asian Values: Restraining the Logic of Capitalism?', 215. Also see generally Chua Beng-Huat, *Communitarian Ideology and Democracy in Singapore.*
120 Chan, 'An Alternative View', 37.
121 Cf. Noor, 'Values in the Dynamics of Malaysia's Internal and External Political Relations', 151: 'Asian Values exist because Asians exist' – an argument based on the thought of the later Wittgenstein.
122 Osman Bakar, 'Asian Values or Universal Values Championed by Asia?', 172.
123 Bell, 'The East Asian Challenge', 667.

2 The Real Asian Values Debate

1 In the wake of the Enlightenment, religion became a phenomenon to be studied, not a legitimate premise from which to study other phenomena. In addition, and more directly, there is the influence of Weber on the social sciences, which resulted in the attempt to divorce facts from values and to engage in 'value-free' social science. This project today is most loudly criticised by those in the diverse conglomerate named (often against their will) 'postmodernists', and has been criticised by the more longstanding critics of modernism such as (on the left) the Frankfurt School and (on the right) George Parkin Grant, Eric Voegelin, Leo Strauss, and others. Of Strauss, Robert Pippin says, 'His attacks on the self satisfaction of post-Enlightenment culture, his doubts about the benefits of technological mastery, about the attempted avoidance of any public reliance on religion, and about the modern confidence in the power of enlightened self-interest in the formation of a polity ... have now suddenly reappeared, more quietly but insistently, on the agendas of neo-Aristotelians, critical theorists, communitarians, and postmodernists'. Pippin, 'The Modern World of Leo Strauss', 139. Within the Western tradition, a powerful re-invocation of the role of theology can be found in works emanating from what might loosely be called the Cambridge School, such as Milbank, *Theology and Social Theory*; Blond (ed.), *Post-Secular Philosophy*; and Milbank et al. (eds), *Radical Orthodoxy*. See also Forrester, *Christian Justice and Public Policy*. Works which undertake social analysis from within the assumptions of Islam are referenced throughout this chapter. See also Camilleri and Chandra Muzaffar (eds), *Globalisation.*
2 Between fifty and sixty people participated in discussions about Asian conceptions of human rights. Slightly more of these came from Indonesia than from Malaysia and Singapore. The people interviewed were academics, government researchers, human rights commissioners, NGO personnel, lawyers, Islamic leaders, theologians, think-tank officers, theatre artists, public intellectuals and taxi drivers. A policy of anonymity for interviewees was assumed.
3 Verbatim quotes: a Singapore academic, interview, March 1998; analyst, Malaysian Government think-tank, interview, March 1998; researcher, Indonesian Government think-tank, interview, February 1998; columnist, former Malaysian Government think-tank employee, interview, March 1998; analyst, Malaysian Government think-tank, interview, March 1998; spokesperson for Indonesian National Commission on Human Rights, interview, February 1998; Malaysian women's NGO leader, interview, March 1998.
4 A Singaporean academic, interview, March 1998. See also Cotton, 'State and Society in Singapore'.

5 Women's activist and NGO leader, Jakarta, interview, March 1998.

6 Analyst, Malaysian Government think-tank, interview, March 1998.

7 It is, again, a particularly liberal view of the world which presupposes that particular religions are merely expressions of some more fundamental religious urge found in humans, which in turn can be explained reductively – by biology, or social constructivism, or Freudian psychology, and so on.

8 Researcher, Indonesian Government think-tank, interview, February 1998.

9 Catholic Church leader and educator, Jakarta, interview, February 1998.

10 Leader of a private Islamic think-tank in Kuala Lumpur, interview, March 1998.

11 Law academic, University of Malaya, interview, March 1998; Muhammadiyah adviser and ICMI leader, interview, March 1998; see also, among his other writings, Chandra Muzaffar, *Human Rights and the New World Order*, 40; *Dominance of the West over the Rest*, ch. 7.

12 Indonesian academic, Salatiga, interview, January 1998. Cf. discussion of 'Eclectic Ijtihad' in Abdullah Saeed, '*Ijtihad* and Innovation in Neo-Modernist Islamic Thought in Indonesia', 285.

13 Researcher, Indonesian Government think-tank, interview, February 1998.

14 Columnist, former Malaysian Government think-tank employee, interview, March 1998.

15 Indonesian journalist and human rights researcher, interview, February 1998.

16 Director, Malaysian women's NGO, interview, March 1998.

17 Catholic Church leader and educator, Jakarta, interview, February 1998. For more on Javanese culture, see Mochtar Pabottingi, 'Indonesia: Historicizing the New Order's Legitimacy Dilemma', 237–9.

18 Masdar F. Mas'udi, director, Perhimpunan Pengembangan Pesantren Dan Masyarakat (P3M), Indonesian community development NGO, interview, February 1998.

19 As Philip Eldridge notes, there are few institutional relationships between the UN human rights infrastructure and Southeast Asia. This means that relationships can easily become difficult when the United Nations criticises countries in the region, as there is no mechanism by which to manage conflict and proceed with dialogue. Eldridge, 'Human Rights and Democracy in Indonesia and Malaysia', 4.

20 Masdar F. Mas'udi, interview, February 1998.

21 Malaysian academic, interview, March 1998.

22 Representative, Centre for Information and Development Studies, Indonesia, interview, February 1998.

23 Singaporean academic, interview, March 1998.

24 MacIntyre, *Whose Justice? Which Rationality?* This theme has been taken up by many thinkers in different fields. In Asian studies, for example, see M. Bambang Pranowo, 'Which Islam and Which Pancasila'.

25 Ghai, 'Human Rights and Governance', 14 at note 33. Serious questions can also be asked at this point about the psychology of certain forms of sport and recreation which routinely cause pain and injury: cricket, football, and so on. People engage in these activities fully cognisant that they will cause pain, injury and sometimes death. They are wilfully inflicted upon children, some of whom have been coerced into involvement against their wishes by, for example, the school system (this author's experience!).

26 Malaysian academic, interview, March 1998.
27 Leader of a private Islamic think-tank in Kuala Lumpur, interview, March 1998.
28 Leader of a private Islamic think-tank in Kuala Lumpur, interview, March 1998.
29 Malaysian academic and NGO supporter, interview, March 1998.
30 Law academic, University of Malaya, interview, March 1998.
31 Academic, International Islamic University, Malaysia, interview, March 1998. For an account of further traditionalist arguments, see Othman, 'Grounding Human Rights in Non-Western Culture', 181.
32 Indonesian journalist and human rights researcher, interview, February 1998; Stewart, 'Malaysia Gets Tough on Western Decadence'.
33 Cf. Bowen, 'Abortion, Islam, and the 1994 Cairo Population Conference', 164.
34 Leader of a private Islamic think-tank in Kuala Lumpur, interview, March 1998.
35 Malaysian academic and NGO supporter, interview, March 1998.
36 Researcher, Indonesian Government think-tank, interview, February 1998.
37 Columnist, former Malaysian Government think-tank employee, interview, March 1998.
38 Researcher, Indonesian Government think-tank, interview, February 1998. An increasing number of books are being published which seek to do precisely this. In addition to the publications of Sisters in Islam (see below), there are works such as Leila Ahmed, *Women and Gender in Islam*, and Asghar Ali Engineer, *The Rights of Women in Islam*.
39 Columnist, former Malaysian Government think-tank employee, interview, March 1998.
40 Leader of a private Islamic think-tank in Kuala Lumpur, interview, March 1998. A position, it should be noted, that is strongly contested.
41 Women's activist and NGO leader, Jakarta, interview, March 1998.
42 Interviews were conducted with two members of Sisters in Islam, including Norani Othman, whose writings are quoted below.
43 Representative from Muhammadiyah, Jakarta, interview, February 1998.
44 Ismail (ed.), *Hudud in Malaysia*, back cover.
45 Othman (ed.), *Shari'a Law and the Modern Nation-State*, 151.
46 See generally Othman, *Shari'a and the Citizenship Rights of Women in a Modern Nation State*.
47 Columnist, former Malaysian Government think-tank employee, interview, March 1998.
48 Feillard, 'Indonesia's Emerging Muslim Feminism', 93. The issue of who has the 'right' understanding of any doctrine is essentially the same issue as that dealt with in chapter 6, where the 'doctrine' under discussion is justice.
49 Othman, *Shari'a and the Citizenship Rights of Women*, 50–1.
50 Director, Malaysian women's NGO, interview, March 1998.
51 See also Othman, 'Grounding Human Rights in Non-Western Culture', 186–7.
52 Director, Malaysian women's NGO, interview, March 1998.
53 See also Coomaraswamy, 'Reinventing International Law: Women's Rights as Human Rights in the International Community', esp. 181–2.
54 Masdar F. Mas'udi, interview, February 1998. See also Mas'udi et al., 'Learning from Islam'.

55 S. H. Alatas, 'Core Concepts and Asian Traditions', 42.
56 Academic, International Islamic University, Malaysia, interview, March 1998.
57 Representative, Centre for Information and Development Studies, Indonesia, interview, February 1998.
58 Columnist, former Malaysian Government think-tank employee, interview, March 1998.
59 Catholic Church leader and educator, Jakarta, interview, February 1998; Indonesian academic, Salatiga, interview, January 1998.
60 Political scientist, NGO affiliate (various), Malaysia, interview, March 1998.
61 Altman, 'Commentary One', 311.
62 Interview with Chua Beng-Huat; see also his works quoted in the previous chapter. For yearly accounts of Singapore's human rights observation record, see Human Rights Watch and Amnesty International.
63 Singaporean academic, interview, March 1998.
64 Homosexual activist, Singapore, interview, March 1998.
65 Altman, untitled comments. See also his 'Rupture or Continuity?'.
66 Political scientist, NGO affiliate (various), Malaysia, interview, March 1998. Other commentators are more ambivalent. Cf. Muhammad As Hikam, 'Islam and Human Rights', 3: 'Islam … may or may not be compatible with the secular-based universal principles of human rights'.
67 Ketua, NU (Nahdlatul Ulama), interview, February 1998; Representative from Muhammadiyah, Jakarta, interview February 1998. 'But', as Liddle observes, 'the political values, beliefs and attitudes of Indonesian Muslims have historically been diverse, as has been their expression in organisations such as Muhammadiyah and Nahdlatul Ulama'. Liddle, 'The Islamic Turn in Indonesia', 631. As noted above, Indonesian Islam characteristically allows more diversity of opinion than Malaysian Islam.
68 Political scientist, NGO affiliate (various), Malaysia, interview, March 1998. See An-Na'im, 'The Cultural Mediation of Human Rights', 157, where he argues that the imposition of the death penalty for those who leave Islam denies the reality of freedom of religion in its standard human rights sense. He argues that rights that do exist under Shari'a law are not the same as human rights because they are premised on sex and religion, rather than existing inalienably by virtue of being human.
69 Representative from Muhammadiyah, Jakarta, interview, February 1998.
70 Leader of a private Islamic think-tank in Kuala Lumpur, interview, March 1998; Islamic academic, Jakarta, interview, January 1998.
71 Although it should be noted that the Shari'a courts function to adjudicate proper interpretations and social arrangements.
72 Zifirdaus Adnan, 'Islamic Religion', 447.
73 Researcher, Malaysian church leader, and representative of an affiliation of non-Islamic religious leaders, interview, March 1998; Malaysian academic, interview, March 1998. See also Jayasankaran, 'Forbidden Love'.
74 Malaysian academic, interview, March 1998.
75 Spokesperson for Indonesian National Commission on Human Rights, interview, February 1998.
76 Researcher, Indonesian Government think-tank, interview, February 1998.
77 Human rights NGO member, former academic, Salatiga, interview, January 1998.
78 For an account of different approaches to Islam in Indonesia, see Zifirdaus Adnan, 'Islamic Religion', 458–66.

79 See Abdullah Saeed, '*Ijtihad* and Innovation in Neo-Modernist Islamic Thought in Indonesia'.
80 Othman, *Shari'a and the Citizenship Rights of Women*, 52–3.
81 Director, Malaysian women's NGO, interview, March 1998.
82 See An-Na'im, 'The Cultural Mediation of Human Rights'.
83 See also Meuleman, 'Reaction and Attitudes towards the Darul Arqam Movement in Southeast Asia'.
84 *New Straits Times*, 'Shi'ite Sect against Our Monarchy, Says Hamid'.
85 Zailani Ahmad, 'Hamid: Govt Aims To Keep Muslims United', *Star*, 9 November 1997.
86 An-Na'im, 'The Cultural Mediation of Human Rights', 163.

3 Human Rights: Political Reality, Philosophical Problem

1 Taylor, *Sources of the Self*, 11.
2 Weissbrodt, 'Human Rights: An Historic Perspective', 1.
3 Burgers, 'The Road to San Francisco', 468.
4 See, for example, Patterson, 'Freedom, Slavery and the Modern Construction of Rights', 156; and Burns H. Weston, 'Human Rights', in Weston and Claude (eds), *Human Rights in the World Community*, 15.
5 Zechenter, 'In the Name of Culture', 319; Burgers, 'Road to San Francisco', 450; and Weston and Claude, 'Human Rights as a Challenge to State Sovereignty', in Weston and Claude (eds), *Human Rights in the World Community*, 4.
6 Hausermann, 'Myths and Realities', 132.
7 Chris Brown makes particular note of the rhetorical power of the human rights discourse, despite its conceptual weaknesses, to be reviewed below. He says, 'Perhaps fortunately, most people are not political philosophers, and are less likely to be worried about the conceptual inadequacies associated with the liberal position on human rights than they are to be attracted by the obvious benefits of living in a political system based on or influenced by it'. This is a strong point, but it must be balanced by the consideration that when the conceptual issues find political application, as they increasingly do in pluralist societies, they threaten the capacity of the discourse to maintain the legitimacy of the political system. Brown, 'Human Rights', 474.
8 See, for example, the work of Amnesty International, Human Rights Watch, Christian Solidarity International, the Red Cross, and countless other NGOs.
9 Chesterman, 'Human Rights as Subjectivity', 97.
10 Mayer gives some examples of this within Islamic discourse in her *Islam and Human Rights*.
11 Kamenka, 'The Anatomy of an Idea', 6.
12 Tuck, *Natural Rights Theories*, 2.
13 Ibid., 13. The significance of the idea of the passive right is discussed at length by Tuck because, in his view, it threatens to undermine the whole enterprise of rights language – to render it 'nugatory'. To have a passive right is to 'be given or allowed something by someone else, while to have an active right is to have the right to do something oneself'. The boundaries between these two are admittedly fuzzy. The key point is that the notion of a passive right leads to the modern rights theory that all rights entail duties. This is where rights-talk threatens to become pointless, for 'if any right can be completely expressed as a more or less complex set of duties on other people towards the possessor of the right, and those duties can in turn be explained

in terms of some higher-order moral principle, then the point of a separate language of rights seems to have been lost, and with it the explanatory or justificatory force possessed by reference to rights'. Ibid., 6.

14 Ibid., 15. Tuck argues that this is not surprising, given that these developments were bound up with the development of canon and ecclesiastical law, these being concerned with general questions of welfare, the claims made on those well endowed by the poor or deserving.

15 Ibid., 66–7.

16 See also Tuck, *Hobbes*, 21–4.

17 Shapiro, *The Evolution of Rights in Liberal Theory*, 3, 48.

18 Kamenka, 'The Anatomy of an Idea', 1. See also Bobbio, *Liberalism and Democracy*, 6–7.

19 Kamenka, 'The Anatomy of an Idea', 2–5.

20 Minogue, 'Natural Rights, Ideology and the Game of Life', 13.

21 Kamenka, 'The Anatomy of an Idea', 9.

22 Haakonssen, *Natural Law and Moral Philosophy*, 5.

23 Waldron (ed.), *Nonsense upon Stilts*, 13.

24 Ibid., 18.

25 Gay, *The Enlightenment*, 458. Knud Haakonssen moderates this position somewhat. He argues for an interpretation of the Enlightenment that sees it less as a turning-point in the history of ideas, and more as a social process involving local and national communities. At issue here are the relative roles of the history of ideas and intellectual history. Haakonssen, 'Enlightened Dissent', 1.

26 Talk of natural rights seems to be a case which well illustrates MacIntyre's point (see note 48). John Phillip Reid, for example, argues that in using the language of natural rights the Americans 'went off the constitutional deep end'. By this, according to James H. Hutson, Reid means 'that because natural rights ... were unwritten and hence undefined, they could be used to dignify any desire, to package any prejudice ... A term so protean could not help introducing confusion and contradiction into the rights discourse.' He instances claims of natural rights that public office should be limited to Protestants, that church ministers had natural rights to be paid by state legislators, that judges violated the natural rights of the people by being paid by the king, and so forth. Reid is quoted from his *Constitutional History of the American Revolution*, 88, in Hutson, 'The Bill of Rights and the American Revolutionary Experience', 67.

27 Haakonssen, 'From Natural Law to the Rights of Man', 61. Pufendorf produced the first sketch of the history of modern moral philosophy in his 1672 *Law of Nature and Nations*.

28 Vincent, *Human Rights and International Relations*, 38.

29 Bentham, 'Anarchical Fallacies', 53.

30 Vincent, *Human Rights and International Relations*, 39.

31 Waldron (ed.), *Nonsense upon Stilts*, 126.

32 Rosen, *The Mask of Enlightenment*, 1.

33 Gray, *Enlightenment's Wake*, 123.

34 Maran, *Torture*, 3.

35 Pufendorf held, for example, that rights derived from duties, which were in turn derived from a natural law. This natural law was prescriptive (as opposed to causal, like physical laws), and the idea of a prescriptive law implies a legislator: God. This is quite different from the theories of subjective right which

were devised by Grotius and Hobbes, in which rights were features of human nature. Haakonssen argues that Hobbes' and Grotius' position was so radical that few understood it properly. Pufendorf's restatement of a strong natural law theory of rights eclipsed these movements towards a strong subjective rights theory, although he maintained (for 'prudential' reasons) that he was continuing the natural law tradition established by Grotius. Haakonssen, 'From Natural Law to the Rights of Man', 23–9.

36 Henkin, *Rights of Man Today*, 5.
37 Turner, 'Human Rights, Human Difference', 279.
38 Gaete, 'Postmodernism and Human Rights', 153.
39 Gaete, *Human Rights and the Limits of Critical Reason*, 106.
40 Quoted in Gay, *The Enlightenment*, 456–7.
41 See Grant, *English Speaking Justice*, 74; and Shestack, 'The Philosophic Foundations of Human Rights', 206.
42 Grant, *English Speaking Justice*, 77. The reference in Grant's words is to Rawls, *A Theory of Justice*.
43 Nietzsche, *Thus Spoke Zarathustra*, quoted in Grant, *English Speaking Justice*, 77. See also note 84 below.
44 Tinder, 'Can We Be Good without God', 165.
45 The foremost American exponent of anti-foundationalism is Richard Rorty. See, in particular, his *Philosophy and the Mirror of Nature; Contingency, Irony and Solidarity*; and, specifically on human rights, 'Human Rights, Rationality, and Sentimentality'. For a critique of the latter, see Langlois, 'Redescribing Human Rights'.
46 Oden, *After Modernity ... What?*, 43.
47 Gray, *Liberalism*, 51.
48 MacIntyre, *After Virtue*, 60.
49 MacIntyre, *Three Rival Versions of Moral Enquiry*, 8.
50 Gray, *Liberalisms: Essays in Political Philosophy*, 240.
51 See Gray's *Liberalisms* and his *Post-Liberalism*.
52 Ortega y Gasset, *The Revolt of the Masses*, 83, in Gray, *Liberalism*, 90.
53 Dworkin, *A Matter of Principle*, 191.
54 Kymlicka, 'Liberal Individualism and Neutrality', 168. Kymlicka refers to Raz, *The Morality of Freedom*.
55 George Sher, in a major recent contribution to the literature on the subject of liberal neutrality, argues that such a position is also undesirable. He says, of his conclusions, that the most important are 'first, that governments may and should take an active interest in the goodness of their citizens' lives, and second, that many of the value-claims that have long been regarded as fundamental – claims about the importance of excellence, knowledge, certain preferred modes of interaction among persons, and the traditional virtues – really are so. Taken together, these conclusions imply that both governments and individual political agents often have good reason to promote the favoured traits and activities.' Sher, *Beyond Neutrality*, 19. Sher thus supports a traditionalist perfectionist position. He notes that even liberal theorists such as Rawls have withdrawn from a completely neutral position and argues that, while perfectionist reasons are not the only grounds for political decisions and should not necessarily be dominant reasons, they do nonetheless have a vital role to play. While Rawls still maintains that perfectionist reasons should not influence our thinking on basic justice or constitutional essentials, Sher persuasively argues that even this position cannot be sustained and that per-

fectionist reasons have proper application here also. Ibid., 247. This, from a different angle, is because, as Simon Caney argues, 'The problem … is that the reasoning anti-perfectionists invoke to defend liberal neutrality also implies that the state is prohibited from enacting principles of justice – a highly counterintuitive outcome'. Caney calls this the anti-perfectionist dilemma, arguing that the same factors which cause people to diverge about the good will also cause them to diverge about the right, the right being that which anti-perfectionists take to be the concern of justice. Caney, 'Liberal Legitimacy, Reasonable Disagreement and Justice', 23.

56 Gray, *Liberalism*, 90.
57 Holt, *Wittgenstein, Politics and Human Rights*, 9.
58 Mulhall and Swift, *Liberals and Communitarians*, 54–5.
59 Marshall, 'Liberalism, Pluralism and Christianity', 156–7.
60 Ibid.
61 Rawls, 'Fairness to Goodness', 549.
62 Waldron, 'Theoretical Foundations of Liberalism', 57.
63 Holt, *Wittgenstein, Politics and Human Rights*, 81.
64 In his later *Political Liberalism*, Rawls still holds to the position that there is 'but one public reason', 230.
65 Ivison, 'The Secret History of Public Reason', 144. See also his 'Postcolonialism and Political Theory'.
66 Mulhall and Swift, *Liberals and Communitarians*, 237–9.
67 See Fish, 'Why We Can't All Just Get Along'.
68 Grant, *English Speaking Justice*, 6.
69 Fish, 'Why We Can't All Just Get Along', 248.
70 Ibid., 254.
71 Fish, 'Liberalism Doesn't Exist', 136.
72 Liberalism makes out that we need not structure society according to any one narrative or story that is true. It claims thus to be doing something other than what all narratives have done in the past. Liberalism pretends to be other than a new story which claims that we do not need stories in order to live as free and rational creatures, tempting us to believe that freedom and rationality are independent of narrative. It is, ironically, a story that claims we need no story. Hauerwas, *A Community of Character*, 12, 149. It is because of a conception of truth that depends on Reason and an Olympic or Archimedean standpoint that story and narrative are dismissed as legitimate means for truth-seeking. Beiner argues that what we may call storied theory 'will seek to tell true stories that help us to see our nature more clearly, and it will serve to disclose (or remind us of) possibilities of human life that are hidden from us by our immersion in the needs and preoccupations of the present'. Beiner, *What's the Matter with Liberalism?*, 10. That an increasing number of theorists (MacIntyre, Stout, Hauerwas, Taylor, Oakeshott, Schklar, and others) tell the development of liberalism as a historic narrative points again to the role of narrative, tradition and particularist reasons in our truth-seeking endeavours.
73 Fish, 'Liberalism Doesn't Exist', 137–8.
74 Larmore, *The Morals of Modernity*, 51. Larmore argues that this can be demonstrated by examining the work of Leo Strauss. Strauss was a vehement critic of what he called 'historicism' and yet was unable, despite arguing prolifically for the maintenance of a belief in a Platonic rationality, to use it to furnish us with a content-filled politico-moral philosophy. See *The Morals of Modernity*, ch. 3.

75 Kamenka, *Human Rights*, 6.
76 Which claim 'exhibits the structural similarity of liberalism to the evangelizing Christianity of which it is the illegitimate offspring'. Gray, *Liberalisms*, 239.
77 Kothari, 'Human Rights', quoted in Turner, 'Human Rights, Human Difference', 284. This is particularly the case when translated into economic policy terms. Gray argues, for example, that one effect of the neo-liberal economic ideology is to undermine the traditional local values which sustain communities and provide the social resources for developing communities in which the poor and marginalised are empowered. See, generally, Gray, *Endgames*. This argument is also made in Taylor, *The Ethics of Authenticity*, generally, but especially ch. 10.
78 Shue, *Basic Rights*.
79 Turner, 'Human Rights: From Local Cultures to Global Systems', 12.
80 Turner, 'Outline of a Theory of Human Rights', 504.
81 Camilleri, 'Human Rights, Cultural Diversity and Conflict Resolution', 21.
82 Grant, *English Speaking Justice*, 22.
83 Ibid., 30.
84 As Nietzsche says, 'I do not wish to be mixed up and confused with these preachers of equality. For, to *me* justice speaks thus: "Men are not equal." Nor shall they become equal!' *Thus Spoke Zarathustra*, 101. (The vogue in recent political theory for using Nietzsche as a bolster for democracy by virtue of his emphasis on difference fails to recognise that his difference is in the form of a spiritual aristocracy. It is anything but egalitarian (Abbey and Appel, 'Nietzsche and the Will to Politics').) See Grant on this point in part IV of *English Speaking Justice*. Perry asks, 'Why is it that the good of every human being is worth pursuing in its own right?' His response: 'One answer – the answer that informs the international law of human rights – is that the good of every human being is an end worth pursuing in its own right *because every human being is sacred* … there might be no intelligible secular version of that answer – that is, no intelligible secular version of the conviction that every human being is sacred.' Perry, 'Are Human Rights Universal?', 466. See also Perry, *The Idea of Human Rights*, in which this essay is reproduced with three others, one of which is entitled 'Is the Idea of Human Rights Ineliminably Religious?' – his answer is yes.
85 For example, that millions of rats die prematurely from inadequate food resources, disease, abuse by human rat-eradication programs, and so on, does not automatically generate moral opprobrium nor a universally accepted rat-right to life. The only reason human needs are treated differently is because of the metaphysical and normative assumptions we have about the nature and status of humans and therefore of the moral significance of their needs. This significance depends on traditions of thought, not just on the existential awareness of needs. This is implicitly supported by Gray's assertion that 'humanism is indefensible without resort to the Judaeo-Christian tradition which grounds the supreme value of human personality in its kinship with a divine personality which animates the universe'. Gray calls the forms of humanism found in secular liberalism an 'atavistic anomaly' and a 'relic of theism'. Despite the polemic, it is clear that the issue revolves around social norms which have been retained despite the apparent obsolescence of their original philosophical justifications. Gray, *Post-Liberalism*, 307.
86 Cf. Wendt, *Social Theory of International Politics*, 122–5. 'Beliefs define and direct material needs', 123. This includes our most basic needs, which

depend on beliefs to give content to what is desirable – beliefs are ideas which come from our wider frameworks, the narratives given by the human traditions.

87 MacIntyre, *After Virtue*, 68.
88 Ibid., 69.
89 Cf. Mervyn Frost, who also argues (although in a more constructive manner) against 'all rights-based theories', that one does not have rights outside of those relationships with social and political institutions that constitute one as a rights-bearer. Frost, *Ethics in International Relations*, 138.
90 Gray, *Liberalisms*, 263.

4 Human Rights as Incompletely Theorised Agreement

1 Freeman, 'The Philosophical Foundations of Human Rights', 498.
2 Campbell, *Truth and Historicity*, 12.
3 Taylor, 'A World Consensus on Human Rights?', 21.
4 Kamenka, 'Anatomy of an Idea', 12.
5 This does not rule out the possibility that only one of the human traditions may finally be 'the truth'. I am attending here to the political reality of many such contending claims owned by communities of people who would not automatically change their belief systems, even if there were knock-down philosophical arguments. One still has to live with the people who do not or cannot believe the truth.
6 I am deeply indebted to Dr Christine Parker for drawing Sunstein's work to my attention.
7 Sunstein, 'Incompletely Theorized Agreements', 1734.
8 Ibid., 1748.
9 Ibid., 1734.
10 Ibid., 1735.
11 Sunstein, *Legal Reasoning and Political Conflict*, 37.
12 Sunstein, 'Practical Reason and Incompletely Theorized Agreements', 1.
13 Sunstein, 'Incompletely Theorized Agreements', 1739.
14 Ibid., 1739.
15 Ibid., 1737.
16 Ibid., 1738.
17 Ibid.
18 Sunstein, *Legal Reasoning*, 43.
19 Sunstein, 'Practical Reason', 2.
20 Ibid., 6.
21 Sunstein, 'Incompletely Theorized Agreements', 1738.
22 Sunstein, *Legal Reasoning*, 44.
23 Sunstein, 'Practical Reason', 6.
24 Ibid., 7.
25 Ibid.
26 Ibid.
27 See, in particular, his *A Theory of Justice* and *Political Liberalism*.
28 Sunstein, 'Practical Reason', 8.
29 Ibid.
30 See section 'On the Use of Abstract Conceptions' in Rawls, *Political Liberalism*, 43–6.
31 Ibid., 46.
32 Sunstein, 'Practical Reason', 9.

33 Rawls, quoted in Sunstein, 'Practical Reason', 9.
34 Sunstein, 'Practical Reason', 9.
35 Sunstein, *Legal Reasoning*, 50.
36 Sunstein, 'Incompletely Theorized Agreements', 1738.
37 Sunstein, *Legal Reasoning*, 54.
38 Ibid., 56.
39 Ibid., 60.
40 Sunstein, 'Incompletely Theorized Agreements', 1771–2.
41 Ibid., 1748.
42 Mayer, *Islam and Human Rights*, 50.
43 Taylor, 'Conditions of an Unforced Consensus on Human Rights', 136.
44 Adams, *Life, the Universe and Everything*.
45 Maritain, 'The Possibilities for Co-operation in a Divided World', in Guinness, *The American Hour*, 251.
46 Sunstein, 'Practical Reason', 1.
47 See, for example, Alston and Steiner, *International Human Rights in Context*; and Alston (ed.), *The United Nations and Human Rights*.
48 For differing views on this in the international law context, see Bruno Simma and Philip Alston, 'The Sources of Human Rights Law: Custom, Jus Cogens, and General Principles', *Australian Year Book of International Law*, Vol. 12, 1992, 82–108; and J. S. Watson, 'Legal Theory, Efficacy and Validity in the Development of Human Rights Norms in International Law', *University of Illinois Law Forum*, Vol. 3, 1979, 609–41.
49 John Charvet exemplifies the commonly made mistake that agreement among state elites says much about genuine global agreement: 'Since most states have signed up to these covenants, it would seem that there already exists a world ethical consensus, even if there remain substantial problems of securing compliance with the norms' (p. 523). In many cases the problem with compliance exists precisely because antithetical norms to those signed by state elites are held with mass legitimacy by the average citizen. He mentions the issue of non-compliance again (p. 529) but chooses not to give it detailed attention. When one considers NGOs, corporations, religious organisations, cultural groupings, philosophical traditions – that is, non-state agents – 'world ethical consensus' looks a long way off. See Charvet, 'The Possibility of a Cosmopolitan Ethical Order Based on the Idea of Universal Human Rights'.
50 Bell, 'Minority Rights', 38–9.
51 Berting et al. (eds), *Human Rights in a Pluralist World*.
52 Van Ness, 'Introduction', and Coomaraswamy, 'Reinventing International Law', in Van Ness (ed.), *Debating Human Rights*, 10, 178.
53 See Cranston, *What Are Human Rights*, esp. ch. 8, 65–71.
54 Alston, 'A Proposal for Quality Control'.
55 Van Ness, 'Introduction', in Van Ness (ed.), *Debating Human Rights*, 10.
56 Sunstein, 'Practical Reason', 9.
57 Ivison, 'The Secret History of Public Reason', 146.
58 A claim which many took Rawls to be making with his *Theory of Justice*, but from which he distances himself in *Political Liberalism*, where he appears to address his theory to modern democratic societies. Rawls, *Political Liberalism*, xvi. Cf. Kukathas and Pettit, who comment that the later Rawls addresses his question 'how can people settle on a conception of justice "that is (most) reasonable for them in virtue of how they conceive of their persons and construe

the general features of social cooperation among persons so regarded"? … This is, more specifically, a question addressed to American society which, on Rawls's reading of its particular history, conceives of moral persons as "free and equal", but enjoys "no agreement about the way basic social institutions should be arranged to conform to the freedom and equality of citizens as moral persons".' Kukathas and Pettit, *Rawls*, 126. They quote from Rawls, 'Kantian Constructivism in Moral Theory', 517. This article appears revised as 'Political Constructivism', ch. 3 of *Political Liberalism*. Thus, in his later work, Rawls appears to eschew the universalism commonly attributed to his intentions, to focus on what justice might mean for the liberal American polity. However, it is not clear that Rawls can evade the criticisms levelled against his universalism by limiting the scope of this universalism to those in the liberal American polity, for it surely would be a mistake to see this polity as co-extensive with the American polity at large, let alone the 'West'. On the other hand, it is this change in approach on Rawls' part which has led some to defend him against the communitarians, with their critique of his universalist unencumbered self, by arguing that in fact Rawls' position is one of 'communitarian liberalism' developed on the basis of a historical tradition, an experience of political community and a concretely lived mode of common life as found in liberal democracies such as America.

59 Walzer, *Thick and Thin*, 15.
60 Walzer, *Spheres of Justice*, 6.
61 Mulhall and Swift, *Liberals and Communitarians*, 154.
62 Gray, *Endgames*, 162.

5 The Return of Politics and Human Rights

1 I am deeply indebted to Dr C. J. Wee Wan-ling for drawing Mouffe's work to my attention.
2 Hopgood, 'Reading the Small Print in Global Civil Society'.
3 Taylor, 'Conditions of an Unforced Consensus', 137–8.
4 Brown, 'International Theory and International Society', 192. Brown is specifically talking about states here, whereas Taylor's argument (and the point to follow, from Gray) draws more widely on other groups within society. Gray talks of communities, not just states, and Taylor's argument was illustrated by drawing on themes in Buddhist literature, theology, and social movements. The wider argument of this book agrees with Brown, however, in thinking that actual consensus on values, especially values which are to change the behaviour of states and citizens, is much harder to achieve than nominal adherence to 'unspecific norms'.
5 Gray, *Enlightenment's Wake*, 129.
6 Mouffe, *The Return of the Political*, 13.
7 Shih Chih-yu, 'Human Rights as Identities', 146.
8 Ibid., 160–1.
9 See also Narramore, 'The Politics of Rights and Identity in Japan'.
10 Gray, *Endgames*, 54.
11 Ibid., 40.
12 Nikhil Aziz, 'The Human Rights Debate in an Era of Globalisation', in Van Ness (ed.), *Debating Human Rights*, 40.
13 Hauerwas, *In Good Company*, 177, particularly the chapter 'Casuistry in Context: The Need for Tradition', 169–83.

14 Stout, *The Flight from Authority*, 262–3, and ch. 12, 'Explicating Historicism'.
15 Ibid., 266.
16 Hauerwas, *Wilderness Wanderings*, 117. See also his *Dispatches from the Front*.
17 Gaita, *A Common Humanity*, 14, 22. He refers to Cavell, *The Claim of Reason*.
18 Holt, *Wittgenstein, Politics and Human Rights*, 20.
19 Mouffe, *The Return of the Political*, 6.
20 Van Ness, *Debating Human Rights*, 10.
21 Benhabib, *Situating the Self*, 73. It is this that Benhabib takes to be the central insight of Habermas' project. However, Benhabib is strongly critical of Habermas' rationalism and his focus on a strong deontological interpretation of ethics.
22 Crawford, 'Postmodern Ethical Conditions and a Critical Response', 121.
23 Mouffe, *The Return of the Political*, 14–15.
24 See, generally, Campbell, *Truth and Historicity*.
25 Hauerwas, *Against the Nations*, 6. His quotations are from Lindbeck, *The Nature of Doctrine*, 130 and 131, respectively.
26 For his latest such attempt, see Rawls, *The Law of Peoples* (1999).
27 Stout, 'On Having a Morality in Common', 224. See also his *Ethics after Babel* and *The Flight from Authority*.
28 Gray, *Endgames*, 41.
29 Mouffe, *The Return of the Political*, 53.
30 Gray, *Endgames*, 177.
31 Barber, *The Conquest of Politics*, 18, in Benhabib, *Situating the Self*, 102.
32 Pritchard, 'The Jurisprudence of Human Rights', 11.
33 Hauerwas, *Against the Nations*, 6.
34 Dworkin, *Taking Rights Seriously*, 176.
35 Donnelly, 'Human Rights: A New Standard of Civilization?'. For a brief critique of the ambiguities in Donnelly's position, see O'Manique, 'Universal and Inalienable Rights'.
36 Freeman, 'The Philosophical Foundations of Human Rights', 493.
37 George, 'Realist "Ethics", International Relations, and Post-Modernism: Thinking beyond the Egoism–Anarchy Thematic', 215. See also his *Discourses of Global Politics*.
38 Linklater, *The Transformation of Political Community*, 48.
39 Mouffe, *The Return of the Political*, 15. The work of Zygmunt Bauman (*Postmodern Ethics*) is but a particularly cogent example of a postmodernism which urges that morality is not relativistic.
40 William A. Galston refers to this relativism as 'Cartesianism with a minus sign', his point being that such relativism results only if one remains within the horizon of Cartesian presuppositions. Galston, *Liberal Purposes*, 34.
41 Taylor, *Sources of the Self*, 27.
42 Reeder, 'Foundations without Foundationalism', 201.
43 Mouffe, *The Return of the Political*, 52.
44 Booth, 'Three Tyrannies', 40.
45 Van Ness, *Debating Human Rights*, 17.
46 Nikhil Aziz, 'The Human Rights Debate in an Era of Globalisation', in Van Ness (ed.), *Debating Human Rights*, 39.
47 Mouffe, *The Return of the Political*, 147.
48 An-Na'im, 'The Cultural Mediation of Human Rights', 153.
49 Camilleri, 'Regional Human Rights Dialogue in Asia Pacific', 177.
50 Taylor, 'Conditions of an Unforced Consensus', 136.

51 The first was Bell's *Communitarianism and Its Critics.*
52 Bell, *East Meets West,* 11.
53 Ibid., 9.
54 Ibid., 1.
55 De Bary, *Asian Values and Human Rights,* 11.
56 Ibid., 13
57 Ibid., 15.
58 Woodiwiss, *Globalisation, Human Rights and Labour Law in Pacific Asia,* 1.
59 Ibid., 4.
60 Ibid., 14.

Conclusion

1 Lev, 'Introduction', xiv.
2 For example, Charvet, 'Cosmopolitan Ethical Order', 529.
3 Kothari, 'Human Rights: A Movement in Search of a Theory'.
4 Fish, 'Why We Can't All Just Get Along', 248.
5 See, generally, Campbell, *Truth and Historicity;* Larmore, *The Morals of Modernity.*
6 Dworkin, *Taking Rights Seriously.*
7 In his *Political Liberalism.*
8 MacIntyre, *After Virtue,* 69.
9 Katongole's *Beyond Universal Reason* appeared too late to interact with the argument of this work. However, it provides a systematic and comprehensive guide to a number of the ideas which animate my thinking and exemplifies the philosophical tradition in which I would locate myself.
10 Hauerwas, *A Community of Character,* 149.
11 Stout, *The Flight from Authority,* 262–3.
12 Gaita, *A Common Humanity,* 14, 22.
13 Cavell, *The Claim of Reason,* quoted by Gaita, ibid.
14 Translation of the Indonesian '*Orang Kecil*'.
15 Stout, *The Flight from Authority,* 266.
16 Hauerwas, *Dispatches from the Front,* 150.
17 Stout, *The Flight from Authority,* 266.
18 See, generally, Rorty, 'Human Rights, Rationality, and Sentimentality'.
19 Gaita, *A Common Humanity,* 14, 22; Hauerwas, *Wilderness Wanderings,* 117.
20 Gray, *Enlightenment's Wake,* 15–16.
21 In Southeast Asia, see the critiques by Chandra Muzaffar and Anwar Ibrahim against secularism. See also, with respect to Western thought, Milbank, *Theology and Social Theory.*
22 Rorty, 'Human Rights, Rationality, and Sentimentality', 112.
23 Gaete, 'Postmodernism and Human Rights', 149.
24 Mouffe, *The Return of the Political,* 15.
25 Maran, *Torture,* 3.
26 Hauerwas, *Against the Nations,* 6.
27 Campbell, *Truth and Historicity,* 434.
28 Hauerwas, *In Good Company,* 172.
29 The phrase 'Justice as Fairness' is from Rawls' *A Theory of Justice.*
30 Campbell, *Truth and Historicity,* 437.

Bibliography

A. B. Shamsul. 'Debating about Identity in Malaysia: A Discourse Analysis', *Tonan Ajia Kenkyu (Southeast Asian Studies)*, Vol. 34, No. 3, December 1996, 476–99.

Abbey, Ruth and Fredrick Appel. 'Nietzsche and the Will to Politics', *Review of Politics*, Vol. 60, No. 1, Winter 1998, 83–114.

Abdullah Saeed. '*Ijtihad* and Innovation in Neo-Modernist Islamic Thought in Indonesia', *Islam and Christian–Muslim Relations*, Vol. 8, No. 3, 1997, 279–95.

Abubakar Eby Hara. The Claims of 'Asian Values' and 'Asian Democracy': Some Implications for International Society, with Special Attention to Singapore, Malaysia and Indonesia, PhD thesis, Australian National University, 1999.

Adams, Douglas. *Life, the Universe and Everything*, London: Pan Books, 1982.

Ahmed, Leila. *Women and Gender in Islam*, New Haven: Yale University Press, 1992.

Ali Alatas. Statement to Second World Conference on Human Rights, Vienna, 14 June 1993, http://www.dfa-deplu.go.id/english/ham_stmt.htm (accessed 23.1.97).

—— Keynote address at Indonesia–Canada Colloquium on Human Rights, Jakarta, 28 October 1997; http://www.dfa-deplu.go.id/english2/menlu281097.htm (accessed 29.7.98).

—— Address at inaugural meeting of Indonesia Council on World Affairs, Jakarta, 2 December 1997.

Alston, Philip. 'A Proposal for Quality Control', *American Journal of International Law*, 1984, Vol. 78, No. 3, 607–21.

—— (ed.). *The United Nations and Human Rights: A Critical Appraisal*, Oxford: Clarendon Press, 1992.

Alston, Philip and Henry J. Steiner. *International Human Rights in Context: Law, Politics, Morals*, Oxford: Clarendon Press, 1996.

Alston, Philip and Karel Vasak (eds). *The International Dimensions of Human Rights*, Westport: Greenwood Press, 1982.

Altman, Dennis. 'Rupture or Continuity? The Internationalization of Gay Identities', *Social Text*, Fall 1996, 77–94.

—— 'Commentary One', *Social Semiotics*, Vol. 8, Nos 2/3, August–December 1998, 309–13.

Anderson, Walter Truett (ed.). *The Truth about the Truth: De-confusing and Re-constructing the Postmodern World*, New York: Tarcher/Putnam, 1995.

An-Na'im, Abdullahi Ahmed. 'The Cultural Mediation of Human Rights: The Al-Arqam case in Malaysia', in Bauer and Bell (eds), *The East Asian Challenge for Human Rights*, 147–68.

—— (ed.). *Human Rights in Cross-Cultural Perspectives: A Quest for Consensus*, Philadelphia: University of Pennsylvania Press, 1992.

Anwar Ibrahim. Speech at conference on Islam in Southeast Asia, Petaling Jaya Hilton, 5 March 1996; http://www.smpke.jpm.my/ucapan.tpm/1996/960305.htm (accessed 25.8.97).

—— 'Asian Renaissance and the Reconstruction of Civilisation', speech, University Loyola Heights, Quezon City, Philippines, 2 May 1996; http://www.smpke.jpm.my/ucapan.tpm/1996/960502.htm (accessed 25.8.97).

—— Speech at International Conference on the Philippine Revolution and Beyond, Manila, 23 August 1996; http://www.smpke.jpm.my/ucapan.tpm/1996/960823.htm (accessed 25.8.97).

—— *The Asian Renaissance*, Kuala Lumpur: Times Books International, 1996.

Aryeh Neier. 'Asia's Unacceptable Standard', *Foreign Policy*, No. 92, Fall 1993, 42–52.

Asghar Ali Engineer. *The Rights of Women in Islam*, London: C. Hurst and Co., 1992.

Barber, Benjamin. *The Conquest of Politics: Liberal Philosophy in Democratic Times*, Princeton, NJ: Princeton University Press, 1988.

Bartley, Robert et al. *Democracy and Capitalism: Asian and American Perspectives*, Singapore: ISEAS, 1993.

Bauer, Joanne R. and Daniel A. Bell (eds). *The East Asian Challenge for Human Rights*, Cambridge: Cambridge University Press, 1999.

Bauman, Zygmunt. *Postmodern Ethics*, Oxford: Blackwell Publishers, 1993.

Baylis, John and Steve Smith (eds). *The Globalization of World Politics: An Introduction to International Relations*, Oxford: Oxford University Press, 1997.

Beiner, Ronald. *What's the Matter with Liberalism?*, Berkeley: University of California Press, 1992.

Bell, Daniel A. *Communitarianism and Its Critics*, Oxford: Oxford University Press, 1993.

—— 'Minority Rights: On the Importance of Local Knowledge', *Dissent*, Summer 1996, 36–41.

—— 'The East Asian Challenge to Human Rights: Reflections on an East West Dialogue', *Human Rights Quarterly*, Vol. 18, No. 3, 1996, 641–67.

—— *East Meets West: Human Rights and Democracy in East Asia*, Princeton, NJ: Princeton University Press, 2000.

Bellamy, Richard and Martin Hollis (eds). *Pluralism and Liberal Neutrality*, London: Frank Cass Publishers, 1999.

Benhabib, Seyla. *Situating the Self: Gender, Community and Postmodernism in Contemporary Ethics*, Cambridge: Polity Press, 1992.

Bentham, Jeremy. 'Anarchical Fallacies: Being an Examination of the Declaration of Rights Issued during the French Revolution', in Waldron (ed.), *Nonsense upon Stilts*, 46–76.

Berlin, Isaiah. *Four Essays on Liberty*, Oxford: Oxford University Press, 1969.

Berting, Jan et al. (eds). *Human Rights in a Pluralist World: Individuals and Collectives*, Westport: Meckler, 1990.

Bilahari Kausikan. 'Asia's Different Standard', *Foreign Policy*, No. 92, Fall 1993, 24–41.

—— 'Governance That Works', *Journal of Democracy*, Vol. 8, No. 2, 1997, 24–34.

Birch, David. 'Constructing Asian Values: National Identities and "Responsible" Citizens', *Social Semiotics*, Vol. 8, Nos 2/3, August–December 1998, 177–202.

Black, Ian. 'Rights for All Still Remain a Dream', *Guardian Weekly*, 13 December 1998, 7.

Blond, Phillip (ed.). *Post-Secular Philosophy: Between Philosophy and Theology*, London: Routledge, 1998.

Bobbio, Norberto. *Liberalism and Democracy*, trs. M. Ryle and K. Soper, London: Verso, 1990.

—— *The Age of Rights*, trs. Allan Cameron, Cambridge: Polity Press, 1996.

Booth, Ken. 'Human Wrongs and International Relations', *International Affairs*, Vol. 71, No. 1, 1995, 103–26.

—— 'Three Tyrannies', in Dunne and Wheeler (eds), *Human Rights in Global Politics*, 31–70.

Boucher, David and Paul Kelly (eds). *Social Justice: From Hume to Walzer*, London: Routledge, 1998.

Bourchier, David. 'Indonesianising Indonesia: Conservative Indigenism in an Age of Globalisation', *Social Semiotics*, Vol. 8, Nos 2/3, August–December 1998, 203–14.

Bowen, Donna Lee. 'Abortion, Islam, and the 1994 Cairo Population Conference', *International Journal of Middle East Studies*, Vol. 29, 1997, 161–84.

Brems, Eva. 'Enemies or Allies? Feminism and Cultural Relativism as Dissident Voices in Human Rights Discourse', *Human Rights Quarterly*, Vol. 19, No. 1, 1997, 136–64.

Brown, Chris. *International Relations Theory: New Normative Approaches*, Hemel Hempstead: Harvester Wheatsheaf, 1992.

—— 'International Theory and International Society: The Viability of the Middle Way?', *Review of International Studies*, Vol. 21, No. 2, April 1995, 183–96.

—— 'Human Rights', in Baylis and Smith (eds), *The Globalization of World Politics*, 469–82.

—— 'Universal Human Rights: A Critique', in Dunne and Wheeler (eds), *Human Rights in Global Politics*, 103–27.

Budiman, Arief (ed.). *State and Civil Society in Indonesia*, Monash Papers on Southeast Asia, No. 22, Melbourne: Monash University, 1990.

Bull, Hedley. *The Anarchical Society: A Study of Order in World Politics*, London: Macmillan, 1977.

Bull, Hedley and A. Watson. *The Expansion of International Society*, Oxford: Clarendon Press, 1984.

Burgers, Jan Herman. 'The Road to San Francisco: The Revival of the Human Rights Idea in the Twentieth Century', *Human Rights Quarterly*, Vol. 14, No. 4, 1992, 447–77.

Caballero-Anthony, Mely. 'Human Rights, Economic Change and Political Development: A Southeast Asia Perspective', in Tang (ed.), *Human Rights and International Relations in the Asia–Pacific Region*, 39–53.

Camilleri, Joseph A. 'Human Rights, Cultural Diversity and Conflict Resolution: The Asia Pacific Context', *Pacifica Review*, Vol. 6, No. 2, 1994, 17–41.

—— 'Regional Human Rights Dialogue in Asia Pacific: Prospects and Proposals', *Pacifica Review*, Vol. 10, No. 3, October 1998, 167–85.

Camilleri, Joseph A. and Chandra Muzaffar (eds). *Globalisation: The Perspectives and Experiences of the Religious Traditions of Asia Pacific*, Petaling Jaya: International Movement for a Just World, 1998.

Campbell, Richard. *Truth and Historicity*, Oxford: Clarendon Press, 1992.

Camroux, David. 'State Responses to Islamic Resurgence in Malaysia: Accommodation, Co-option, and Confrontation', *Asian Survey*, Vol. XXXVI, No. 9, September 1996, 852–68.

Caney, Simon. 'Liberal Legitimacy, Reasonable Disagreement and Justice', in Bellamy and Hollis (eds), *Pluralism and Liberal Neutrality*, 19–36.

Case, William. 'Malaysia: Aspects and Audiences of Legitimacy', in Muthiah Alagappa (ed.), *Political Legitimacy in Southeast Asia*, 69–107.

Cavell, Stanley. *The Claim of Reason*, Oxford: Clarendon Press, 1979.

Cerna, Christina M. 'Universality of Human Rights and Cultural Diversity: Implementation of Human Rights in Different Socio-Cultural Contexts', *Human Rights Quarterly*, Vol. 16, No. 4, 1994, 740–52.

Chan Heng Chee. 'Democracy: Evolution and Implementation: An Asian Perspective', in Bartley et al. (eds), *Democracy and Capitalism*, 1–26.

Chan, Joseph. 'The Task for Asians: To Discover Their Own Political Morality for Human Rights', *Human Rights Dialogue*, Vol. 4, March 1996, 5–6.

—— 'An Alternative View', *Journal of Democracy*, Vol. 8, No. 2, 1997, 3–48.

—— 'A Confucian Perspective on Human Rights for Contemporary China', in Bauer and Bell (eds), *The East Asian Challenge for Human Rights*, 212–37.

Chandra Muzaffar. 'Ethnicity, Ethnic Conflict and Human Rights in Malaysia', in Welch and Leary (eds), *Asian Perspectives on Human Rights*, 107–41.

—— *Human Rights and the New World Order*, Penang: JUST, 1993.

—— 'From Human Rights to Human Dignity', *Bulletin of Concerned Asian Scholars*, Vol. 27, No. 4, October–December 1995, 6–8.

—— *Dominance of the West over the Rest*, Penang: JUST, 1995.

—— 'Towards Human Dignity', in Chandra Muzaffar (ed.), *Human Wrongs*, 268–75.

—— 'Removal from the University of Malaya', *Commentary*, No. 22, March 1999, 5–9.

—— (ed.). *Human Wrongs: Reflections on Western Global Dominance and Its Impact upon Human Rights*, Penang: JUST, 1996.

Chaplin, Jonathan and Paul Marshall (eds). *Political Theory and Christian Vision: Essays in Memory of Bernard Zylstra*, Maryland: University Press of America, 1994.

Charlesworth, Hilary. 'Feminist Critiques of International Law and Their Critics', *Third World Legal Studies 1994*, published by International Third World Legal Studies Association and Valparaiso University School of Law.

—— 'Worlds Apart: Public/Private Distinctions in International Law', in Margaret Thornton (ed.), *Public and Private: Feminist Legal Debates*, Melbourne: Oxford University Press, 1995, 243–59.

Charvet, John. 'The Possibility of a Cosmopolitan Ethical Order Based on the Idea of Universal Human Rights', *Millennium: Journal of International Studies*, Vol. 27, No. 3, 1998, 523–41.

Chen, Selia. 'Liberal Justification: A Typology', *Politics*, Vol. 18, No. 3, 1998, 189–96.

Chesterman, Simon. 'Human Rights as Subjectivity', *Millennium: Journal of International Studies*, Vol. 27, No. 1, May 1998, 97–118.

Chew, Melanie. 'Human Rights in Singapore: Perceptions and Problems', *Asian Survey*, Vol. XXXIV, No. 11, November 1994, 933–48.

Cho-Oon Khong. 'Singapore: Political Legitimacy through Managing Conformity', in Mochtar Pabottingi, 'Indonesia', 108–35.

Christie, Kenneth. 'Human Rights Agendas and Southeast Asia', paper presented at ASEAN Inter-University Seminars on Social Development, Universiti Kebangsaan Malaysia/National University of Singapore, November 1993.

—— 'Regime Security and Human Rights in Southeast Asia', *Political Studies*, Vol. XLIII, Special Issue, 1995, 204–18.

Chua Beng-Huat. *Communitarian Ideology and Democracy in Singapore*, London: Routledge, 1995.

—— *Culture, Multiracialism, and National Identity in Singapore*, Singapore: Department of Sociology, National University of Singapore, 1995.

—— 'Asian Values: Restraining the Logic of Capitalism?', *Social Semiotics*, Vol. 8, Nos 2/3, August–December 1998, 215–26.

—— 'Culturalisation of Economy and Politics in Singapore', in Robison (ed.), *Pathways to Asia*, 87–107.

Clammer, John. 'Deconstructing Values: The Establishment of a National Ideology and Its Implications for Singapore's Political Future', in Rodan (ed.), *Singapore Changes Guard*, 34–51.

Clark, Ian. *Globalization and Fragmentation: International Relations in the Twentieth Century*, Oxford: Oxford University Press, 1997.

Cohen, Margot. 'Man of Many Parts', *Far Eastern Economic Review*, 4 November 1999, 20–1.

Colls, Robert. 'Ethics Man: John Gray's New Moral World', *Political Quarterly*, Vol. 69, No. 1, January–March 1998, 59–71.

Cook, Michael (ed.). *The New Imperialism: World Population and the Cairo Conference*, Sydney: Little Hill Press, 1994.

Coomaraswamy, Radhika. 'Reinventing International Law: Women's Rights as Human Rights in the International Community', in Van Ness (ed.), *Debating Human Rights*, 167–83.

Cotton, James. 'On the Identity of "Confucianism": Theory or Practice?', *Political Theory Newsletter*, No. 3, 1991, 113–21.

—— 'Political Innovation in Singapore: The Presidency, the Leadership and the Party', in Rodan (ed.), *Singapore Changes Guard*, 3–15.

—— 'State and Society in Singapore', *Pacific Review*, Vol. 9, No. 2, 1996, 278–82.

Cranston, Maurice. *What Are Human Rights*, London: Bodley Head, 1973.

Crawford, Neta C. 'Postmodern Ethical Conditions and a Critical Response', *Ethics and International Affairs*, Vol. 12, 1998, 121–40.

Crouch, Harold. 'Malaysia: Neither Authoritarian nor Democratic', in Hewison et al. (eds), *Southeast Asia in the 1990s*, 135–57.

—— *Government and Society in Malaysia*, Ithaca, NY: Cornell University Press, 1996.

—— 'Indonesia's "Strong" State', in Dauvergene (ed.), *Weak and Strong States in Asia–Pacific Societies*, 93–113.

Dauvergne, Peter (ed.). *Weak and Strong States in Asia–Pacific Societies*, Sydney: Allen & Unwin, 1998.

Davies, Norman. *Europe: A History*, London: Pimlico, 1996.

Davies, Peter (ed.). *Human Rights*, London: Routledge, 1988.

Davis, Michael C. 'Chinese Perspectives on Human Rights', in Davis (ed.), *Human Rights and Chinese Values*, 3–23.

—— (ed.). *Human Rights and Chinese Values: Legal, Philosophical and Political Perspectives*, Hong Kong: Oxford University Press, 1995.

de Bary, William Theodore. *The Liberal Tradition in China*, New York: Columbia University Press, 1983.

—— *Asian Values and Human Rights: A Confucian Communitarian Perspective*, Cambridge, MA: Harvard University Press, 1998.

Delhaise, P. F. *Asia in Crisis: What Went Wrong and Why*, Singapore: John Wiley and Sons Inc., 1998.

Donnelly, Jack. 'Human Rights and Human Dignity: An Analytic Critique of Non-Western Conceptions of Human Rights', *American Political Science Review*, Vol. 76, No. 2, June 1982, 303–16.

—— *International Human Rights in Theory and Practice*, Ithaca, NY: Cornell University Press, 1989.

—— 'Human Rights: A New Standard of Civilization?', *International Affairs*, Vol. 47, No. 1, January 1998, 1–24.

—— 'Human Rights and Asian Values: A Defense of "Western Universalism"', in Bauer and Bell (eds), *The East Asian Challenge for Human Rights*, 60–87.

—— 'The Social Construction of International Human Rights', in Dunne and Wheeler (eds), *Human Rights in Global Politics*, 71–102.

Dunn, John. *The History of Political Theory and Other Essays*, Cambridge: Cambridge University Press, 1996.

Dunne, Tim and Nicholas J. Wheeler (eds). *Human Rights in Global Politics*, Cambridge: Cambridge University Press, 1999.

Dworkin, Ronald. *Taking Rights Seriously*, London: Duckworth, 1981.

—— *A Matter of Principle*, Cambridge, MA: Harvard University Press, 1985.

Economist, 'Why Voting Is Good for You', 27 August 1994, 15.

—— 'New Leader, New Indonesia?', 23 October 1999, 31–2.

—— 'A Blind Seer Points the Way', 30 October 1999, 27–8.

Eide, A. and A. Schou. *International Protection of Human Rights*, New York: Interscience Publishers, 1968.

Eldridge, Philip. 'Human Rights and Democracy in Indonesia and Malaysia: Emerging Contexts and Discourses', paper presented at 20th Anniversary Conference of Asian Studies Association of Australia, La Trobe University, Melbourne, July 1996.

Elshtain, Jean Bethke. 'Really Existing Communities', *Review of International Studies*, Vol. 25, 1999, 141–6.

Falk, Richard A. 'Cultural Foundations', in An-Na'im (ed.), *Human Rights in Cross-Cultural Perspectives*, 44–64.

—— 'The Challenge of Genocide and Genocidal Politics in an Era of Globalisation', in Dunne and Wheeler (eds), *Human Rights in Global Politics*, 177–94.

—— *Human Rights Horizons: The Pursuit of Justice in a Globalizing World*, New York: Routledge, 2000.

Fareed Zakaria. 'Culture Is Destiny: A Conversation with Lee Kuan Yew', *Foreign Affairs*, Vol. 73, No. 2, 109–26.

Feillard, Andree. 'Indonesia's Emerging Muslim Feminism: Woman Leaders on Equality, Inheritance and Other Gender Issues', *Studia Islamica*, Vol. 4, No. 1, 1997, 83–111.

Ferrara, Alessandro. 'Universalisms: Procedural, Contextualist and Prudential', in Rasmussen (ed.), *Universalism vs. Communitarianism*, 11–38.

Finnis, John. *Natural Law and Natural Rights*, Oxford: Clarendon Press, 1980.

Fish, Stanley. 'Liberalism Doesn't Exist', in Fish, *There's No Such Thing as Free Speech*.

—— *There's No Such Thing as Free Speech and It's a Good Thing Too*, Oxford: Oxford University Press, 1994.

—— 'Why We Can't All Just Get Along', in S. Fish, *The Trouble with Principle*, Cambridge, MA: Harvard University Press, 1999, 243–62.

Forrester, Duncan B. *Christian Justice and Public Policy*, Cambridge: Cambridge University Press, 1997.

Forrester, Geoff (ed.). *Post-Soeharto Indonesia: Renewal or Chaos?*, Bathurst, NSW: Crawford House Publishing, 1999.

Forrester, Geoff and R. J. May (eds). *The Fall of Soeharto*, Bathurst, NSW: Crawford House Publishing, 1999.

Foster, M. B. 'The Christian Doctrine of Creation and the Rise of Modern Natural Science', *Mind*, Vol. 43, 1934, 446–68.

Freeman, Michael. 'The Philosophical Foundations of Human Rights', *Human Rights Quarterly*, Vol. 16, No. 3, 1994, 491–514.

—— 'Human Rights: Asia and the West', in Tang (ed.), *Human Rights and International Relations in the Asia–Pacific Region*, 13–24.

—— 'Human Rights, Democracy and Asian Values', *Pacific Review*, Vol. 9, No. 3, 1996, 352–66.

Friedman, Edward. 'What Asia Will or Won't Stand For: Globalizing Human Rights and Democracy', *Asian Thought and Society*, Vol. XXII, No. 65, May–August 1997, 85–113.

—— 'Asia as a Fount of Universal Human Rights', in Van Ness (ed.), *Debating Human Rights*, 56–79.

Friedman, Jeffrey. 'Pluralism or Relativism', *Critical Review*, Vol. 11, No. 4, Fall 1997, 469–79.

Frost, Mervyn. *Ethics in International Relations: A Constitutive Theory*, Cambridge: Cambridge University Press, 1996.

Fukuyama, Francis. *The End of History and the Last Man*, London: Hamish Hamilton, 1992.

Gaete, Rolando. 'Postmodernism and Human Rights: Some Insidious Questions', *Law and Critique*, Vol. II, No. 2, 1991, 149–70.

Gaete, Rolando. *Human Rights and the Limits of Critical Reason*, Dartmouth: Aldershot, 1993.

Gaita, Raimond. *A Common Humanity: Thinking about Love and Truth and Justice*, Melbourne: Text Publishing, 1999.

Galston, William A. *Justice and the Human Good*, Chicago: University of Chicago Press, 1980.

—— *Liberal Purposes: Goods, Virtues, and Diversity in the Liberal State*, Cambridge: Cambridge University Press, 1991.

—— 'Practical Philosophy and the Bill of Rights: Perspectives on Some Contemporary Issues', in Lacey and Haakonssen (eds), *A Culture of Rights*, 215–65.

Galtung, Johan. *Human Rights in Another Key*, Cambridge, MA: Polity Press, 1994.

Gay, Peter. *The Enlightenment: An Interpretation: The Science of Freedom*, London: Weidenfeld and Nicolson, 1969.

George, Jim. *Discourses of Global Politics: A Critical (Re)Introduction to International Relations*, Boulder, CO: Rienner, 1994.

—— 'Realist "Ethics", International Relations, and Post-Modernism: Thinking beyond the Egoism–Anarchy Thematic', *Millennium: Journal of International Studies*, Vol. 24, No. 2, 1995, 195–223.

Geras, Norman. 'The View from Everywhere', *Review of International Studies*, Vol. 25, 1999, 157–63.

Ghai, Yash. 'Human Rights and Governance: The Asia Debate', Occasional Paper No. 1, San Francisco: Center for Asian Pacific Affairs, Asia Foundation, November 1994.

—— 'Asian Perspectives on Human Rights', in Tang (ed.), *Human Rights and International Relations in the Asia–Pacific Region*, 54–67.

—— 'Rights, Social Justice, and Globalization in East Asia', in Bauer and Bell (eds), *The East Asian Challenge for Human Rights*, 241–63.

Gough, Leo. *Asia Meltdown: The End of the Miracle*, Oxford: Capstone, 1998.

Grant, George Parkin. *English Speaking Justice*, Notre Dame, IN: University of Notre Dame Press, 1985.

Gray, John. *Liberalism*, Milton Keynes: Open University Press, 1986.

—— *Liberalisms: Essays in Political Philosophy*, London: Routledge, 1989.

—— *Post-Liberalism: Studies in Political Thought*, London: Routledge, 1993.

—— *Enlightenment's Wake*, London: Routledge, 1995.

—— *Berlin*, London: Fontana, 1995.

—— *Endgames: Questions in Late Modern Political Thought*, Cambridge: Polity Press, 1997.

Gress, David. *From Plato to Nato: The Idea of the West and Its Opponents*, New York: The Free Press, 1998.

Griswold Jr, Charles L. 'Rights and Wrongs: Jefferson, Slavery, and Philosophical Quandaries', in Lacey and Haakonssen (eds), *A Culture of Rights*, 144–214.

Guinness, Os. *The American Hour: A Time of Reckoning and the Once and Future Role of Faith*, New York: The Free Press, 1993.

Haakonssen, Knud. 'From Natural Law to the Rights of Man: A European Perspective on American Debates', in Lacey and Haakonssen (eds), *A Culture of Rights*, 19–61.

—— 'Enlightened Dissent: An Introduction', in Haakonssen (ed.), *Enlightenment and Religion*, 1–11.

—— *Natural Law and Moral Philosophy*, Cambridge: Cambridge University Press, 1996.

—— (ed.). *Enlightenment and Religion*, Cambridge: Cambridge University Press, 1996.

Han Sung-Joo (ed.). *Changing Values in Asia: Their Impact on Government and Development*, Tokyo: Japan Center for International Exchange, 1999.

Hauerwas, Stanley. *A Community of Character: Toward a Constructive Christian Social Ethic*, Notre Dame, IN: University of Notre Dame Press, 1981.

—— *Against the Nations: War and Survival in a Liberal Society*, Notre Dame, IN: University of Notre Dame Press, 1992.

—— *Dispatches from the Front: Theological Engagements with the Secular*, Durham, NC: Duke University Press, 1994.

—— *In Good Company: The Church as Polis*, Notre Dame, IN: University of Notre Dame Press, 1995.

—— *Wilderness Wanderings: Probing Twentieth-Century Theology and Philosophy*, Boulder, CO: Westview Press, 1997.

Hausermann, Julia. 'Myths and Realities', in Davies (ed.), *Human Rights*, 126–54.

Hefner, Robert W. 'Modernity and the Challenge of Pluralism: Some Indonesian Lessons', *Studia Islamica*, Vol. 2, No. 4, 1995, 21–45.

Henderson, C. *Asia Falling: Making Sense of the Asian Crisis and Its Aftermath*, Singapore: McGraw Hill Co., 1998.

Henkin, Louis. *Rights of Man Today*, Boulder, CO: Westview Press, 1978.

—— *The Age of Rights*, New York: Columbia University Press, 1990.

Hewison, Kevin, Richard Robison and Gary Rodan (eds). *Southeast Asia in the 1990s: Authoritarianism, Democracy and Capitalism*, Sydney: Allen & Unwin, 1993.

Hill, Michael. *The Politics of Nation Building and Citizenship in Singapore*, London: Routledge, 1995.

Holt, Robin. *Wittgenstein, Politics and Human Rights*, London: LSE/Routledge, 1997.

Hopgood, Stephen. 'Reading the Small Print in Global Civil Society: The Inexorable Hegemony of the Liberal Self', *Millennium*, 29(1), 2000, 1–25.

Hsiung, James C. (ed.). *Human Rights in East Asia: A Cultural Perspective*, New York: Paragon House Publishers, 1985.

Hufton, Olwen (ed.). *Historical Change and Human Rights: The Oxford Amnesty Lectures 1994*, New York: Basic Books, 1995.

Huntington, Samuel. *The Clash of Civilisations and the Remaking of World Order*, New York: Simon & Schuster, 1996.

Hussin Mutalib. *Islam and Ethnicity in Malay Politics*, Singapore: Oxford University Press, 1990.

Hutson, James H. 'The Bill of Rights and the American Revolutionary Experience', in Lacey and Haakonssen (eds), *A Culture of Rights*, 62–97.

Ingleson, John. 'The Asian Values Debate: Accommodating Dissident Voices', *Social Semiotics*, Vol. 8, Nos 2/3, August–December 1998, 227–38.

Inoue Tatsuo. 'Liberal Democracy and Asian Orientalism', in Bauer and Bell (eds), *The East Asian Challenge for Human Rights*, 27–59.

Ismail, Rose (ed.). *Hudud In Malaysia: The Issues at Stake*, Kuala Lumpur: SIS Forum (Malaysia) Berhad, 1995.

Ivison, Duncan. 'The Secret History of Public Reason: Hobbes to Rawls', *History of Political Thought*, Vol. XVIII, No. 1, Spring 1997, 125–47.

—— 'Postcolonialism and Political Theory', in Vincent (ed.), *Political Theory*, 154–71.

Jabri, Viviene. 'Restyling the Subject of Responsibility in International Relations', *Millennium: Journal of International Studies*, Vol. 27, No. 3, 1998, 591–611.

Jacobson, Michael. 'Workshop Report: Human Rights and Asian Values', *NIAS-nytt*, No. 3, 1997, 12–14.

Jakarta Post. 'Government Accused of Poor Human Rights Development', 2 January 1992, 2.

Jayasankaran, S. 'Forbidden Love: Cross-Cultural Romance Sparks Muslim Anger', *Far Eastern Economic Review*, 5 February 1998, 21.

Jenson, Robert W. 'How the World Lost Its Story', in Wolfe (ed.), *The New Religious Humanists*, 135–49.

Jones, Alan. *Sovereign Statehood: The Basis of International Society*, London: Allen & Unwin 1986.

Jones, Eric. 'Asia's Fate: A Response to the Singapore School', *National Interest*, Spring 1994, 18–28.

Jones, L. Gregory and Stephen E. Fowl (eds). *Rethinking Metaphysics*, Oxford: Blackwell, 1995.

Jones, Sidney. 'The Impact of Asian Economic Growth on Human Rights', paper written for Council on Foreign Relations Asia Project, January 1995.

Juwono Sudarsono. 'Human Rights: An Indonesian View', paper presented at Conference on Contemporary Indonesia, organised by Carleton University and Embassy of Indonesia, Ottawa, 25 February 1997, http://www.dfa-deplu.go.id/english2/juwono.htm (accessed 29.7.98).

—— 'The Diplomatic Scam called Human Rights', *Jakarta Post*, 11 April 1997, http://www.dfa-deplu.go.id/english/juwono.htm (accessed 29.7.98).

Kahn, Joel S. 'Malaysian Modern or Anti-Anti Asian Values', *Thesis Eleven*, No. 50, August 1997, 15–33.

Kamenka, Eugene. 'The Anatomy of an Idea', in Kamenka and Tay (eds), *Human Rights*, 1–12.

Kamenka, Eugene and Alice Erh-Soon Tay (eds). *Human Rights*, Port Melbourne: Edward Arnold (Australia), 1978.

Kanishka Jayasuria. 'Review Essay: Legalism and Social Control in Singapore', *South East Asia Research*, Vol. 4, No. 1, March 1996, 85–94.

Kartashkin, Vladimir. 'Economic, Social and Cultural Rights', in Alston and Vasak (eds), *The International Dimensions of Human Rights*, 111–34.

Katongole, Emmanuel. *Beyond Universal Reason: The Relation between Religion and Ethics in the Work of Stanley Hauerwas*, Notre Dame, IN: University of Notre Dame Press, 2000.

Kelly, David and Anthony Reid (eds). *Asian Freedoms: The Idea of Freedom in East and Southeast Asia*, Cambridge: Cambridge University Press, 1998.

Khoo Boo Teik. *Paradoxes of Mahathirism: An Intellectual Biography of Mahathir Mohamad*, Kuala Lumpur: Oxford University Press, 1995.

Kielmansegg, Peter Graf et al. (eds). *Hannah Arendt and Leo Strauss: German Emigres and American Political Thought after World War II*, Cambridge: Cambridge University Press, 1995.

Kim Dae Jung. 'Is Culture Destiny?', *Foreign Affairs*, Vol. 73, No. 6, November–December 1994, 189–94.

Kingsbury, Damien and Greg Barton (eds). *Difference and Tolerance: Human Rights Issues in Southeast Asia*, Melbourne: Deakin University Press, 1994.

Kishore Mahbubani. 'The West and the Rest', *National Interest*, Summer 1992, 3–12.

—— *Can Asians Think?*, New York: Times Editions, 1998.

—— 'An Asian Perspective on Human Rights and Freedom of the Press', in Van Ness (ed.), *Debating Human Rights*, 80–97.

Kothari, R. 'Human Rights: A Movement in Search of a Theory', in S. Kothari and H. Sethi (eds), *Rethinking Human Rights: Challenges for Theory and Action*, Delhi: Lokayan, 1991.

Kraar, Louis. 'A Blunt Talk with Singapore's Lee Kuan Yew', *Fortune*, 4 August 1997, http://www.pathfinder.com/fortune/1997/970804/yew.html (accessed 13.7.98).

Kukathas, Chandran. 'Liberalism, Multiculturalism and Oppression', in Vincent (ed.), *Political Theory*, 132–53.

Kukathas, Chandran and Philip Pettit. *Rawls: A Theory of Justice and Its Critics*, Cambridge: Polity Press, 1990.

Kymlicka, Will. 'Liberal Individualism and Neutrality', in Shlomo Avineri and Avner de Shalit (eds), *Communitarianism and Individualism*, Oxford: Oxford University Press, 1992, 165–85.

Kyong-Dong Kim. 'Confucianism, Economic Growth and Democracy', *Asian Perspective*, Vol. 21, No. 2, Fall 1997, 77–97.

Lacey, Michael J. and Knud Haakonssen (eds). *A Culture of Rights: The Bill of Rights in Philosophy, Politics and Law – 1791 and 1991*, Cambridge: Woodrow Wilson International Center for Scholars and Cambridge University Press, 1991.

Langlois, Anthony J. 'Redescribing Human Rights', *Millennium: Journal of International Studies*, Vol. 27, No. 1, 1998, 1–22.

Larmore, Charles. *The Morals of Modernity*, Cambridge: Cambridge University Press, 1996.

Lauterpacht, Hersch. *International Law and Human Rights*, New York: Garland Publishing, 1973.

Lawson, Stephanie. 'Occidentalising Democracy', *Pacific Research*, November 1995–February 1996, 7–9.

—— 'Cultural Relativism and Democracy: Political Myths about "Asia" and the "West"', in Robison (ed.), *Pathways to Asia*, 108–28.

—— 'Confucius in Singapore: Culture, Politics and the PAP State', in Dauvergne (ed.), *Weak and Strong States in Asia–Pacific Societies*, 114–34.

—— 'Democracy and the Problem of Cultural Relativism: Normative Issues for International Politics', *Global Society*, Vol. 12, No. 2, 1998, 251–70.

Leary, Virginia A. 'The Asian Region and the International Human Rights Movement', in Welch and Leary (eds), *Asian Perspectives on Human Rights*, 12–27.

—— 'Postliberal Strands in Western Human Rights Theory', in An-Na'im (ed.), *Human Rights in Cross-Cultural Perspectives*, 105–32.

Lev, Daniel S. 'Human Rights NGOs in Indonesia and Malaysia', in Welch and Leary (eds), *Asian Perspectives on Human Rights*, 142–61.

—— 'Introduction', in Todung Mulya Lubis, *In Search of Human Rights*, xi–xv.

Liddle, R. William. 'The Islamic Turn in Indonesia: A Political Explanation', *Journal of Asian Studies*, Vol. 55, No. 3, August 1996, 613–34.

Lim, Linda Y. C. 'Singapore's Success: The Myth of the Free Market Economy', *Asian Survey*, Vol. XXIII, No. 6, June 1983, 752–63.

Lindbeck, George. *The Nature of Doctrine: Religion and Theology in a Postliberal Age*, Philadelphia: Westminster, 1984.

Lindholm, Tore. 'Prospects for Research on the Cultural Legitimacy of Human Rights: The Case of Liberalism and Marxism', in An-Na'im (ed.), *Human Rights in Cross-Cultural Perspectives*, 387–435.

Linklater, Andrew. *The Transformation of Political Community: Ethical Foundations of the Post-Westphalian Era*, Cambridge: Polity Press, 1998.

—— 'Transforming Political Community: A Response to the Critics', *Review of International Studies*, Vol. 25, 1999, 165–75.

Little, David. 'The Nature and Basis of Human Rights', in Outka and Reeder (eds), *Prospects for a Common Morality*, 73–92.

Lukes, Steven. 'Making Sense of Moral Conflict', in Rosenblum (ed.), *Liberalism and the Moral Life*, 127–42.

M. Bambang Pranowo. 'Which Islam and Which Pancasila: Islam and the State in Indonesia: A Comment', in Budiman (ed.), *State and Civil Society in Indonesia*, 479–502.

MacIntyre, Alasdair. *After Virtue*, Notre Dame, IN: University of Notre Dame Press, 1981.

—— *Whose Justice? Which Rationality?*, Notre Dame, IN: University of Notre Dame Press, 1988.

—— *Three Rival Versions of Moral Enquiry: Encyclopaedia, Genealogy, and Tradition*, Notre Dame, IN: University of Notre Dame Press, 1990.

Mahathir bin Mohamad. *The Malay Dilemma*, Singapore: D. Moore, 1970.

—— 'Keynote Address', in Chandra Muzaffar (ed.), *Human Wrongs*, 5–12.

—— 'The Future of Asia and the Role of Japan: Challenges of the 21st Century to Youth', speech at Wasenda University, Tokyo, 27 March 1997, http://www.smpke.jpm.my/ucapan.pm/1997/970327.htm (accessed 3.9.97).

—— Speech to summit level meeting on Cooperation for Development, Istanbul, 15 June 1997, http://www.smpke.jpm.my/gn-data/ucapan.pm/1997/970615.htm (accessed 3.9.97).

Mahathir bin Mohamad and Shintaro Ishihara. *The Voice of Asia: Two Leaders Discuss the Coming Century*, Tokyo: Kodansh International Ltd, 1995.

Maran, Rita. *Torture: The Role of Ideology in the French–Algerian War*, New York: Praeger, 1989.

Maritain, Jacques. 'The Possibilities for Co-operation in a Divided World', inaugural address to Second International Conference of Unesco, 6 November 1947.

Marshall, Paul. 'Liberalism, Pluralism and Christianity', in Chaplin and Marshall (eds), *Political Theory and Christian Vision*, 143–62.

Mas'udi, Masdar F., Rosalia Sciortino and Lies Marcoes. 'Learning from Islam: Advocacy of Reproductive Rights in Indonesian *Pesantren*', *Studia Islamica*, Vol. 4, No. 2, 1997, 83–104.

Masakazu Yamazaki. 'Asia, a Civilisation in the Making', *Foreign Affairs*, July/August 1996, Vol. 75, No. 4, 106–18.

Masykuri Abdillah. 'Theological Responses to the Concepts of Democracy and Human Rights: The Case of Contemporary Indonesian Muslim Intellectuals', *Studia Islamica*, Vol. 3, No. 1, 1996, 1–41.

Mauzy, Diane. 'The Human Rights and "Asian Values" Debate in Southeast Asia: Trying to Clarify the Key Issues', *Pacific Review*, Vol. 10, No. 2, 1997, 210–36.

—— 'The Realm of Values in Southeast Asia: Globalisation or Western Domination', in Rodolphe de Koninck and Christine Veilleux (eds), *L'Asia du Sud-Est Face à la Mondialisation: Les Nouveaux Champs d'Analyse*, Quebec: Institute Quebecois des Hautes Etudes Internationales, 1997, 37–51.

Mayer, Ann Elizabeth. *Islam and Human Rights: Tradition and Politics*, Boulder, CO: Westview Press, 1991.

McBeth, John and Margot Cohen. 'Unlikely Victor', *Far Eastern Economic Review*, 28 October 1999, 12–13.

McBeth, John and Dan Murphy. 'Balancing Act', *Far Eastern Economic Review*, 4 November 1999, 18–19.

McLeod, R. and R. Garnaut (eds). *East Asia in Crisis: From Being a Miracle to Needing One?*, London: Routledge, 1998.

Mehta, Pratap B. 'Pluralism after Liberalism?', *Critical Review*, Vol. 11, No. 4, Fall 1997, 503–17.

Messer, Ellen. 'Pluralist Approaches to Human Rights', *Journal of Anthropological Research*, Vol. 53, No. 3, Fall 1997, 293–317.

Meuleman, Johan Hendrik. 'Reaction and Attitudes towards the Darul Arqam Movement in Southeast Asia', *Studia Islamica*, Vol. 3, No. 1, 1996, 43–78.

Milbank, John. *Theology and Social Theory: Beyond Secular Reason*, Oxford: Blackwell, 1993.

Milbank, John, Catherine Pickstock and Graham Ward (eds). *Radical Orthodoxy: A New Theology*, London: Routledge, 1999.

Milner, Anthony. *The Invention of Politics in Colonial Malaya: Contesting Nationalism and the Expansion of the Public Sphere*, Cambridge: Cambridge University Press, 1995.

—— (ed.). 'Perceiving Human Rights', Australian–Asian Perceptions Project Working Paper No. 2, Kensington: Academy of the Social Sciences in Australia and Asia–Australia Institute, University of New South Wales, 1993.

Minogue, K. R. 'Natural Rights, Ideology and the Game of Life', in Kamenka and Tay (eds), *Human Rights*, 13–35.

Mochtar Lubis. 'Asian Cultures and Human Rights', in Berting et al. (eds), *Human Rights in a Pluralist World*, 125–32.

Mochtar Pabottingi. 'Indonesia: Historicizing the New Order's Legitimacy Dilemma', in Muthiah Alagappa (ed.), *Political Legitimacy in Southeast Asia*, 224–56.

Mohamad S. El-Awa. *Punishment in Islamic Law*, Indianapolis: American Trust Publications, 1982.

Mohamed El Sayed Said. 'Islam and Human Rights', in Warner (ed.), *Human Rights and Humanitarian Law*, 3–28.

More, Thomas. *Utopia*, Harmondsworth: Penguin, 1973.

Morris, David Paul. 'Interview: Anwar on Currency Woes, Elders and Asian Values', *Time Asia*, 6 October 1997, Vol. 150, No. 14, http://www.pathfinder.com/time/magazine/1997/int/971006/interview.html (accessed 13.7.98).

Mouffe, Chantal. *The Return of the Political*, London: Verso, 1993.

Muhammad As Hikam. 'Islam and Human Rights: Tensions and Possible Cooperations: The Case of Indonesia', *A Report from the Asia Foundation*, No. 24, February 1997, 1–7.

Mulhall, Stephen and Adam Swift. *Liberals and Communitarians*, 2nd edn, Oxford: Blackwell, 1996.

Muntarbhorn, Vitit. *Human Rights in Southeast Asia: A Challenge for the 21st Century*, Bangkok: Chaiyong Limthongkul Foundation, 1993.

—— 'Asia, Human Rights and the New Millennium: Time for a Regional Human Rights Charter?', *Transnational Law and Contemporary Problems*, Vol. 8, Fall 1998, 407–18.

Muthiah Alagappa (ed.). *Political Legitimacy in Southeast Asia: The Quest for Moral Authority*, Stanford: Stanford University Press, 1995.

Nagel, Thomas. *The View from Nowhere*, Oxford: Oxford University Press, 1986.

Narramore, Terry. 'The Politics of Rights and Identity in Japan', *Pacific Review*, Vol. 10, No. 1, 1997, 39–56.

Neher, Clark D. 'Asian Style Democracy', *Asian Survey*, Vol. XXXIV, No. 11, November 1994, 949–61.

New Straits Times. 'Shi'ite Sect against Our Monarchy, says Hamid', 8 November 1997.

Ng, Margaret. 'Are Rights Culture Bound?', in Davis (ed.), *Human Rights and Chinese Values*, 59–71.

—— 'Why Asia Needs Democracy', *Journal of Democracy*, Vol. 8, No. 2, 1997, 10–23.

Nietzsche, Friedrich. (Walter Kaufmann, trs.) *Thus Spoke Zarathustra: A Book for None and All*, London: Penguin, 1966.

Nikhil Aziz. 'The Human Rights Debate in an Era of Globalisation: Hegemony of Discourse', *Bulletin of Concerned Asian Scholars*, Vol. 27, No. 4, October–December 1995, 9–23.

—— 'The Human Rights Debate in an Era of Globalisation', in Van Ness (ed.), *Debating Human Rights*, 32–55.

Noor, Farish A. 'Values in the Dynamics of Malaysia's Internal and External Political Relations', in Han Sung-Joo (ed.), *Changing Values in Asia*, 146–76.

Noordin Sopiee. 'Asia and the West: A Malaysian's View of a Controversial Debate', *Asia Week*, 12 December 1997.

Nozick, Robert. *Anarchy, State and Utopia*, Oxford: Oxford University Press, 1974.

O'Hagan, Jacinta. Conceptions of the West in International Relations Thought: From Oswald Spengler to Edward Said, PhD thesis, Australian National University, 1998.

O'Manique, John. 'Universal and Inalienable Rights: A Search for Foundations', *Human Rights Quarterly*, Vol. 12, No. 4, 1990, 465–85.

Oden, Thomas. *After Modernity ... What?*, Michigan: Zondervan, 1990.

Onuma Yasuaki. 'Toward an Intercivilizational Approach to Human Rights', in Bauer and Bell (eds), *The East Asian Challenge for Human Rights*, 103–23.

Ortega y Gasset, Jose. *The Revolt of the Masses*, London: Allen & Unwin, 1932.

Osman Bakar, 'Asian Values or Universal Values Championed by Asia? Implications for East–West Understanding', *Social Semiotics*, Vol. 8, Nos 2/3, August–December 1998, 169–76.

Othman, Norani. *Shari'a and the Citizenship Rights of Women in a Modern Nation State: Grounding Human Rights Arguments in Non-Western Cultural Terms*, Bangi: Universiti Kebangsaan Malaysia (IKMAS), 1997.

—— 'Grounding Human Rights in Non-Western Culture: *Shari'a* and the Citizenship Rights of Women in a Modern Islamic State', in Bauer and Bell (eds), *The East Asian Challenge for Human Rights*, 169–92.

—— (ed.). *Shari'a Law and the Modern Nation-State: A Malaysian Symposium*, Kuala Lumpur: SIS Forum (Malaysia) Berhad, 1994.

Outka, Gene and John P. Reeder, Jr (eds), *Prospects for a Common Morality*, Princeton, NJ: Princeton University Press, 1993.

Panikkar, Raimon. 'The Defiance of Pluralism', *Soundings*, Vol. 79, Nos 1–2, Spring/Summer 1996, 167–91.

Patterson, Orlando. 'Freedom, Slavery and the Modern Construction of Rights', in Hufton (ed.), *Historical Change and Human Rights*, 131–78.

Perry, Michael J. 'Are Human Rights Universal? The Relativist Challenge and Related Matters', *Human Rights Quarterly*, Vol. 19, No. 3, 1997, 461–509.

—— *The Idea of Human Rights: Four Inquiries*, Oxford: Oxford University Press, 1998.

Peters, Julie and Andrea Wolper (eds). *Women's Rights Human Rights: International Feminist Perspectives*, New York: Routledge, 1995.

Pheng Cheah. 'Posit(ion)ing Human Rights in the Current Global Conjuncture', *Public Culture*, Vol. 9, No. 2, Winter 1997, 233–65.

Pippin, Robert B. 'The Modern World of Leo Strauss', in Kielmansegg et al. (eds), *Hannah Arendt and Leo Strauss*, 139–60.

Preis, Ann-Belinda S. 'Human Rights as Cultural Practice: An Anthropological Critique', *Human Rights Quarterly*, Vol. 18, No. 2, 1996, 286–315.

Pritchard, Sarah. 'The Jurisprudence of Human Rights: Some Critical Thoughts and Developments in Practice', *Australian Journal of Human Rights*, Vol. 2, No. 1, 1995, 3–38.

Radio National. 'Doing Human Rights in Asia', *Background Briefing* Transcript, 24 August 1997, http://www.abc.net.au/rn/talks/bbing/bb970824.htm (accessed 2.9.97).

Rasmussen, David M. (ed.). *Universalism vs. Communitarianism: Contemporary Debates in Ethics*, Cambridge, MA: MIT Press, 1990.

Rawls, John. *A Theory of Justice*, Oxford: Oxford University Press, 1971.

—— 'Fairness to Goodness', *Philosophical Review*, Vol. 84, 1975, 536–54.

—— 'Kantian Constructivism in Moral Theory', *Journal of Philosophy*, Vol. 88, 1980, 515–72.

—— 'The Law of Peoples', in Shute and Hurley (eds), *On Human Rights*, 41–82.
—— *Political Liberalism*, New York: Columbia University Press, 1993.
—— *The Law of Peoples*, Cambridge, MA: Harvard University Press, 1999.
Raz, Joseph. *The Morality of Freedom*, Oxford: Oxford University Press, 1986.
Reeder, Jr, John P. 'Foundations without Foundationalism', in Outka and Reeder (eds), *Prospects for a Common Morality*, 191–214.
Reid, John Phillip. *The Constitutional History of the American Revolution: The Authority of Rights*, Madison: University of Wisconsin Press, 1986.
Renteln, Alison Dundes. *International Human Rights: Universalism versus Relativism*, Newbury Park: Sage, 1990.
Robison, Richard. 'Indonesia: Tensions in State and Regime', in Hewison et al. (eds), *Southeast Asia in the 1990s*, 41–74.
—— 'Introduction', *Pacific Review*, Vol. 9, No. 3, 1996, 305–8.
—— 'The Politics of "Asian Values"', *Pacific Review*, Vol. 9, No. 3, 1996, 309–27.
—— (ed.). *Pathways to Asia: The Politics of Engagement*, Sydney: Allen & Unwin, 1996.
Rodan, Gary. 'Preserving the One-Party State in Contemporary Singapore', in Hewison et al. (eds), *Southeast Asia in the 1990s*, 77–108.
—— 'The Internationalisation of Ideological Conflict: Asia's New Significance', *Pacific Review*, Vol. 9, No. 3, 1996, 328–51.
—— (ed.), *Singapore Changes Guard: Social, Political and Economic Directions in the 1990s*, New York: Longman Cheshire, 1993.
—— 'Civil Society and Other Political Possibilities in Southeast Asia', *Journal of Contemporary Asia*, Vol. 27, No. 2, 1997, 156–78.
Rodan, Gary and Kevin Hewison. 'A "Clash of Cultures" or the Convergence of Political Ideology?', in Robison (ed.), *Pathways to Asia*, 29–55.
Rorty, Richard. *Philosophy and the Mirror of Nature*, Princeton, NJ: Princeton University Press, 1979.
—— *Contingency, Irony and Solidarity*, Cambridge: Cambridge University Press, 1989.
—— 'Human Rights, Rationality, and Sentimentality', in Shute and Hurley (eds), *On Human Rights*, 111–34.
Rosen, Stanley. *The Mask of Enlightenment: Nietzsche's Zarathustra*, Cambridge: Cambridge University Press, 1995.
Rosenblum, Nancy L. (ed.). *Liberalism and the Moral Life*, Cambridge, MA: Harvard University Press, 1989.
Roy, Denny. 'Singapore, China, and the "Soft Authoritarian" Challenge', *Asian Survey*, Vol. XXXIV, No. 3, March 1994, 231–42.
S. H. Alatas. 'Core Concepts and Asian Traditions', in Tay (ed.), *In Search of Universal Human Rights*, 41–4.
Sajoo, Amyn B. *Pluralism in 'Old Societies and New States': Emerging ASEAN Contexts*, Singapore: ISEAS, 1994.
Sarmiento, Rene V. 'Asian Views of Human Rights', in Tay (ed.), *In Search of Universal Human Rights*, 1–6.
Sen, Amartya. 'Thinking about Human Rights and Asian Values', *Human Rights Dialogue*, Vol. 4, March 1996, 2–3.
—— *Human Rights and Asian Values*, New York: Carnegie Council on Ethics and International Affairs, 1997.
—— 'Human Rights and Economic Achievements', in Bauer and Bell (eds), *The East Asian Challenge for Human Rights*, 88–99.
Sen, Amartya and Jean Dreze. *Hunger and Public Action*, Oxford: Clarendon Press, 1989.

Seow, Francis T. *To Catch a Tartar: A Dissident in Lee Kuan Yew's Prison*, Monograph 42, New Haven: Southeast Asian Studies, Yale University, 1994.

Shapiro, Ian. *The Evolution of Rights in Liberal Theory*, Cambridge: Cambridge University Press, 1986.

Sher, George. *Beyond Neutrality: Perfectionism and Politics*, Cambridge: Cambridge University Press, 1997.

Sheridan, Greg. *Asian Values Western Dreams: Understanding the New Asia*, Sydney: Allen & Unwin, 1999.

Shestack, Jerome J. 'The Philosophic Foundations of Human Rights', *Human Rights Quarterly*, Vol. 20, No. 2, 1998, 201–34.

Shih Chih-yu. 'Human Rights as Identities: Difference and Discrimination in Taiwan's China Policy', in Van Ness (ed.), *Debating Human Rights*, 144–63.

Shue, Henry. *Basic Rights*, Princeton, NJ: Princeton University Press, 1980.

Shute, Stephen and Susan Hurley (eds). *On Human Rights: The Oxford Amnesty Lectures 1993*, London: Basic Books, 1993.

Sisters in Islam, *Are Muslim Men Allowed To Beat Their Wives*, Kuala Lumpur: Sisters in Islam, 1991.

Skinner, B. F. *Walden Two*, New York: Macmillan, 1962.

Stammers, Neil. 'Human Rights and Power', *Political Studies*, Vol. XLI, 1993, 70–82.

Steadman, John M. *The Myth of Asia*, London: Macmillan, 1969.

Stewart, Ian. 'Malaysia Gets Tough on Western Decadence', *Australian*, 16 June 1997, 6.

—— 'Mahathir's Allies Go West', *Australian*, 5 August 1998, 8.

Stout, Jeffrey. *The Flight from Authority: Religion, Morality and the Quest for Autonomy*, Notre Dame, IN: University of Notre Dame Press, 1981.

—— *Ethics after Babel: The Languages of Morals and Their Discontents*, Boston: Beacon Press, 1988.

—— 'On Having a Morality in Common', in Outka and Reeder (eds), *Prospects for a Common Morality*, 215–32.

Straits Times. 'The Democracy Debate – SM', 17 June 1993.

Suharto. Speech at 1992 NAM Summit, gopher://gopher.igc.apc.org:2998/OREG-INDONESIA/r 858312554.26677.353 (accessed 14.3.97).

Sunstein, Cass R. 'Incompletely Theorized Agreements', *Harvard Law Review*, Vol. 108, No. 7, May 1995, 1733–72.

—— 'Practical Reason and Incompletely Theorized Agreements', paper presented at Law Program, Research School of Social Sciences, Australian National University, Canberra, 1996.

—— *Legal Reasoning and Political Conflict*, New York: Oxford University Press, 1996.

Syed Husin Ali. *Two Faces: Detention without Trial*, Kuala Lumpur: INSAN, 1996.

Tan, Kevin Y. L. 'Human Rights in East Asia: Developments in Legal Reform in Singapore and Taiwan', ms, an edited version of which appears as 'Economic Development, Legal Reform, and Rights in Singapore and Taiwan', in Bauer and Bell (eds), *The East Asian Challenge for Human Rights*, 264–84.

Tang, James T. H. (ed.). *Human Rights and International Relations in the Asia–Pacific Region*, London: Pinter, 1995.

Tariq Modood, 'Racial Equality: Colour, Culture, Justice', in Boucher and Kelly (eds), *Social Justice*, 200–14.

Tay, Simon S. C. 'The Singapore Example', *McGill Law Journal/Revue De Droit De McGill*, Vol. 41, No. 4, 1996, 744–80.

—— (ed.). *In Search of Universal Human Rights: An Ongoing Dialogue between Europe and ASEAN*, conference papers from Friedrich-Ebert-Stiftung's Office for Regional Activities in Southeast Asia, Singapore, 1997.

Taylor, Charles. *Sources of the Self*, Cambridge: Cambridge University Press, 1989.

—— *The Ethics of Authenticity*, Cambridge, MA: Harvard University Press, 1991.

—— *Multiculturalism and 'The Politics of Recognition'*, Princeton, NJ: Princeton University Press, 1992.

—— 'A World Consensus on Human Rights?', *Dissent*, Summer 1996, 15–21.

—— 'Conditions of an Unforced Consensus on Human Rights', in Bauer and Bell (eds), *The East Asian Challenge for Human Rights*, 124–44.

Teson, Fernando. 'International Human Rights and Cultural Relativism', *Virginia Journal of International Law*, Vol. 25, No. 4, 1985, 894–5.

Thio, Li-ann. 'Asian Values and Human Rights: At the Periphery of ASEAN–EU Relations?', paper presented at CUESP Third International Conference, Bangkok, 13 February 1997.

Tibi, Bassam. *The Crisis of Modern Islam*, Salt Lake City: University of Utah Press, 1988.

Time Australia. 'I'm Not a King, I'm Just Like You', interview with B. J. Habibie, 10 August 1998, No. 32, 53–9.

Tinder, Glenn. 'Can We Be Good without God', in Wolfe (ed.), *The New Religious Humanists*, 150–76.

Todung Mulya Lubis. 'Human Rights Standard Setting in Asia: Problems and Prospects', *Indonesia Quarterly*, Vol. XXI, No. 1, 1993, 25–37.

—— *In Search of Human Rights: Legal–Political Dilemmas of Indonesia's New Order, 1966–1990*, Jakarta: PT Gramedia Pustaka, 1993.

Topper, Keith. 'Richard Rorty, Liberalism and the Politics of Redescription', *American Political Science Review*, Vol. 89, No. 4, 1995, 954–65.

Tremewan, Christopher. *The Political Economy of Social Control in Singapore*, Basingstoke: Macmillan, 1994.

—— 'Singapore in the Asian Human Rights Debate: The Pragmatic Pursuit of Ideology', in Wilkinson (ed.), *Culture, Ethnicity and Human Rights in International Relations*, 55–68.

Tu Wei-Ming. *Confucian Ethics Today*, Singapore: Federal Publications, 1984.

Tuck, Richard. *Natural Rights Theories: Their Origin and Development*, Cambridge: Cambridge University Press, 1979.

—— *Hobbes*, Oxford: Oxford University Press, 1989.

Turner, Bryan S. 'Outline of a Theory of Human Rights', *Sociology*, Vol. 27, No. 3, August 1993, 489–512.

—— 'Human Rights: From Local Cultures to Global Systems', in Kingsbury and Barton (eds), *Difference and Tolerance*, 5–19.

Turner, Terrence. 'Human Rights, Human Difference: Anthropology's Contribution to an Emancipatory Cultural Politics', *Journal of Anthropological Research*, Vol. 53, No. 3, 1997, 273–91.

Van Ness, Peter (ed.). *Debating Human Rights: Critical Essays from the United States and Asia*, London: Routledge, 1999.

Vincent, Andrew (ed.). *Political Theory: Tradition and Diversity*, Cambridge: Cambridge University Press, 1998.

Vincent, John. *Human Rights and International Relations*, Cambridge: Cambridge University Press, 1986.

Waldron, Jeremy. 'Theoretical Foundations of Liberalism', in Waldron, *Liberal Rights*, 35–62.

—— *Liberal Rights: Collected Papers 1981–1991*, Cambridge: Cambridge University Press, 1993.

—— (ed.). *Theories of Rights*, Oxford: Oxford University Press, 1984.

—— (ed.). *Nonsense upon Stilts: Bentham, Burke and Marx on the Rights of Man*, London: Methuen, 1987.

Walker, R. B. J. *One World, Many Worlds: Struggles for a Just World Peace*, Boulder, CO: Rienner, 1988.

—— 'The Concept of Culture in the Theory of International Relations', in Jong-suk Chay (ed.), *Culture and International Relations*, New York: Praeger, 1991, 3–17.

Walzer, Michael. *Spheres of Justice*, New York: Basic Books, 1983.

—— *Thick and Thin: Moral Argument at Home and Abroad*, Notre Dame, IN: University of Notre Dame Press, 1994.

Warner, Daniel (ed.). *Human Rights and Humanitarian Law: The Quest for Universality*, The Hague: Martinus Nijhoff Publishers, 1997.

Weissbrodt, David. 'Human Rights: An Historic Perspective', in Davies (ed.), *Human Rights*, 1–20.

Welch, Claude E. Jr, and Virginia A. Leary (eds). *Asian Perspectives on Human Rights*, Boulder, CO: Westview Press, 1990.

Wellman, Carl. 'A New Conception of Human Rights', in Kamenka and Tay (eds), *Human Rights*, 48–58.

Wendt, Alexander. *Social Theory of International Politics*, Cambridge: Cambridge University Press, 1999.

Weston, Burns H. and Richard Pierre Claude (eds). *Human Rights in the World Community: Issues and Action*, Philadelphia: University of Pennsylvania Press, 1989.

Wielgal, George. 'Are Human Rights Still Universal?', *Commentary*, February 1995, 41–5.

Wilkinson, Rorden (ed.). *Culture, Ethnicity and Human Rights in International Relations*, Auckland: NZIIA, 1997.

Williams, Jeremy B. 'Capitalist Development and Human Rights: Singapore under Lee Kuan Yew', *Journal of Contemporary Asia*, Vol. 22, No. 3, 1992, 360–72.

Wittgenstein, L. *Philosophical Investigations* (trs. G. E. M. Anscombe), Oxford: Basil Blackwell, 1974.

Wolfe, Gregory (ed.). *The New Religious Humanists: A Reader*, New York: The Free Press, 1997.

Woodiwiss, Anthony. *Globalisation, Human Rights and Labour Law in Pacific Asia*, Cambridge: Cambridge University Press, 1998.

Wuthnow, Robert et al. *Cultural Analysis: The Work of Peter L. Berger, Mary Douglas, Michel Foucault and Jurgen Habermas*, London: Routledge, 1984.

Yeo, George. 'Keep Bridging Cultural Boundaries', *Asian Business*, September 1997, 14.

Zechenter, Elizabeth M. 'In the Name of Culture: Cultural Relativism and the Abuse of the Individual', *Journal of Anthropological Research*, Vol. 53, No. 3, Fall 1997, 319–48.

Zifirdaus Adnan. 'Islamic Religion: Yes, Islamic (Political) Ideology: No! Islam and the State in Indonesia', in Budiman (ed.), *State and Civil Society in Indonesia*, 421–77.

Index

Abdurrahman Wahid, 17
Aborigines, 170
abortion, 5, 43, 56, 58, 64, 65, 127, 136
absolutes, 75
Ackerman, Bruce, 163
activists, 4, 20, 41, 48, 70–1, 129, 160
Africa, 1, 35
Allah, 5, 86
Altman, Dennis, 67
America, 1, 14, 76
Amish community, 90
Amnesty International, 2, 71, 150
Analects, 155
antagonism, 9–10, 125, 128–30, 133, 138,
    141, 143, 149, 158
anthropology, 82, 94–6
Anwar Ibrahim, 3, 15–16
arbitrary, 43, 58, 115, 121, 125–6, 135–7,
    140–2, 146, 148, 150–2, 163, 166, 167,
    170, 173
Archimedean point, 83, 126, 129, 134, 139,
    142–3, 145, 150, 167, 171
ASEAN, 39
Asian Renaissance, 3, 15
Asian values, 3–5, 12–17, 22–32, 39, 41,
    43–9, 72, 121, 152, 154, 159–60,
    165–6
authoritarianism, 20, 23, 25, 28, 34–6,
    38–9, 44, 126, 136–7, 153–4
authority, 2, 9, 10, 13, 16, 27–9, 31, 67, 82,
    84, 90, 95, 128, 134, 138, 142, 164
autonomy, 14, 16, 21, 68, 78, 89, 90
axiology, 46, 97, 98, 113, 145

Bangkok Declaration, 39
barbarism, 82
beauty pageant, 57
behavioural norms, 47, 61, 123, 132, 134
Beiner, Ronald, 164
Bell, Daniel, 44, 152–5
Benhabib, Seyla, 125, 139, 147
Bentham, Jeremy, 6, 79, 80
Berlin, Isaiah, 93
Bilahari Kausikan, 21, 22, 23, 24
British Isles, 1
Burke, Edmund, 78, 79
Burma, 3, 35

Campbell, Richard, 172
Cavell, Stanley, 136, 166
Chandra Muzaffar, 15, 174
Chesterton, Simon, 75
Chinese populations, 25, 36, 37, 57, 152,
    155
Christ, 60
Christianity, 14, 41, 43, 51, 60, 67, 74, 77,
    82, 84, 85, 111, 113, 114
Chua Beng-Huat, 66
church, 77, 81, 128
circle, vicious/virtuous, 11, 150
citizens, 4, 17, 22, 25, 33–5, 71, 103, 107,
    133, 140
civilisation, 7, 15, 60, 64, 75, 81–2, 84,
    155
Cold War, 155
colonialism, 17, 49
communitarianism, 18, 25, 128

Habibie, B. J., 17
Hauerwas, Stanley, 125, 136–7, 140, 164, 172
hegemony, 6, 10, 128, 142–3, 150
Hercules, 108–9, 115–17, 121
heterogeneity, 28, 103, 104, 144
Hinduism, 67
historicity, 54, 60, 63, 73, 79
Holocaust, the Jewish, 74
Holt, Robin, 90–1, 138
homosexuality, 43, 64, 65, 66, 127
Hong Kong, 34, 156
human dignity, 50–3, 87
human flourishing, 94, 129
human frailty, 96–7
human rights, 1–12, 14, 17–20, 23–5, 29, 32–4, 36–56, 60–75, 77, 79–80, 82–3, 85–7, 90–1, 94–103, 110–66, 168–73
Human Rights Watch, 2
human traditions, 6–10, 100, 102, 125, 134–7, 147, 151, 153–4, 156–7, 159–62, 172
humanitarian intervention, 40
Hume, David, 82
hypocrisy, 3, 14, 17, 18, 20

identity, 6, 10, 18, 26, 30–1, 50, 61, 65, 66, 68–9, 83, 89, 129–32, 141, 146, 167, 169
ideology, 2, 26, 30, 41, 43, 45, 74, 83, 87, 102, 129, 173, 186
imitation, 138
imperialism, 17, 33, 80, 170
incommensurability, 125–6
incompletely theorised agreement, 8–9, 101, 103–16, 118–24, 173
indigenism, 30
individualism, 13, 15–16, 23, 31, 79, 128, 133, 134, 163, 164
Indonesia, 2–3, 12, 16, 17–20, 24, 27–30, 34–9, 48, 58, 62, 64, 68–9, 175–82
intellectuals, 1, 4, 41–3, 48, 71, 105, 129, 178
investment, 31, 33
Islam, 12–13, 16, 18, 26, 41, 47, 49–51, 56–64, 67–70, 111, 114–15, 132, 137, 175–82, 188
Ismail, Rose, 59, 180

Javanese people and culture, 5, 53, 64, 179
Jones, Sidney, 36
Jose Ortega y Gasset, 88, 184

justice, 7, 9–11, 16, 41–2, 45, 55, 59–62, 69, 71, 76, 79, 84, 90–1, 97, 100–1, 103, 107–8, 110–11, 113, 118–20, 125–6, 130, 132–3, 135–6, 139, 141–4, 147–8, 150–4, 156–7, 163, 165–6, 168, 172–3, 180, 184–9
justification, 3, 13, 19, 23, 26, 35, 39, 42, 50, 52, 54, 56, 65, 80, 84, 89, 95, 99, 114, 116, 119, 122, 136, 140, 141, 154, 162, 163
Juwono Sudarsono, 20, 175

Kamenka, Eugene, 94
Kant, Emmanuel, 85
Kantianism, 104, 114
Kishore Mahbubani, 21
Koran, 5, 58, 59, 60, 111

language, 1–2, 9, 20, 47, 50–3, 64, 74–7, 82, 98, 100, 102, 111, 117, 121, 126, 128, 136–8, 140, 145–6, 160–1, 164–5, 168
Larmore, Charles, 93, 163
law, international, 3, 7, 38, 40, 80, 116, 121, 124, 161, 186, 188
Lee, Kuan Yew, 3, 18, 22–3, 31, 45, 152
legal instrumentalities, 42, 102, 116
legitimation, 1–2
Lev, Daniel, 42
liberalism, 7, 14, 28–9, 31, 42, 67, 71, 80, 87–95, 107, 114, 118–19, 128–9, 132, 137–8, 147, 150, 153–5, 157, 160, 162, 165, 167, 169, 171–2
liberals, 31, 41, 44, 64, 78, 90, 91, 95, 128–9, 141, 162
liberty, 29, 79, 84, 104, 113, 126, 128–9, 141, 146–8
'little people', 47, 167
Locke, John, 75–8, 80, 162
loyalty, 173

MacIntyre, Alasdair, 85–6, 98, 164
Mahathir bin Mohammad, 3, 13–16, 18, 45, 48, 137
majoritarianism, 135
Malays, 29, 37, 61
Malaysia, 2–3, 12–19, 24, 27–31, 35–7, 39, 48, 58–9, 61–2, 64–5, 68–70, 132, 137, 156
marriage, 14, 16, 43, 66, 132, 133
Marxism, 79
materialism, 16